T0243763

Patton's Madness

The Dark Side of a Battlefield Genius

Jim Sudmeier

STACKPOLE
BOOKS
Guilford, Connecticut

Published by Stackpole Books
An imprint of The Rowman & Littlefield Publishing Group, Inc.
4501 Forbes Blvd., Ste. 200
Lanham, MD 20706
www.rowman.com

6 Tinworth Street, London SE11 5AL, United Kingdom
Distributed by NATIONAL BOOK NETWORK
800-462-6420

British Library Cataloguing in Publication Information Available

Library of Congress Cataloging-in-Publication Data Available

ISBN 978-0-8117-3854-5 (hardcover)
ISBN 978-0-8117-6898-6 (e-book)

∞™ The paper used in this publication meets the minimum requirements of American National Standard for Information Sciences—Permanence of Paper for Printed Library Materials, ANSI/NISO Z39.48-1992.

To all the "dogfaces" of World War II
who lived with the terror of war without the glory,
to the replacements who performed their duty
without a single buddy, and to the combat leaders
who made the tough calls and took action
without the accolades of history.

Contents

List of Illustrations

List of Maps

List of Tables

Preface

Among the many heroic characters who have occupied the American stage, General George S. Patton Jr. is one I find irresistible. For decades, I have been drawn to the aura of this flamboyant, handsome, charismatic, and outrageous celebrity. An innovator in the use of combined arms, the American general officer most feared by the Germans, Patton was unsurpassed as a battlefield commander in rapidly moving, fluid situations. He was almost always on the attack and by sheer willpower and force of personality, he made things happen. In staking out the role of America in World War II, initially subordinate to the Brits, Patton was a major force in political infighting. During the depths of World War II, news reports about General Patton, including two *Life* magazine cover stories, lifted the spirits of a nation. Patton had "star quality" aplenty and gave the American GI a name and a face. It was also beneficial that he fired up the troops to overcome their Judeo-Christian taboos against killing the enemy.

At the same time, I have been repelled by Patton's shameless abuse, bullying, and belittling of others, his egotism, snobbishness, racism, and xenophobia. He was extremely callous about the needs of his colleagues and subordinates, including many American soldiers who were needlessly killed or wounded under his command. It is most cruel that the names and reputations of many fine officers who served beside Patton's star—a star that sometimes shone too brightly—have suffered virtual oblivion.

The elements that make Patton such an enigmatic figure—his mercurial temper, his battlefield courage and brilliance, his abuses of subordinates, his ability to train and inspire the troops, his political gaffes—all sprang from his *own kind of madness*. Patton possessed the rare attribute among general officers of being *attracted* to danger—not a normal human response. Since war is a form of collective insanity, the idea that leaders who are mentally ill will rise to the top in war or similar crises has been argued by Tufts and Harvard University psychiatrist Professor Nassir Ghaemi.[1]

Patton's psychological instability was well known to his commanders. General Eisenhower, who had known Patton since 1919, reported him as "a problem child,"[2] "my mentally unbalanced officer,"[3] and "just like a time bomb."[4] "Brilliantly insane,"[5] says military historian Edward Lengel. Biographer Ladislas Farago considered him "if not actually mad, at least highly neurotic."[6] Historian Brig. Gen. S. L. A. Marshall described Patton as "about half mad," and said, "Any man who thinks he is the reincarnation of Hannibal or some such isn't quite possessed of all his buttons."[7]

Military historian Dan Crosswell hypothesized that Patton suffered from bipolar disorder, a condition he claims both Patton's father and aunt suffered from.[8] However, as I will show, Patton's mood swings were directly linked to the state of his career, in cycles often lasting many years, and lacked the sudden randomness typical of bipolar disorder. Blumenson first,[9] later D'Este[10] and others since[11] have attributed Patton's anomalous behaviors to the learning disorder dyslexia. But after first attending school at age eleven, Patton became a voracious reader. Blumenson also suggested that the problem was attention deficit disorder (ADD), although starting as a teenager Patton developed intense focus. I've heard the suggestion that Patton's behavior was caused by traumatic brain injuries and/or posttraumatic stress disorder (PTSD).

The present book is the first to diagnose Patton using the psychiatrist's manual rather than guesswork or conjecture. I will show that the same "craziness" that made Patton dangerous to the enemy sometimes made him dangerous to his own soldiers and fellow officers.

The story of Patton's life has been written by some excellent biographers, among them Martin Blumenson, Carlo D'Este, Stanley Hirshson, Ladislas Farago, John Rickard, Roger Nye, Charles Whiting, Patton's grandson Robert Patton, and Patton's daughter Ruth Ellen Patton Totten. "What made Patton tick emotionally?" is the subject of this psychobiographical study of the man. This book does not introduce new stories about Patton's life. Instead, I cite quotations and retell stories that best reveal Patton's psychological characteristics, while supplying an abundance of new analyses, context, and insights.

One could question the validity of psychoanalyzing a person long dead. To the contrary, Professor Ghaemi claims that the dead can be better subjects than the living, who sometimes try to obstruct their analysts and biographers.[12] Patton made it a daily habit to write in his diary, which he used in part as an outlet for his frustrations, replete with obscenities. During separations (most of World War I and World War II) from his wife, Beatrice, he wrote frank and revealing letters to her almost daily. Convinced even in his twenties of his future greatness, he made certain that his essays, letters, and poems were preserved. These writings and his post–World War II memoir, *War as I Knew It*, richly augmented after his death by revelations of family members and comrades in arms, provide extraordinary source material on Patton's psychology.

Psychiatric disorders in the United States today are classified in the *Diagnostic and Statistical Manual of Mental Disorders*, fifth edition (DSM-5)—a consensus published in 2013 by the American Psychiatric Association.[13] Using the DSM-5, I will present herein the justification for my conclusion that General Patton suffered from pathological, overt, narcissistic personality disorder (NPD). Thus he was an emotionally arrested, pre-moral, adult toddler who wielded the almost godlike power to command a half million soldiers in battle. Such a diagnosis makes it possible to understand the general's enigmatic personality and to rationalize his seemingly irrational behavior.

The main point of this book is to deal with Patton's mental problems, and thus I will spend more time discussing his weaknesses than his many virtues—the latter already well covered in numerous biographies. While dealing with Patton's emotional problems, my admiration for the man and his unique gifts remains steadfast. In the final analysis, Patton's actions must be viewed against the backdrop of the wars he was trying to win.

The authors of DSM-5 say that "it is 'not advised' that nonclinical, nonmedical, or otherwise *insufficiently trained* individuals use DSM-5 to assess for the presence of a mental disorder" (italics mine). They also state, "The definition of a mental disorder that is included in DSM-5 was designed for clinicians, public health professionals, and *researchers*"[14] (italics mine). I am using the DSM-5 for historical research. One more author's opinion cannot cause undue harm to a public figure when he or she is long since dead. A career academic, I trust that readers of this book will judge it based on the plausibility of my arguments, the quality of my discussion, and my command of the material (i.e., *sufficiency of training*).

For many people, the 1970 Oscar-winning movie *Patton* cast the man's carefully crafted, ultra-macho image in stone, thus doing a disservice to a full-dimensional understanding of his character, with all his volatility and self-doubt. For starters, the Hollywood facade, by substituting the strongly masculine, gravel voice of the actor George C. Scott, concealed Patton's incongruously high-pitched voice,[15] which he tried to overcome in his speeches by using shock and excess profanity. Aware that something was awry in Patton's character, the moviemakers focused on his belief in reincarnation, playing an eerie theme song every time the matter arose—and totally missing the mark.

Any objective analysis of Patton's character today has the task of overcoming mountains of heroic myths in readers' minds, consciously or subconsciously built up over decades by the general's own press corps, headline news stories, magazine cover stories, newsreels, a smash Hollywood film, mostly flattering biographies, and the public's addiction to the "star system." As British psychologist Norman Dixon wrote some forty years ago, "Judging by the attitude of some historians . . . a putting together of psychology and military history is positively indecent. . . . Since there are few things more annoying than having one's behavior explained, there exists a natural distaste for explanations of historical figures with whom one perhaps identifies."[16]

Today the Patton legend is so strong that we have gurus in print and on the web, even presidential candidates, recommending how his "principles of leadership" can be used to solve the world's problems, running corporations (though Patton held businessmen in disdain) or combating terrorism.[17] How many people have bought into the idea that to be a hairy-chested "he-man" is to act like the authoritarian Patton? Or that to be like Patton means to be a "winner" or a patriotic American? These myths and stereotypes will be challenged here.

Thousands of World War II veterans (and their progeny, including President Obama) state with pride, "I was with Patton," the name of a book by D. A. Lande presenting some of their stories.[18] These ordinary soldiers were among the real war heroes and deserve more of the spotlight.

We live in an age when showmanship, media hype, or outrageous behavior often pass for excellence. Will history record that Liberace was the greatest pianist that ever lived? Bobby Knight the greatest basketball coach? Donald Trump the greatest businessman? I hope that this analysis of General Patton's emotional makeup will help to clarify his standing in the pantheon of great American military leaders.

Acknowledgments

I wish to thank the staffs of the US Army Military History Institute in Carlisle Barracks, Pennsylvania; the Infantry Museum, Fort Benning, Georgia; the National Archives at College Park, Maryland; the Manuscript Division, Library of Congress, Washington, DC; and the Patton Museum, Fort Knox, Kentucky, for helpful assistance during my visits that started in 2002. Thanks to the Boston and Los Angeles Public Library research departments, and the archivists at Virginia Military Institute and the US Military Academy at West Point. I am also thankful to Colleen Allen and Jill Glover at the library in Luck, Wisconsin, for their dependable, resourceful service.

Thanks to author Dr. Edward Lengel for helpful consultations on the World War I battles and to World War II authors Martin Blumenson, Carlo D'Este, Henry G. Phillips, Belton Cooper, Leo Barron, Joe W. Wilson Jr., Brig. Gen. Albin F. Irzyk, Lewis Sorley, and Rick Atkinson for valuable communications. Thanks for encouragement and advice from Dr. John B. Shirley, Alan Tomkins, and Gen. Manton S. Eddy aides Ben Hardaway and John Wessmiller. Thanks to Dr. Sandy Hotchkiss, psychoanalyst, narcissism expert, and author for helpful discussions on this book. Thank you, Dr. Meryl Botkin, psychoanalyst and author, for clarification on separation-individuation theory. Thank you philosopher and author Aaron James for clarification on "assholeness." Thanks also to Dr. Anthony Weinhaus, director of human anatomy, University of Minnesota, and Dr. Zeke McKinney for valuable discussions on bullet trajectories and Patton's World War I wound at Cheppy, France.

I am very grateful to Lt. Col. Peter Domes and M. Sgt. Martin Heinlein, German collaborators on our Houston Film Festival first-prize-winning 2006 screenplay, *Patton's Secret Mission*. They maintain the website http://www.taskforcebaum.de and have written the definitive work on the Hammelburg raid in German (*Alarm! Die Panzerspitze Kommt!!!*)—soon to be available in English (*Task Force Baum: Behind Enemy Lines!*). I am thankful for valuable discussions with Hammelburg raid veterans Bill Nutto, W. C. Henson, Norm Hoffner, Irv Solotoff, Robert Zawada, Bob Thompson, Milt Koshiol, Tony Desanto, and the raid leader, Abe Baum. Nutto and Baum made several corrections and suggestions for improving the screenplay. I am indebted to other 4th Armored veterans Simon Kulinich, Stan Lyons, Jimmie Leach, and Harold Cohen for valuable communications and insights.

Thanks to editors Barbara Price and John Lindley, friends Jim Muir, Peter Bullock, Jere Briggs, and Cargill Hall, brother Paul Sudmeier, and cousin Steve Wangsness for encouragement and proofreading. Thank you, Karel Margry and my daughter Karen Sudmeier-Rieux, for helping to find some of the photos. Special thanks to my wife, Jilly, whose ideas, proofreading, patience, and unflagging love and support contributed greatly to the writing of this book. Any error of fact or interpretation is my sole responsibility.

• 1 •

Mexican Trophy Hunt

> You are probably wondering if my conscience hurts me for killing a man [at home in front of his family]. It does not.[1]
>
> —Patton, from letter to his wife, Beatrice, May 17, 1916

Three Dodge open touring cars come speeding across the desert, raising clouds of dust in the afternoon heat. They arrive at the field headquarters[2] of Brig. Gen. John J. "Black Jack" Pershing, the commanding officer of Fort Bliss, Texas.

NAMIQUIPA, MEXICO, MAY 14, 1916

The sentry recognizes in the lead car 2nd Lt. George S. Patton Jr., one of the general's acting aides, and he waves ahead the cars bristling with rifles and fifteen occupants. Strapped to the hood and fenders are three blood-soaked bodies punctured with bullet holes, looking for all the world like prize game trophies.[3]

Lieutenant Patton exits the convertible, enters General Pershing's tent, and salutes smartly, reporting, "I know where we can get 2,000 bushels of corn and a hundred tons of hay. We also got three Mexican bandits."

Pershing said, "What do you mean?"

Patton answered, "They're on my car if you want to see them."[4] One of the three bodies belonged to Col. Julio Cárdenas, second in command to the primary target of US troops in Mexico, the revolutionary General Francisco "Pancho" Villa. General Pershing's pleasure at the military coup must have been tempered by the grisly sight and smell of the rapidly decomposing bodies. The corpses were soon buried after a mock funeral ceremony. Lieutenant Patton was allowed to keep Cárdenas' saber, spurs, and silver-bedecked saddle.

Setting aside all conventions of war (e.g., Article 15 of the First Geneva Convention of 1864 forbidding the despoiling of the dead), why would a man treat his fallen enemies with such utter contempt? Only two years earlier, Pancho Villa, a notorious bandit with a Robin Hood reputation, had been supported by the US government, was a darling of Hollywood filmmakers and a guest of General Pershing at Fort Bliss.

When US policy changed, Villa was no longer able to purchase weapons from America for his revolution. In retaliation, Villa made the strategic error of pillaging military supplies from American border towns in 1915, resulting in the deaths of twenty or thirty American soldiers and civilians. In return, President Wilson dispatched 4,800 US troops called the "Punitive Expedi-

Gen. Pancho Villa and Gen. John J. Pershing near Fort Bliss, Texas, 1914 (one year before Patton arrived). Library of Congress.

tion" to Mexico with the express purpose of capturing or killing Pancho Villa and his troops.[5]

Thirty-year-old 2nd Lt. George S. Patton Jr., almost seven years out of West Point, was a man with a mission and a flair for publicity—determined to make a name for himself. The purpose of bringing back the bodies was not for identification—already confirmed by eyewitnesses at the gun battle—but to flaunt the successful battle and to capture headlines. "As you have probably seen in the paper, I have at last succeeded at getting into a fight," Patton wrote home exuberantly on May 14, 1916, to his wife, Beatrice. He had pestered General Pershing to be included as a special aide in Pershing's latest raid in Mexico.[6] "George S. Patton Shoots Villista Captain," blared the *Pasadena News*. "Patton the Bandit-Killer" became an instant celebrity across America. Frank Elser, a *New York Times* reporter befriended by Patton, wrote a flattering account, calling the incident "one of the prettiest fights of the campaign." Patton was quoted as saying, "Cárdenas had nerve, even if he was a Mexican."[7]

Patton's status as aide and protégé of General Pershing was now guaranteed. He was promoted to first lieutenant on May 23, 1916. Pershing too was promoted in 1916—to major general, no doubt aided by the minor victory and the ensuing publicity, despite the fact that the Punitive Expedition failed in its eleven-month campaign to eliminate Pancho Villa.

What actually happened during the fifteen-minute gun battle? As in later episodes of personal combat in World War I, Patton wrote several versions of the event, but here is the most probable chronology: Twelve days before the shootout, Patton and his men came to Cárdenas' hacienda in San Miguelito near the Villa stronghold of Rubio. Cárdenas escaped, but they found his uncle and tortured him by repeatedly hanging him up by his arms. The man fainted several times before he cooperated. Patton wrote, "The uncle was a very brave man and nearly died before he would tell me anything."

At high noon of May 14, 1916, Patton, along with ten soldiers, two civilian guides, and two chauffeurs, returned in three automobiles to Cárdenas' hacienda. Cárdenas was home that day with his wife, baby, mother, and grandparents. Knowing the layout, the Americans blocked all exits from the hacienda and entered. A fierce gun battle erupted. Three Mexican men tried to escape on horseback. Patton was credited with a pistol shot that felled the horse of Pvt. Juan Gaza, who was then killed by multiple rifle shots. Patton was also one of several who shot rifles, killing Capt. Isador Lopez. Cárdenas himself had been shot several times on horseback but took off on foot and was finally dispatched by the civilian guide, E. L. Holmdahl, an ex-Villista. Cárdenas had faked surrender and then opened fire on Holmdahl, who won the face-to-face gunfight.[8]

1915 Dodge touring car of type used in raid on Colonel Cárdenas.
West Point Museum, photo courtesy of http://www.williammaloney.com

With so many Americans shooting simultaneously, it is likely that Patton had a hand in wounding Cárdenas and wounding or killing the other two. He killed one horse but is hardly entitled to claim credit for killing all three Mexicans. In a letter to General Pershing on September 24, 1920, then Major Patton wrote the following: "I trust you will excuse the personal vanity which emboldens me to intrude this upon your valuable time. But as I am one of the few officers who has ever registered hits on a human target I am very anxious to have that fact on my record." Patton enclosed his own recounting of the "Rubio Affair." Pershing forwarded it to the adjutant general, and Patton was rewarded with a Silver Star decoration for his part in the event.[9] The Silver Star is supposed to be awarded for acts of gallantry performed with marked distinction, displaying exceptional valor while engaged in military combat operations against an enemy force.

The incident raised the question of how Patton felt about killing a man at home in the presence of his mother, wife, and baby, "even if he was a Mexican," in Patton's words. His answer came in a letter to Bea on May 17: "You are probably wondering if my conscience hurts me for killing a man. It does not. I feel about it just as I did when I got my sword fish [*sic*], surprised at my luck."[10] This remarkably unfeeling response was preceded by a letter to Bea on April 13, 1916, in which Patton expressed his contempt for the Villista Mexicans. "They are much lower than the Indians. . . . They have absolutely no morals and there have been no marriages for five years. Imagine that any woman would sell what elsewhere would be called her virtue for a peso or less and a girl could be bought for about 20 pesos."[11]

In World Wars I and II, Patton would show more respect for his Aryan-blooded German enemies than for his Mexican opponents in 1916. Yet estimates are that more than 500,000 Hispanic Americans served in uniform in World War II and, unlike African Americans, were fully integrated with other soldiers. Like other American soldiers, they fought and died, earning every decoration, including thirteen Medals of Honor.[12]

• 2 •

Charging into the Million-Dollar Wound

> I think I killed one man [American soldier] here, he would not work so I hit him over the head with a shovel.[1]
>
> —Patton, from letter to his wife, Beatrice, September 28, 1918

Lieutenant Colonel Patton had worked himself into a frenzy. Almost single-handedly over the previous year, he had built from scratch America's first and only tank force.

BOURG, FRANCE, 1918

He and his 304th Tank Brigade of some eight hundred men learned to drive, maintain, and deploy in battle several hundred of these experimental weapons of war. No officer ever worked more diligently than Patton, no matter what the task. He had to train and discipline the troops, write the manuals, and figure out who should lead the way in combat—the men or the tanks? His 6.5-ton, thirty-five-horsepower, French-made Renault FT-17 tanks were proving extremely unreliable, noisy, and uncomfortably hot. Poor visibility left the two-man crews virtually blind. Nor did the men have any way to communicate with their commanders or with each other. But they hoped that the trench-hopping, barbed wire-ripping, machine gun-deflecting tank could break the stalemate of trench and gas warfare.[2]

The end of World War I was in sight, and Patton was desperate to get into a battle where he could prove himself and win glory. He and the 304th had been in one notable day of combat—closing the salient at Saint-Mihiel, France, on September 12, 1918. That eight-mile trip from Beaumont, penetrating north through Essey and Pannes in five hours, had gone almost too smoothly against territory lightly defended by the Germans.[3]

The most significant event that day for Patton was a chance meeting with legendary fellow West Pointer (first captain and top student academically, class of 1903), Brig. Gen. Douglas MacArthur. A regimental commander of the 42nd Infantry "Rainbow" Division, MacArthur was conspicuously walking around on the front lines in Essey, nonchalantly smoking his pipe—the only soldier not ducking from the German artillery—that is, except for Lieutenant Colonel Patton, who was also smoking a pipe. As a creeping artillery barrage came toward them, each man probably wanted to leave but hated to say so. MacArthur remembered Patton flinching as one shell came over and said: "Don't worry, Major; you never hear the one that gets you."[4] Patton got permission from MacArthur to order his tanks ahead to Pannes, which he soon captured.

Patton knew that MacArthur was the youngest US soldier ever promoted to the rank of general, that he had been twice recommended for the Medal of Honor, and that he had already received the first of his seven Silver Stars for action in World War I.[5] Patton, in contrast, had taken five years (six if you count a "warm-up" year at Virginia Military Institute) to graduate from West Point, class of 1909, where he graduated 46th in his class of 103 cadets. He had no close friends—in fact was unpopular, known as a "quilloid" (a cadet who is ready to curry favor by "skinning" other cadets) and a "bootlicker."[6] While MacArthur had been leading doughboys in combat since February, Patton had gambled his entire career on a single unknown—the success of the tank.

Renault model FT-17 tank (top speed 6 mph) of type used by Patton's 304th Tank Brigade. It could cross trenches of up to about six feet. Courtesy of Jesus Dapena.

CHEPPY, FRANCE, MEUSE-ARGONNE, SEPTEMBER 26, 1918

Now, in the early morning hours of September 26, 1918, Patton would finally get his day of reckoning as America launched the battle of the Meuse-Argonne. The next six weeks would include the biggest and bloodiest battle in American history until that time. It involved 1.2 million men and resulted in 120,000 casualties, of whom 26,000 were killed. Starting in the village of Neuvilly, France, Patton's assignment was to run four companies and eighty of his Renault tanks northward on the east side of the Aire River. They were to follow the inexperienced, poorly led, and poorly trained 35th "Santa Fe" Infantry Division.[7] This force would attempt to break through enemy trench lines just north of Boureuilles, un-cracked by the French for three years, and then try advancing to the German-held villages of Varennes, Cheppy, and beyond.[8]

The 35th Division artillery barrage commenced at 2:30 a.m. More explosives were fired in the next three hours ($180 million worth in 1918 dollars) by some three thousand guns than had been expended in four years in the US Civil War.[9] The two-hundred-man artillery battery commanded by future president Capt. Harry S. Truman occupied a hilltop less than one thousand yards west of Lieutenant Colonel Patton.[10] Truman's battery alone fired over three thousand rounds from his French-made 75 mm howitzers until their barrels were red hot and Truman was "deaf as a post."[11] At 5:30 a.m., the 35th Infantry Division pushed off into a valley dense with fog, supported by an artillery barrage rolling at four hundred feet per minute ahead of them.[12] Patton's first two companies followed right behind and by 6:30 a.m., Patton himself took off. Hoping to stay in touch with HQ, he was accompanied by two communications officers, a dozen runners, some carrier pigeons, field telephones, and rolls of telephone wire. The fog was so thick that he needed to use his compass and had to follow his tankers' tracks parallel to the main road, Route 46.

At 10:00 a.m., Patton and his group reached a major intersection about five hundred yards south of Cheppy village, where he paused and sent a carrier pigeon reporting his position. When the fog lifted, the Germans opened fire with artillery and machine guns on the American troops and tanks. Patton had outrun these tanks due to their getting stuck in some old German trench works several hundred yards to his rear. He and his party found relief in an earthen cut for a narrow-gauge railway. The 35th Infantry was leaderless, disoriented from the fog and the intense bombardment, and had begun to unravel. The bombardment became so intense that Patton and scores of 35th Infantry stragglers had to retreat behind a hill some two hundred yards to the south.

The brigade's tanks were needed in order to head off a disaster, but a mixture of light and heavy tanks were mired in the trench works below and presented a tempting target for the Germans. Patton sent an officer down the slope to tell the tankers to dig their way out and get moving. Later, he sent his orderly, or "striker," Pfc. Joseph T. Angelo, but the tanks still didn't come forward. Patton was getting increasingly frustrated, and decided to go in person. When he discovered both French and American tankers sitting in the trench with their shovels, doing nothing, he blew his top. Bellowing and raging, he ordered the infantry to get up and dig them out. Enemy fire swept the area, with aerial spotters to direct their artillery and machine gun fire. Some of the diggers were hit. Patton and one of his company commanders, Capt. Math L. English, directed the work from exposed positions on the parapet to extract the tanks stuck in the muddy trench works. "To hell with them—they can't hit me," Patton shouted several times.[13] Those who did not obey immediately discovered that with Patton around it was more dangerous to stay under cover than to brave the enemy shells.[14]

As he described to his wife, Beatrice, on September 28, 1918,[15]

> I decided to do business. . . . So I went back and made some Americans hiding in the trenches dig a passage. I think I killed one man here he would not work so I hit him over the head with a shovel.[16] It was exciting for they shot at us all the time but I got mad and walked on the parapet.

As Edward Lengel phrased it, Patton "split the skull of a terrified American soldier with his shovel."[17] Could he have been exaggerating to his wife in this letter? Joking? Boasting? What soldier would commit such a brutal act against a fellow soldier—or exaggerate, or joke, or boast about it if he didn't do it? Biographers Blumenson and D'Este[18] cited the letter to Beatrice and the incident reported therein, but without comment. In writing to his wife, whom he often used as Mother Confessor, Patton may have been seeking atonement and forewarning her in case he should be court-martialed or forced to pay hush money. If he made any attempt to investigate the matter or to make amends, there is no mention of it in any biographies or letters. Because Patton was such a darling of General Pershing, because the victim might have been a member of his own tank brigade, and thus easier to cover up, and because of what happened to Patton next, there were no consequences for the vicious act. Even if the victim survived his head wounds, for an officer to attack an enlisted man was a court-martial offense. Had justice been carried out, Patton's career might have ended there.

> At last we got [Captain English's] Five tanks accross [*sic*] and I started them forward and yelled and cussed and waved my [walking] stick and said

> come on. About 150 dough boys started but when we got to the crest of the hill the fire got fierce right along the ground. We all lay down. (Letter of September 28, 1918, to Beatrice)

At this point, Patton trembled with fear until he claimed to see his ancestors looking at him from a cloud over the German lines. He became calm and said out loud, "It's time for another Patton to die."

> I could not go back so I yelled who comes with me. A lot of dough boys yelled but only six of us started. My striker, me, and 4 doughs. . . . Soon there were only three but we could see the machine guns right ahead so we yelled to keep our courage and went on. Then the third man went down. (Letter of September 28, 1918, to Beatrice)

"We are alone," Private Angelo said. (Angelo was armed with a rifle, but Patton was smoking a pipe and armed only with a cane. His pistol was holstered.) "Come on anyway," said Patton.[19]

> And I felt a blow in the leg but at first I could walk so went about 40 ft when my leg gave way. My striker . . . yelled "Oh god the colonels hit and there aint no one left." He helped me to a shell hoel [*sic*] and we lay down and the Bosch [Germans] shot over the top as fast as he could. He was very close. The tanks began getting him and in about an hour it was fairly clear. Some of my men carried me out under fire which was not at all plesant [*sic*]. Finally I got to a hospital at 3:30. I was hit at 11:15. The bullet went into the front of my left leg and came out just at the crack of my bottom about two inches to the left of my rectum. It was fired at about 50 meters so made a hole about the size of a silver dollar where it came out. (Letter of September 28, 1918, to Beatrice)

Private Angelo dragged Patton to a shell hole, sliced his pants open, stopped the bleeding, and refused to leave his side until he reached the field hospital. Patton probably spent about two hours lying in the shell hole. The village of Cheppy was secured by about 1:30 p.m.,[20] approximately the same time as Patton was evacuated. At least one of his tanks stood nearby for protection most of that time.[21] Of course, memories are distorted in the heat of battle, different soldiers had different versions, and the number of Patton's embellishments grew as he began his campaign for the coveted Distinguished Service Cross (DSC) almost immediately. The DSC is the next-to-highest award for battlefield glory, second only to the Medal of Honor.

Private Angelo's recollections in early April 1919 were quite different when he spoke to newsmen in Camden, New Jersey, with Patton present in his new Pierce-Arrow automobile.[22] Angelo said that Patton found some stragglers and "told Angelo to take about 15 riflemen and clear out the machine guns." Angelo did so but soon returned. "They have all been killed," he told Patton.

"We'll clean out the machine gun nests ourselves," Patton said. "We went about 20 yards and the colonel fell with a bullet in his thigh," said Angelo, who assisted Patton into a shell hole and bandaged his wound. According to Angelo, Patton passed out and revived two hours later.

In order to earn the DSC, Patton evidently wanted his story to contain these elements:

1. The German machine guns, said to be as many as twenty-five, were firing at extremely close range, as close as thirty yards.
2. His leadership was essential in rallying and inspiring an otherwise disjointed rabble into charging directly into the jaws of withering machine gun fire in a way that shifted the momentum of the entire battle to the American side.
3. Even after being wounded, he kept on trying to move forward.
4. After being wounded, he remained conscious and continued to direct the battle, to locate German machine gun nests for targeting by the tanks, and to transfer command to his successor.
5. The bullet entered the *front* of his body (left thigh) and exited the *back* (near the rectum), which is to say, he was *advancing*, not *retreating* from fire at the time of the wound. The latter was a possible embarrassment he had contemplated previously.[23]

Private Angelo's testimony casts doubt on item 4. I will disprove item 1 and cast doubt on item 5.

The most negative interpretation of the day's events would be that Patton's hysteria, fanaticism, and desperation for military glory had recklessly led scores of his men to slaughter, and that he had foolishly gotten himself wounded by leading a suicidal infantry charge into overwhelming machine gun fire that he had no realistic chance of stopping.[24] Patton's lying there unconscious for two hours also endangered the life of Private Angelo and others who protected him. The message Patton sent to his battalion commander, Major Brett, to take over his command didn't reach Brett until mid-afternoon, when the battle at Cheppy was essentially finished. Perhaps Patton was so troubled about having just killed a soldier with a shovel that he risked everything, including his men, to escape a court-martial.

If the machine guns were only thirty yards away, as Patton said (or in some early versions, forty or fifty yards) and not too numerous, maybe an infantry charge *could* have wiped them out. But in a letter to his father on

October 28, 1918, Patton said, "Major Brett said that there were 12 machine guns right in front of me at about 150 yards . . . while from 50 to 150 machine guns were firing at us from the flanks."[25]

HOW FAR AWAY WAS THE MACHINE GUN THAT HIT PATTON?

As reported by Major General Peter E. Traub of the 35th Infantry Division, there were ten machine gun emplacements around the village of Cheppy[26] (in essential agreement with Major Brett's statement), distributed mostly east of Buanthe Creek approximately as shown in map 2.1. They were probably standard German water-cooled Machinegewehr 8 mm guns (MG 08, a machine gun used by the Germans also in World War II), shooting four hundred to five hundred rounds per minute of eight-by-fifty-seven Mauser cartridges with a 153-grain bullet and with a muzzle velocity 2,950 feet per second, yielding an effective range of more than two thousand meters.

The intersection Patton initially reached in the fog was some five hundred yards south of Cheppy. Map 2.1 shows the author's interpretation of the location of the ten German machine gun nests and his best guess at the site of

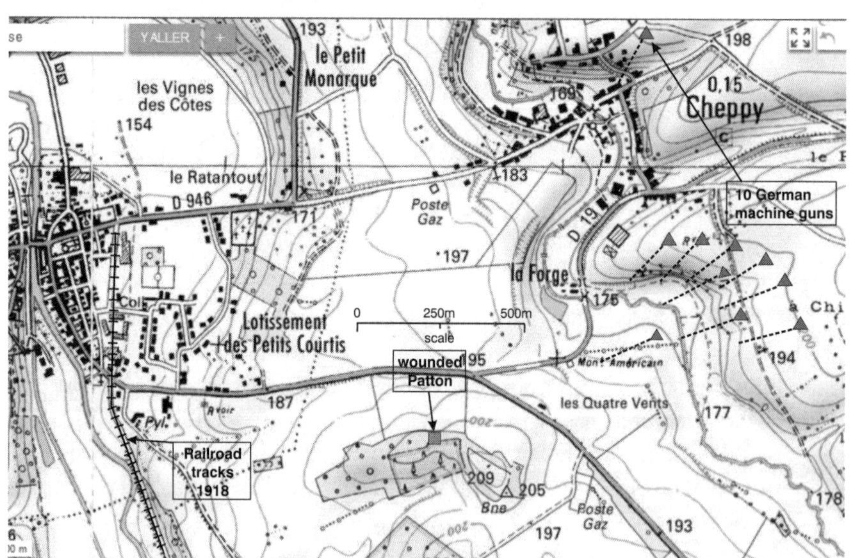

Map 2.1. Cheppy, France, World War I battlefield. Author's interpretation of Gen. Traub's description of ten German machine guns. Author's guess at location of wounded Patton. Hill 209 area was probably denuded of trees in 1918 after three years of French artillery bombardment. The main railroad ran through Varrenes, the village on left.

Patton's wounding on a shoulder of Hill 209. This hill is about two hundred yards south of the intersection and, by viewing Google Earth, the only one that could have afforded much protection from the machine guns.

The narrow-gauge railroad cut where Patton's party initially found shelter was probably close to the road intersection, unrelated to the main (presumably standard-gauge) railway through Varennes, which was more than one thousand meters away from the road intersection. As reported by D'Este, the railroad cut first occupied by Patton's party was about forty yards away from where the wounded Patton ended up.[27] Local narrow-gauge railways were used by the Germans to build and supply their underground fortifications. The intersection and Hill 209 areas no doubt were fortified, as revealed after the battle by one of Patton's officers, who told him, in Patton's words, that "during the fog, we sat on the roof of a dugout that had a battalion of Germans in it. We had only nine men. Some luck."[28]

The main conclusion to draw from map 2.1 is that the machine gun nests that shot Patton and his five men charging on foot were at least seven hundred to one thousand yards away.[29] Patton pretty well confirms this in his 1945 memoir, *War as I Knew It*, in which he states that in the Meuse-Argonne, he and his men had come under "long-range machine-gun and artillery fire."[30]

SHOT IN THE ASS?

Few people would fault Patton, who was notoriously active on the battlefield, for getting shot when his back happened to be turned to the enemy, even momentarily. It was important to Patton, however, that he was shot in the front in order to buttress his image as a warrior always on the attack. After his initial report that the exit wound was near his rectum (presumably meaning anus), later descriptions left room for doubt. A month later he wrote Beatrice, "The hole in my hip is as big as a tea cup and they have to leave it open" to be drained.[31] The use of the word "hip" is ambiguous. If the hole two inches to the left of the rectum was the size of a silver dollar, perhaps the teacup-sized hole was in the front of his left thigh—the actual exit wound. No detailed medical records of the wound survive.

At a lecture in 1942, Patton said, "I was shot in the behind in World War I. I do not want to be hit there again. I got a medal for charging the enemy, but I have had to spend a lot of time explaining how I got shot in the behind!"[32] During a press conference in September 7, 1944, Patton, discussing the Meuse-Argonne battle, stated, "I was shot there that day; I ought to remember it. I was shot in the ass. There was a good story about that, but you mustn't tell it. Some fellows said, 'That God Damn [*sic*] fellow, Patton, was shot in the ass. He must have been going to the rear.'"[33] Was this hyperbole? Was he speaking in jest? Or perhaps a moment of candor?

In any case, Patton received a promotion to colonel, one of the first among his West Point classmates to reach that rank, within three weeks of his wounding.[34] A nomination for a DSC came three days after his wounding but was rejected due to inadequate proof—a rejection that was normally final. Patton wrote to Bea, "I feel like dying. . . . It was the whole war to me."[35] But after writing letters to a number of his top brass connections and getting eleven eyewitness letters of recommendation revised and expanded, Patton had the nomination resubmitted.

Somehow, the second time it worked, and on December 16, 1918, he was awarded the DSC.[36] The citation read: "For extraordinary heroism in action near Cheppy, France, September 26, 1918. He displayed conspicuous courage, coolness, energy, and intelligence in directing the advance of his brigade down the valley of the Aire. Later he rallied a force of disorganized infantry and led it forward behind tanks under heavy machine-gun and artillery fire until he was wounded. Unable to advance farther, he continued to direct the operations of his unit until all arrangements for turning over the command were completed."

Private Angelo also earned a DSC for treating Patton's wounds under fire, staying by his side, and saving his life. Patton on November 7, 1919, was also awarded the Distinguished Service Medal (DSM),[37] the most prestigious noncombat award, for meritorious service in running the Tank School in France for ten months.

GLORY FOR OTHERS, TOO

Partly because Patton was wounded on the first day of the six-week Meuse-Argonne battle, other men in his brigade earned greater military honors than he did.

Cpl. Harold W. Roberts, a tank driver, received the Medal of Honor on October 4 when his tank fell into a shell hole filled ten feet deep with water. Knowing that only one crewmember could escape, Roberts said, "Out you go," and pushed his gunner out the back door, while he himself drowned.

Cpt. Math L. English, tank company commander, earned two DSCs—one for his actions freeing the stuck tanks with Patton on September 26, 1918, and another for combat on October 4, near Exermont, where he left his tank to make a reconnaissance and was killed.

Cpt. Harry Hodges Semmes, a patent lawyer from Washington, DC, was a tank company commander and earned two DSCs in World War I. One for actions on September 12, 1918, near Xifray, France, where he escaped from a tank submerged in water and then dove back in under heavy machine gun fire to rescue the driver. Another for his actions on September 26 near Vauquis, France, where he dismounted to shepherd his tanks through a passage and was shot in the head.[38]

Captain Semmes survived his wound, became a brigadier general in World War II, and earned an unprecedented third DSC in action on November 9, 1943. Although a southerner by birth, Semmes's experience with the segregated 92nd Division in Italy had convinced him that an integrated army was the only policy for America. "I met many brave black soldiers in that division. But overall, their performance on the battlefield was below par. They didn't trust their [white] officers. They suspected they were going to be used as cannon fodder. I saw firsthand the terrible spiritual wounds segregation inflicts." For over a year, Semmes worked with the Pentagon to develop procedures that led to the gradual integration of the US Army. He never received a word of credit for this quiet, largely unofficial job.[39]

LEGEND IN HIS MIND

As World War I came to a close on November 11, 1918, Patton had much to be thankful for. Arriving in France as a captain in June 1917, he served on Pershing's staff and was then transferred in November to the tank service. Promoted to major and then lieutenant colonel within five months through the good graces of General Pershing, he ran the Tank School in perfect comfort and safety until the tankers' first action in September 1918. After two easy days and one serious day of combat in France (September 12, 14, and 26), plus a fifteen-minute gunfight in Mexico, he had become a decorated colonel in the US Army. From Patton's fiery confidence at the start of World War II, most would never have guessed that his total life experience under fire amounted to somewhere between twenty hours and three days.

By way of comparison, General MacArthur, with his seven Silver Stars, two DSCs, and two Medal of Honor nominations, had faced at least ten days of serious combat up to and including World War I (and without any favoritism from General Pershing, who blocked one of the Medal of Honor nominations because of his personal dislike for MacArthur).[40]

In 1965, Maj. H. Norman Schwarzkopf, future mastermind of the victorious Desert Storm I and commander of seven hundred thousand international troops, started his first of two tours in Vietnam trapped in the jungle by two regiments of North Vietnamese Army. He was under mortar attack day and night for ten days, sleeping on the ground and eating the same meager rations as his South Vietnamese paratrooper advisees. In some battles, the group suffered 50 percent casualties.[41] In 1970, while rescuing a black GI bleeding out from stepping on a mine, the six-foot-three-inch, 240-pound Lieutenant Colonel Schwarzkopf went into the minefield, where he was wounded in the chest by shrapnel from another exploding mine, but succeeded in his rescue.[42] General Schwarzkopf did very little schmoozing with the Washington elite[43] and paid his dues in Pentagon staff work for six years.[44] Although his valor in Vietnam was acknowledged via a Silver Star with two Oak Leaf Clusters, a Bronze Star with two Oak Leaf Clusters, and a Purple Heart with Oak Leaf Cluster, there would be no DSC for Schwarzkopf.[45]

• 3 •

Social Climber and People User

She lay [dead] on the floor in a negligée. Pictures of General Patton were strewn about her.[1]

—*Washington Post*, January 9, 1946

To achieve his dreams of glory in the US Army, Patton knew that great wealth would be extremely useful. Taking a page from his father's book, Patton chose the quickest and easiest way to get money—he married it.

MARRY THE MONEY

He had first met Beatrice Ayer, a wealthy heiress from Boston, in 1902 when he was sixteen years old and the Ayers came on vacation to California, Patton's home state. Beatrice was well educated, a talented piano player, and an expert sailboat racer and equestrian. The marriage took place one year after Patton's graduation from West Point, over the strong reservations of Beatrice's father, Frederick. In 1919, the Ayer patent medicine and textile fortune was estimated at $19.2 million, the equivalent of about $265 million in 2015 dollars (inflation of 13.8).[2] This was in contrast to the net worth of $394,000 for Patton's father in 1927 and about $692,000 for Patton's mother, Ruth.[3] Patton had only one sibling, a sister, Anne "Nita," and Beatrice had two siblings—a brother, Frederick, a sister, Katherine—and four stepsiblings. Assuming that all siblings would survive and get equal shares of the inheritance, Beatrice's share of her inheritance would have been worth about $38 million at the time of the marriage, and Patton's share of his inheritance another $7.5 million, all expressed in 2015 dollars. Thus Patton's share of their joint wealth of $45.5 million increased his net worth nominally by about threefold from the marriage.[4]

Patton was cold and calculating about marrying rich girls, as revealed in his correspondence about a girl he almost married, Kate Fowler, a student at Vassar originally from Pasadena. Kate was an only child whose father died in 1904, leaving her $40 million. Patton was aware of the size of her fortune, and he wrote his parents, "With the money [Kate's] I could be a general in no time." A week later he wrote, "This because money seems an excellent tool, not for my own use, but to buy success and if I were unmarried I could get more things by paying attention to daughters of prominent people if necessary by marrying one of them. Now these things are not nice but they are logical."[5] Had he married Kate, his nominal wealth could have increased about seventy-fold, as Kate would have been worth about $1 billion in 2015 dollars (inflation of 26.7).[6]

However, after much soul-searching, Patton found that he was more compatible with Beatrice. She provided motherly comfort and unconditional love, and he could be completely open with her about his fears, self-doubts, and feelings of inferiority. He also revealed to her his grandiose ambitions and was pleasantly surprised that she bought into them.[7] Perhaps he also

Beatrice Ayer Patton, 1918. Patton Museum.

preferred the status of old East Coast money over new West Coast money, but he hedged the bet by staying in touch with Kate for the rest of his life.[8]

Patton's marriage to Beatrice on May 26, 1910, earned him the reputation as the richest and most ostentatious officer in the US Army,[9] able to flaunt his wealth in a dozen ways. Patton always looked great in his tailor-made uniforms and expensive leather boots, and his grooming was immaculate. He exuded confidence and was able to take big risks because of his financial security. Neither ordinary soldiers nor top brass were highly paid, and all were no doubt impressed by Patton's fancy cars, expensive yachts, polo ponies, and world travel. While Bea was back in the United States, Patton, in France during World War I, used her money to buy and ship from America a nifty five-passenger, twelve-cylinder Packard automobile worth more than $80,000 in 2015 currency.[10] He used as a trade-in the car Beatrice had bought for General Pershing when Pershing first arrived in France.[11] The sight of a captain using such a vehicle for commuting a few blocks to work must have raised some eyebrows.

In view of Beatrice's wealth, one might think that Patton would have been careful to treat her unusually well. The contrary was true. In 1935, right before Beatrice's eyes, Patton began a sexual liaison with Beatrice's half-niece, Jean Gordon, that lasted through the rest of his life. The girl was thirty years younger than Patton and had lost her father at an early age. Jean was the same age as Patton's second daughter, Ruth Ellen, and often spent school vacations with the Pattons. While Beatrice stayed in the United States during World War II, Jean was in Europe as a Red Cross donut girl with the man she called "Uncle Georgie." Fluent in French, a debutante with many social graces, she was often present at dinners when Patton entertained top brass. "She's been mine for 12 years," Patton bragged to a West Point classmate, Gen. Everett S. Hughes, on July 9, 1944.[12] If true, it would mean that it started when Jean was only seventeen years old—probably an exaggeration. Wrote Ruth Ellen, regarding her once-close friend, "She had started making a play for Georgie as far back as Bee's [little Beatrice, Patton's oldest daughter] wedding."[13] The wedding of Little Bee and John Waters, at which Jean Gordon was a bridesmaid, took place at a church near the Patton home in Massachusetts on June 27, 1934.

In late January 1945, Hughes and Patton had a late-night bull session: "Until 1:30 we discussed Brad, Ike, Courtney [Hodges], et al., and as usual agreed on their IQs. George also discussed his prowess as a cocksman. He is good—so he says."[14] After spending a long weekend starting May 16, 1945, with Jean in London, Patton told Hughes that he'd had sex with Jean four times in three days, making a total of seventy-one times.[15] Keeping score of his performance so mechanically with a lover tends to make Jean Gordon look rather ill used by her "Uncle Georgie."

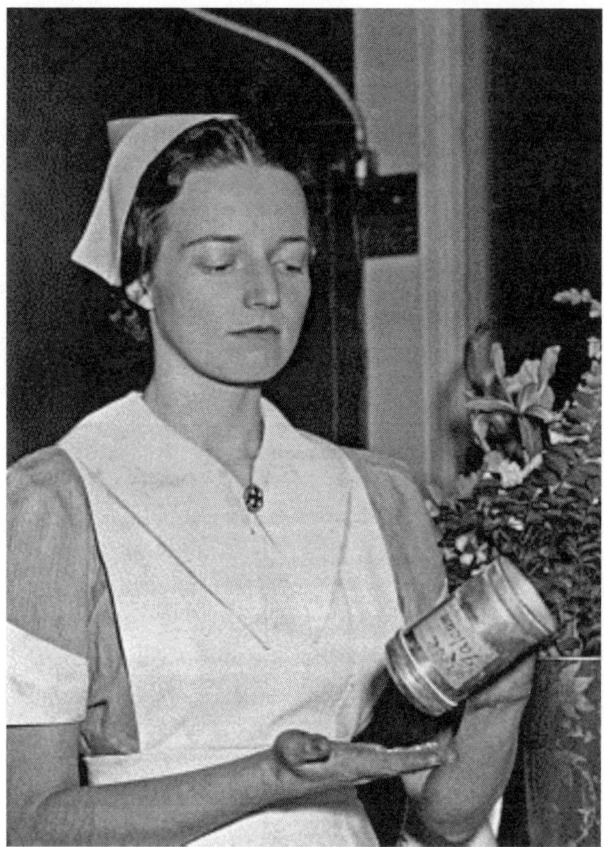

Jean Gordon, half niece of Patton's wife (1916–1946).
Bettmann via Getty Images.

The affair came out in the open in 1936 during the darkest time in Patton's life—when the Pattons were stationed in Hawaii between the world wars,[16] and he was the perfect age for a male midlife crisis. Patton was depressed and abusive to family and colleagues, moody, and drank alcohol to excess.[17] He needed a war in order to realize his destiny and saw nothing like that coming any time soon. When in 1936 Beatrice published a highly acclaimed novel, *Blood of the Shark: A Novel of Old Hawaii*, Patton sulked[18]—envious of his own wife's success.

Throughout his life, Patton used Beatrice to correct his spelling and grammar and to act as a sounding board, literary agent, press agent, and Mother Confessor. In his letters to Beatrice, he was able to brag and boast, to admit his envy and devious plans, and to be brutally honest about most things. But he was evasive in writing about Jean Gordon when Beatrice knew her to be in the European war zone. Patton denied any contact with her, but Beatrice had strong suspicions that the 1936 liaison with Jean in Hawaii was continuing in Europe.

Throughout World War I, Beatrice wanted to come to London to be closer to Patton, but he kept her at bay.[19] When a certain Frenchman accused him of having an affair with his wife,[20] the situation was serious enough that he wrote Beatrice about it, vehemently denying the accusation. He was quite controlling of her, reminding her to cover up her gray hair despite her reluctance to use hair coloring or makeup.[21] He also cautioned her not to get lazy about her weight, lest it show on her chin and tummy.[22] He once wrote, "You are always young and fat, not too fat to me, in my thoughts of you."[23] In a 1912 letter, he criticized Bea's money management, saying, "Your finances are perfectly ridiculous . . . Inspite [*sic*] of your lack of brains I love you more all the time and miss you even here where I am very busy. I love you."[24]

In the height of hypocrisy, Patton once blamed Beatrice for her wealth. Patton was recalled in late 1938 from a cavalry post he liked as commanding officer at Fort Clark, Texas, to take a comparable job at Fort Myer, Virginia—a billet he didn't want at that moment. The demands of social life in the fort adjacent to Washington, DC, were thought to require a commanding officer of independent means. Patton yelled at Beatrice, "You and your money have ruined my career." After arguing with her man who had largely built his career on affluence, horses, yachts, and social connections, Bea threw up her hands and went to bed.[25] In August 1940, as the Pattons were settling into life at Fort Benning, Georgia, Beatrice caught Patton in a sexual affair and abruptly went home to Massachusetts. Months later, Beatrice bit the bullet and returned to live with him.[26]

Patton adored money and everything it could bring, but he expected it to be handed to him on demand and in abundance—his sense of entitlement. He was not only uninterested in but also contemptuous of businessmen and the pursuit of money.[27] He looked down on his maternal grandfather Wilson for a life spent in the accumulation of wealth. He blithely ignored the fact that Wilson's money was responsible for his early life of comfort and ease, and that Ayer's money was responsible for his present luxurious lifestyle.

A few weeks after Patton's death on December 21, 1945, Beatrice paid a visit to Jean in a Boston hotel room with her brother, Frederick, present.[28] Bea's rage came bursting out as she pointed her finger at Jean and delivered the most powerful Hawaiian curse she knew from her years living there. "May the Great Worm gnaw your vitals and may your bones rot joint by little joint." Jean's face turned "from rose to pearl to gray." Frederick was shaken by the tension in the room and left the women alone. Two days later, on January 8, Jean was found dead by suicide in a friend's Manhattan apartment. All four burners on the stove were open, and the apartment was full of gas. She was lying on the floor in a negligée, surrounded by her photos of General Patton.[29]

THE ARMY'S BIGGEST BROWN-NOSER

The seduction and abuse of Beatrice and Jean were not isolated incidents. Anyone with power or resources that could be channeled to Patton's use was a target for his skillful manipulations. His charm, good looks, storytelling ability, humor, wit, flattery, and "military bearing" went very far in the US Army. In every military organization, there is a taboo against currying favor with superiors by using personal favors, known as "bootlicking" or "brown-nosing." Nor is it all right to go "over the head" of your immediate superior, breaking the chain of command. Patton openly violated these norms throughout his career, consistent with his "success at any price" approach.

Patton's first important military conquest was Brig. Gen. John J. Pershing. Already a veteran of the Spanish-American War, General "Black Jack" Pershing, West Point class of 1886 (and first captain), was handsome, dashing, and a strict disciplinarian "whose glacial stare when he was angry could instantly instill fear into even the most veteran trooper."[30] When Patton arrived at Fort Bliss in 1915, he seized on General Pershing as his hero and role model for the rest of his life. He adopted Pershing's ramrod posture, command style, strict discipline, and attention to detail. Pershing was impressed with Patton's physical fitness, his eagerness, and his horsemanship. "Pershing did not hide his fondness for Patton," writes Hirshson.[31] The two of them sometimes went horseback riding in the wilderness.[32]

Patton could not have hitched his wagon to a faster-rising star—a man who after marrying a senator's daughter in 1905 shot from captain directly to brigadier general over the heads of 862 other officers.[33] Patton's quickest routes into combat, both in Mexico and in France, were expeditions led by General Pershing. But it wasn't just Patton's military attributes that caught General Pershing's eye. He was also drawn to Patton's fetching, tall, auburn-haired sister, Nita. Pershing had been widowed in 1915 by a tragic fire that also killed his three daughters. When Nita came to visit her brother at Fort Bliss in March 1916, the mutual attraction between her and Pershing was immediate.[34]

Their affair continued after World War I, when they met in the summer of 1919 in England, where Nita had come as a Red Cross worker to be closer to Pershing. After the meeting, Pershing lost interest,[35] possibly because of his infatuation with Louise Brooks, debutante and J. P. Morgan heiress.[36] Nita never married, and Pershing never remarried (Brooks married General

MacArthur in 1922). To what extent Patton promoted the courtship with Nita, and to what extent Nita may have consciously or subconsciously tried to help her brother's career, can only be speculated upon. However, there can be little doubt that the Pershing-Nita relationship bestowed great favoritism upon Patton, got him plum assignments, and helped get him decorations, promotions, and extrication from trouble.

Patton's wealth gave him a multitude of options for ingratiating himself with his superiors. He and Beatrice traveled in high society with the Harrimans, the show business Lunts, the most powerful people in the US government, and European royalty. Despite his excessive use of profanity and other social gaffes, Patton was tolerated because of his wealth and status, gaining entrance to America's aristocracy. He cultivated Roosevelt's Secretary of War Henry Stimson by offering him unlimited use of his horses and squash court[37] and made it a point to get to know personally every army chief of staff.

Patton routinely wrote letters asking for favors, including medals, from top military brass or government officials. He sometimes offered unsolicited advice, such as his recommendation as a lowly major to General Pershing in 1923 regarding whom Pershing should appoint as the next chief of cavalry.[38] When Gen. George C. Marshall first came to Washington, DC, in 1939 to become the army chief of staff, Patton offered to share his house while Marshall's quarters were being readied. In a letter to Beatrice, Patton bragged that he had "just consumated [*sic*] a pretty snappy move. Gen. George C. Marshall is going to live at our house!!! He and I are batching it. I think that once I can get my natural charm working I won't need any letters from John J.P. [Pershing] or any one else."[39]

In 1940, Lieutenant General Marshall was about to be promoted to full, four-star general. Meanwhile, Patton fretted over his possible promotion to one-star brigadier general, for which he was certified to be eligible. Patton sent Marshall a set of eight silver stars from a jeweler in New York City. Marshall returned a note of appreciation.[40] This obsequious behavior, such as being the first to send various officers their new insignias, was repeated often during Patton's career. These congratulations were two faced because Patton was envious of everyone he considered his rival.[41] They served as a not-very-subtle reminder that, "Hey, I'm here, too. When do I get mine?"

Patton feigned blindness to his habit of seeking personal favors on April 9, 1918, when he wrote to Bea that his Tank Corps supervisor, General Rockenbach (whom Patton brown-nosed incessantly) "threatens to recomend [*sic*] me to be a [full] Colonel. I hope he waits a while or people will accuse me of using 'influence.'"[42] Of course, there is a legitimate purpose for army officers, especially generals, to build relationships built on trust and honest communication. It can provide bonds of mutual assistance which are especially valuable in wartime. Such networking is not the same as the cynical bootlicking engaged in by Patton. His need to ingratiate himself with the top military and political leaders was coldly calculated to provide him with military decorations, rapid promotions, and preferential treatment, including "Get Out of Jail" chits for future misbehavior.

During the depths of the Great Depression in 1932, life was good in the social whirl of Washington, DC, for a glamorous, handsome US Cavalry officer and his wife, such as the Pattons, even with Patton's wartime rank of colonel reduced to major. In 1932–1934, Patton and his wife were masters of the Cobbler Fox Hunt for three seasons. At the start of the third season in 1934, attended by three generals and other top brass, there was a post-hunt barbecue for 2,500 people and a tournament with thirty charging knights. At the end of the season the Pattons resigned, writing that "Beatrice and I both feel that the cost of hunting for the past three years as Masters has been more than offset by the pleasure abtained [*sic*] which no inflation or confiscation can ever take away from us."[43]

Pvt. Joe Angelo (1889–1967). National Archives.

WHAT BECAME OF PRIVATE ANGELO?

Many of the 3.5 million World War I veterans were unemployed and homeless during the Great Depression. The government paid them a bonus after the war in bonds, which could not be cashed until 1945. Considering the poor economy, however, some twenty-five thousand veterans marched peacefully on Washington, DC, in 1932 to lobby Congress for faster payment.

Among the Bonus Marchers was unemployed riveter Pvt. Joe Angelo. The previous year, the 107-pound Angelo had walked to Washington, DC, from his home in Camden, New Jersey—a home he was about to lose due to his inability to pay his property taxes. Angelo wore his uniform, decorated with four medals, including the DSC awarded to him for saving Patton's life. In his testimony before Congress, he said nobody owed him anything for his heroism—he was just doing his duty. All he wanted was a chance to work or to get an advance portion of the $1,424 coming to him for his war service. Patton had quietly sent Private Angelo a few checks over the years,[44] and Angelo had never spoken anything but praise about Patton.[45]

President Herbert Hoover's Congress would not bend to the wishes of the Bonus Marchers, who had established a tent camp across the Anacostia River in southeast Washington, DC. Congress authorized enough money for the marchers' trips back home and then adjourned for its summer recess. Some of the remaining marchers became more desperate and strident, and the movement was said to be infiltrated with communists. On July 28, a paranoid Hoover administration gave the order to disperse the marchers.[46]

Some two hundred cavalrymen, wearing helmets and gas masks, carrying carbines, and with sabers drawn, galloped into DC across the Memorial Bridge, with Major Patton near the front. As executive officer, he was not required to be present, but he couldn't resist taking part. Soon they were met on the Ellipse south of the White House by six hundred infantrymen wearing gas masks and with bayonets fixed. The marchers, armed with only rocks and bricks, were dispersed and forced back to their shantytown by soldiers using tear gas. Against White House orders, General MacArthur, on horseback and in full dress uniform, ordered the veterans' village burned to the ground. Patton was knocked down by a brick in the melee, and he whacked some of the veterans on their butts with the flat side of his saber.

The next day, a tall sergeant asked for Patton. With the sergeant was Pvt. Joseph Angelo. When Major Patton saw them, his face flushed with anger: "Sergeant, I do not know this man. Take him away, and under no circumstances permit him to return!" The sergeant led the downcast man away.[47] The *New York Times* got wind of the story, and the headline ran, "Cavalry Major Evicts Veteran Who Saved His Life in Battle." The story told how Patton "chased out of the camp Joe Angelo . . . who wears four battle decorations."[48]

Now considering himself an expert on crowd control, Major Patton wrote an article, "Federal Troops in Domestic Disturbances." In it he recommended, "Designate in advance certain sharpshooters to kill individual rioters. . . . Gas is paramount. . . . If you must fire do a good job. . . . If they resist they must be killed."[49] Patton displayed once again his rambunctious nature, need for military action, and zeal for the adrenaline high of battle, regardless of whether the quarry were Mexican soldiers, German soldiers, or unarmed American citizens.

The final chapter in the Angelo story came in June 1939. Patton received a letter from a World War I captain who had met Joe Angelo, who was struggling with a menial job and was destitute. Because of Angelo's sunny disposition and the fact that he never asked for any favors, the veteran who wrote asked if Patton could spare something for the man. Perhaps the bad publicity from the Bonus March helped induce Patton to send a check for twenty-five dollars, receiving in return a "Thank You" telegram from Angelo. Patton wrote that "due to changed conditions," that was all he could afford right now. (This was during a week that he and his daughter, Ruth Ellen, had won fourteen ribbons and a reserve championship at horse shows, rejoined the Capital Yacht Club, and had spent the previous month sailing their two-masted schooner from Massachusetts to Washington.)[50]

SCHMOOZING WITH ROYALTY

Once Patton became a general, it would be quite normal for him to socialize with presidents, prime ministers, visiting congressmen, entertainers, movie stars, and European royalty, especially in view of his own celebrity. When in London during World War II, there was nothing unusual about his dining with the Lunts at the Savoy after attending their performance or being invited by Lady Astor to lunch at Claridge's.

But even as a junior captain during World War I, his snobbishness was on full display, as he wrote to Bea on October 5, 1917, about a dance given by nurses: "I have never seen such a lot of horrors in my life . . . and they dance like tons of brick. . . . It is too much work with people out of ones [*sic*] own class who are not dressed up."[51] As Lieutenant Colonel Patton, on August 16, 1918, he wrote to Bea about a dinner dance that was being arranged in his honor: "The guests are rather assorted. One countess two barronnesses [*sic*]. Two reporters' wives of doubtful cast."[52] As Colonel Patton on November 24, 1918, about another dinner dance to which he was invited: "The ladies will not be much class being telephone operators and nurses but that is still better than nothing."[53]

On February 16, 1919, Pershing received a visit from the Prince of Wales, the future King Edward VIII, who would abdicate because of his love for the American divorcee Wallis Simpson. Patton was one of six American officers invited to a reception. The next day, Patton and another officer took His Royal Highness for lunch and a reception; after dinner, Patton danced with him to phonograph music and lost 150 francs to him in a game of craps.[54] During a trip home to Pasadena in 1919, Patton was quoted in an interview with the *Los Angeles Times* as having been an "aide" to the Prince of Wales.[55]

During World War II, Patton spent months in northwest Africa acting as an unofficial diplomat and schmoozing with various local big shots. The surrendering French Admiral Michelier and General Noguès were treated by Patton to champagne and an honor guard in Casablanca. A few days later, Patton went to General Noguès's palace to meet the grand vizier and the sultan of Morocco. Then Patton was introduced to the twelve wise men known as *pashas*. Later he had a second meeting with the sultan at which he met the fourteen-year-old prince imperial. Everybody seemed to be very impressed with everybody else, and Patton felt right at home.[56]

In a lecture on "Why Men Fight," on October 27, 1927, Patton stated that "superiority in all endeavors, particularly in war, was hereditary. A man's class would show in gentlemanly behavior, sacrifice, and leadership. The lower classes had to be schooled to instant and unquestioning obedience to authority." (A Patton colleague read a hard copy of the lecture and commented that "men fight because they see their buddies getting wounded or killed," which corresponds better to sociological research in the intervening years than Patton's lecture.)[57]

MONEY AND CONNECTIONS

When you look at the rapid career rise of General Patton, at every stage you see how little of it could have happened without money and/or personal influence:

1. *West Point.* Getting accepted into the Virginia Military Institute (VMI) and then West Point would never have happened on Patton's merits alone because he was a mediocre student with possible learning disabilities—poor at spelling and poor at math. The fact that his father was a wealthy lawyer, congressman, and former first captain of VMI made both admissions possible after a great deal of lobby-

ing. Including the repetition of his first year at West Point for failing math, it took Patton six years to complete a four-year college program. Rather than working to understand the concepts, Patton relied on memorization,[58] yet he was able to graduate in the class of 1909.[59]

2. *Transfer to Fort Myer.* After two years in the backwater of Fort Sheridan, Illinois, near Chicago, Patton and his friends somehow pulled strings to make the well-timed transfer of George, Bea, and Little Bee to Fort Myer, near Washington, DC, the seat of both power and prestige for government, military, and high society.[60] For a young officer and his wife in 1912, this was the place to be.
3. *Olympics.* The fifth modern Olympic Games in 1912 in Stockholm included these events in the first military modern pentathlon:
   a. fencing
   b. swimming three hundred meters
   c. twenty-five-meter pistol shooting
   d. four-thousand-meter running
   e. five-thousand-meter steeplechase

   Patton had fenced and run at West Point and had swum, shot, and ridden horses since he was a boy.[61] There were no US Olympic trials, and because of his connections with the brass at Fort Myer,[62] Patton was virtually the only nominee, getting three months away from army duties. Perhaps more significant in the selection of Patton was the fact that he could afford the trip to Stockholm at his own expense and, in fact, he brought most of his family. With the help of an illegal injection of performance-enhancing opium, Patton took fourth place in the run, third place in the steeplechase, and fifth place overall.[63] His fame and prestige were greatly enhanced by the press reports about his competitive spirit. His comments later about "the high spirit of sportsmanship" and the "character of the officers" at the games[64] reveal a disconnect with his own use of an illegal drug.
4. *Master of the Sword.* After a prolonged campaign that went to high levels in the War Department, Patton obtained approval for the notion that Fort Riley, Kansas, needed an instructor in swordsmanship and that the instructor should be none other than himself. Thus, he needed to go to Europe for the summer of 1913 at his own expense to study under the best swordsmanship teacher in the world. After the travel was approved, Patton took the whole family to Europe again for the summer and took five weeks of intensive study under the French fencing champion Cléry in Saumur, France. The three-month effort was very successful and resulted in Patton's receiving the prestigious title of Master of the Sword, the only one in the US

> Army. Amazingly, he achieved the honor while at the rank of second lieutenant of the cavalry.[65] Once again, a fine achievement was made possible only because of Patton's personal wealth and connections.

To be fair, the acquisition of social status and money through marriage was a common pursuit among military officers besides Patton. Generals Pershing and MacArthur are examples that come to mind. But no general officer used his status or wealth more effectively or ostentatiously than Patton.

It is strange that General Patton was an important part of an organization as huge as the US Army in World War II and still, as his superiors sometimes noted, he was basically a loner—not a team player.[66] He had many friends and admirers because of his fame and power—his ability to dispense favors and his need to receive them. He attracted hordes of sycophants.[67] Yet it is telling that throughout his life, he did not have a best buddy.

• 4 •

The Spoiledest Boy in the World

> I remember . . . thinking that I must be the happiest boy in the world.[1]
>
> —Patton, from his letter called "My Father," 1927

In 1994, Robert H. Patton, the grandson of General Patton, wrote an excellent character portrait of Patton and his definitive ancestry.[2] His book elucidates in detail the dynamics of the Patton family and the forces that molded Patton's character. The memoir of his aunt, Patton's daughter, Ruth Ellen Patton Totten, followed in 2005.[3] Chapter 8 of Robert's book, which covers Patton's boyhood, is titled "The Happiest Boy in the World." His chapter heading, however, is from the earlier quotation in a letter written by his grandfather[4] and implies no difference of opinion between Robert Patton and me. In fact, Robert Patton discusses at length General Patton's "indulgent upbringing," labeling him at times "childish," "selfish,"[5] and "narcissistic."[6] Patton's nephew, Fred Ayer, who adored his uncle, wrote that there is "not the slightest doubt that the young man was very spoiled, not only by his Aunt Annie but also by his father."[7] I will continue Robert and Ruth Ellen's practice of calling young Patton by the diminutive "Georgie" until he goes off to VMI at age seventeen.

TRIANGLE OF PAIN

It would have been difficult to invent a more dysfunctional family than the household into which Georgie was born—two sisters locked in a bitter struggle for the affection of one man, with only one of the sisters sharing his marriage bed. The man was Georgie's father, George Smith Patton II, a handsome young lawyer, valedictorian of his class and later instructor at VMI, the "West Point of the South." He was a good orator, a natty dresser, Los Angeles' district attorney, and soon to represent California in Washington, DC, as a congressman. Papa's father (Georgie's grandfather), George S. Patton, a colonel in the Confederate Army, had died a hero in battle in the Civil War, as had Papa's uncle, Col. Waller Tazewell Patton.

Mama, age 23. Ruth Wilson Patton (1861–1928). Patton Museum.

Papa, age 21. George Smith Patton II (1866–1927). VMI Archives

"Aunt Nannie." Annie Wilson (1858–1931).

Part of George II pined for a military career, but there were no major wars to fight, and he never served in the army. In reality, he was rather docile and passive, suffered from periodic illness, and drank heavily, especially in his later years. When his father was defeated in his 1916 run for the Senate, Georgie could see that Papa Patton lacked the killer instinct.[8] Georgie worshiped his father despite his weaknesses and vowed to make up for them someday.

The two sisters were Ruth and Annie Wilson, daughters of Benjamin Davis Wilson. An adventurer originally from Tennessee, he was a fur trapper, Indian fighter, successful rancher, orange grower, vintner, and one of the first mayors of Los Angeles. Wilson owned vast acreage in Southern California between what is now the UCLA campus and Riverside.[9] The famous Mount Wilson just north of Pasadena is named after him. Annie Wilson was the older and brighter of the sisters. Described as "edgy and lithe," she dominated her younger sister. Ruth, who would become Georgie's mother, was described as "inscrutable and laconic," "plumply maternal," "on the simple side,"[10] "quiet and strong,"[11] and "strong minded."[12] They were raised on a 1,300-acre ranch called Lake Vineyard in the Los Angeles suburb of San Marino near Pasadena. The estate was like an island paradise, complete with a reservoir, and full of grape vines and citrus trees. They had many servants and wanted for nothing.

The sisters were very close; Annie had written in her diary in 1877 that she never expected to meet a man perfect enough to marry, and she trusted that if she were single, Ruth would likewise remain single so they could always live together.[13] The sisters had both fallen in love with George Patton II even before he entered VMI in 1873.[14] They met him again at their father's funeral in 1878 and at various gatherings afterward. When George Patton II invited Ruth to go dancing, Annie, feeling herself to be prettier and smarter, couldn't believe it. On December 10, 1884, Patton II and Ruth were married. As the couple started off on their honeymoon in New Orleans, Annie's bags were packed. She expected to accompany the newlyweds—a hope which, of course, was dashed. That night, Annie closed the book forever on the diary she had written in every day since her childhood. She was en route to becoming a miserable, strange person and an alcoholic. She was an angry drunk, and her envious rage at Ruth sometimes burst forth in her brandy binges.[15]

The Patton and Wilson families continued living under the same roof at Lake Vineyard while Georgie was growing up. For the rest of her life, Annie, known to Georgie as "Aunt Nannie," never fully accepted the fact that George Patton II was not her husband. She acted out her pain by treating Georgie as her own son. (In 1927, as George Patton II lay dead in his open casket at the family estate, a drunken wail was heard coming from Aunt Nannie's bedroom upstairs: "Wait for me, George! Wait for me! He should have been our child! Georgie should have been ours!" After the funeral, Aunt

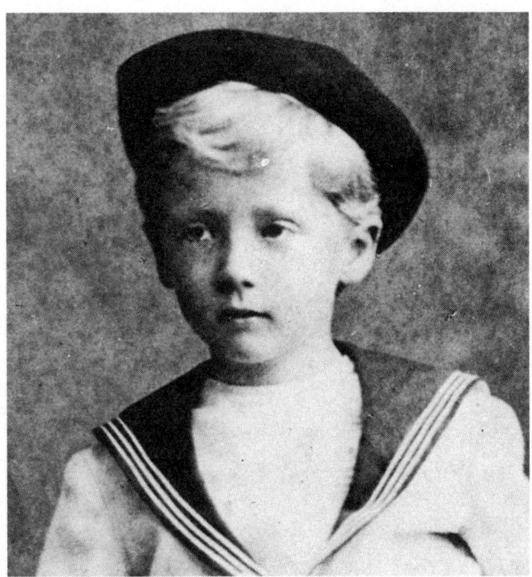

Georgie, age 7. Patton Museum.

Nannie moved out, confirming the only reason she wanted for so many years to live at Lake Vineyard.)[16]

Georgie was born a sickly child[17] on November 11, 1885. Although technically he was George Smith Patton III, he was always called George Smith Patton Jr. In the first few months, he had the croup, and his nurse, Mary Scally, fearing at one point that he would die, had him baptized a Catholic.[18] He also had measles, whooping cough, and chronic tonsillitis.[19] Everyone doted on Baby Georgie, but Aunt Nannie virtually took over his upbringing.[20] She had an almost tyrannical control over the household, partly by feigning illness whenever she didn't get her way.[21] "Nannie often monopolized Georgie's care to the exclusion of his nurse and his mother, but no one doted on him more than his father,"[22] who stayed home for many years, giving up his political ambitions just to be with his son. Whatever maternal bond or authority Ruth had with Georgie was constantly undermined by Aunt Nannie. When Patton was a cadet at VMI and later, West Point, Aunt Nannie rented quarters nearby so that she could be close to the son of the man she loved.[23]

Georgie roamed freely over the massive Lake Vineyard estate. He had a choice of a hundred ponies,[24] a wood shop, guns, and whatever else his heart desired. He had various homemade toy swords and said prophetically to himself, "George S. Patton Jr., lieutenant general."[25] Riding and swordsmanship thus became second nature to Patton at an early age. He played war games and other mischievous activities, sometimes causing damage. Once he killed a number of turkeys with a runaway wagon, for which he received the first punishment of his life—a spanking from his mother. Before the spanking, however, Ruth summoned the doctor, knowing that Aunt Nannie was going to be sick. This kind of manipulative intrusion from Nannie made the punishment so unpalatable that Ruth seldom, if ever, repeated it.[26] Georgie learned that he could get whatever he wanted by playing one of his parental triad off against the other.

A child cannot be spoiled simply by receiving too much love and attention.[27] Little Georgie got attention in abundance, with several adults doting on him constantly. But children also need rules and limits in order to grow up psychologically healthy. Children who are out of their parents' control never learn self-control.[28] In his first eleven years, Georgie got every toy, everything he ever wanted but was seldom taught any discipline or the boundaries of acceptable behavior. Having few playmates, Georgie did not engage in much of the rough-and-tumble with other children. For a child to have no limits placed on his or her behavior can bewilder the child, and parents' caving in to a child's demands teaches the child that rules don't matter.[29] With nobody to challenge his power, Georgie was able to carry into adolescence and adulthood the egocentricity that he, like all babies, learned, but that normal babies outgrow.

GEORGIE'S EDUCATION

Nor was Georgie's near-idyllic childhood ruined by the rigors of having to go to school. He stayed home until age eleven because he was thought too "delicate" by Aunt Nannie, and he was also coddled by his doting, permissive father. Such leniency is not love and can be damaging to children.[30] Instead of learning reading, writing, and arithmetic, he was read stories from classical literature, including the Bible and military history. Aunt Nannie and later Georgie's papa read to him year after year: *The Odyssey*, *The Iliad*, and the stories of Plutarch, Caesar, Alexander the Great, Frederick the Great, Napoleon, and Stonewall Jackson.[31] Aunt Nannie also introduced him to her belief in reincarnation, comforting him for the rest of his life. Whenever fear of dying crept into his consciousness, Patton saw death as nothing but a transition to the next life.

His father also filled him with glorious tales of the Pattons from the Civil and Revolutionary wars. Georgie's grandfather and great-uncle were both colonels in the Confederate Army and actually died, not on the field of battle, as Georgie fantasized, but slowly, in hospitals, from battlefield wounds. Georgie's great-uncle "Taz" was shot in the mouth during Pickett's

George Smith Patton (1833–1864).
VMI Archives.

Waller Tazewell Patton. (1835–1863).
VMI Archives.

charge at Gettysburg in July 1863, which broke facial bones on both sides of the mouth, causing death eighteen days later.[32]

During the third battle of Winchester, Virginia, on September 19, 1864, the Confederate forces were outnumbered three to one by the Union forces. Georgie's grandpa, Col. George Patton I, the brother of "Taz," lost half of his brigade, including all its officers above the rank of captain, during the rout by Gen. George Armstrong Custer. On his horse in a street in Winchester, Virginia, Col. George Patton I was hit in the hip by artillery shrapnel. He was taken to a private home in Winchester, refused amputation of his right leg, and died of gangrene six days later with no family present.[33] By experiencing the deaths of his father and uncle, Papa felt that he had lost a major part of his youth and could never forgive the Yankees.[34] Georgie identified from an early age with these heroic figures, who embodied all of Papa's dreams and aspirations. He resolved to restore the family's dreams of glory—a burden he accepted with relish and enthusiasm.[35]

As a consequence of Georgie's homeschooling, when he was at last sent off shortly before his twelfth birthday to Stephen Clark's Classical School for Boys in Pasadena, he could neither read nor write. Finally, he would be confronted with the bitter truth that his parents had shielded him from. Instead of being coddled, praised, and told how special he was, he suddenly became the object of ridicule. He stuttered through his oral readings and froze up at the blackboard, unable to write simple words and sentences. Georgie took it hard. Conditioned at home to think that he was superior and headed for military glory, he experienced the greatest trauma of his young life. "I am stupid there's no use talking I am stupid," he wrote in a letter. As put by Robert Patton, "The belief that he was 'dum' (he intentionally misspelled it when mocking himself) deeply troubled the formerly confident youth."[36] Even as his reading and writing improved markedly over the next few years, he was never able to spell very well.

Blumenson and D'Este postulated that Patton suffered from the reading disability of dyslexia.[37] Hirshson disputed that, stating that unlike dyslexics, Patton did not see letters or numbers reversed, and "once he learned to read, he read incessantly."[38] Recent research shows that "Dyslexic kids grow up to be dyslexic adults."[39] Blumenson also pointed to a possible learning disability, such as attention deficit disorder (ADD).[40] But by the time Patton entered West Point, his focus was like a laser beam. Obviously, the fact that Georgie started formal schooling so late could, by itself, have greatly impaired his literacy skills.[41] Many brilliant people over the centuries, not all dyslexics, have been poor in spelling without causing them appreciable difficulty in their lives or careers.[42]

Patton was also deficient in science and math. He got by in literature and languages by memorizing the textbooks. He excelled in history, especially military history, which he decided would be his salvation. He astonished his teachers and classmates with the detail of his knowledge in this specialty. Steeped in military history, Patton thenceforward would look to the past for answers both on the battlefield and in his life. The latter, concludes Robert Patton, did not serve him well.[43]

After the initial shock of attending school, a deep-seated sense of inferiority and being an underdog permeated Patton's character. His self-image vacillated between "stupid idiot" and "genius," with very little in between. He would become resourceful in finding ways to succeed. And he would wear a mask so real, so convincing, and so confident that the feelings of inferiority would seldom show through.[44] He used the mask in part to get rid of his giggly laugh and goofy smile, termed by Ruth Ellen as his "sissy-baby smile."[45] He spent hours in front of a mirror practicing his famous "war face,"[46] (now impersonated by Donald Trump). His high-pitched, squeaky voice would be disguised in part by the stream of profanity that he spewed forth when addressing his troops. Another important part of his manufactured macho image was frequent participation in dangerous sports and activities—reckless car driving, horse jumping, fox hunting, steeplechase, polo, transoceanic sailing, or airplane flying, which netted him far more wounds, broken bones, and concussions than all his military battles.[47]

PATTON'S RACISM, XENOPHOBIA, AND SNOBBISHNESS

"You've Got to Be Carefully Taught," goes the Rodgers and Hammerstein song about racism from the musical *South Pacific*. Children are not born racist or xenophobic. But Georgie received full instruction from his Virginia-born elitist papa about racial minorities, and never outgrew it. Papa's bigotry was based on the supposed purity of his Aryan blood. Patton often expressed anti-Semitic and antiblack views, distrusting both groups. A product of his times, he found blacks to be inferior, while he despised Jews for their success.[48]

Georgie even reviled the ancestry of his own mother, Ruth, and his beloved aunt Nannie because his grandpa Wilson was a self-made man, unlike the "aristocratic" Pattons. Papa and hence Georgie also believed that Wilson had disgraced the future Patton family by marrying a Mexican woman, his first wife, who died during childbirth at age twenty-one. Wilson's conversion to Roman Catholicism only made the situation worse. Only the Patton ancestors were glorified, even by "Aunt Nannie" Wilson.[49]

Patton's anti-Semitism was well known to many of his colleagues during his lifetime. His Jewish official biographer, Martin Blumenson, almost dropped the project when he discovered it.[50] Blumenson had been granted exclusive access to the Patton papers by the family and he struggled awkwardly to make excuses for Patton's prejudices.[51] Patton was disgusted by the animal behavior and lack of hygiene of the pitiful Jewish refugees herded into camps after the war. He said, "I have never looked at a group of people who seem to be more lacking in intelligence and spirit. Practically all of them had the flat brownish gray eye common among the Hawaiians which, to my mind, indicates very low intelligence."[52] He also looked down upon the Arabs of North Africa,[53] the Italian peasants of Sicily, and virtually all other poor people.[54] Russians he referred to as a "scurvy race and simply savages"[55] and "recently civilized Mongolian savages" with "devious Oriental minds."[56] He clearly exhibited his Anglophobia of British men,[57] mainly officers,[58] and British females he called "hideous, with fat ankles."[59] He disparaged the "decadence" of the French.[60]

In a letter to his nephew, Fred Ayer, from Sicily in 1943, Patton admitted to some prejudice:

> Sergeant George Meeks, my colored orderly, has it sized up pretty well; he said, "When you and me commanded the 5th Cavalry, them Mexicans was mighty low; then when we got to Morocco, the Arabs was worse; then when we commanded the II Corps in Tunisia, that was worse yet, but when we got back to Algeria, that was the bottom. Now here we is, commanding a Army, and these natives is lower than the bottom!" He is about right.[61]

Ruth Ellen said of her father, "People came in four colors: white, red, yellow, and black—in that order."[62] Her father never became close friends with her husband, James W. Totten, a West Pointer,[63] whom General Patton considered unsuitable because he was Catholic, an artilleryman, and too short (5 feet, 5½ inches).[64] Nor did Patton have anything good to say about politicians, and he wanted jail for any liberal Democrat.[65]

In 1937, while stationed in Hawaii, Patton wrote a paper called "Surprise," predicting, to his credit, with great accuracy the coming attack of the Japanese on Hawaii. But he felt no concern for the rights of the Japanese population of Hawaii, whom he regarded as enemy agents just waiting for orders to commit sabotage.[66] He drew up a brutal plan to arrest and intern certain persons of the "orange race" and retain them as hostages rather than prisoners. He listed them by name and address.[67] He was essentially an American WASP supremacist.

It was quite normal for Patton to refer to American blacks as "niggers." Although he said that many of his black troops in World War II were among the best he had ever seen, he wrote in his memoir in the fall of 1945 that "a colored soldier cannot think fast enough to fight in armor."[68] This must have felt like a slap in the face for his distinguished 761st Tank Battalion (TB),[69] whom he had addressed on November 2, 1944, with: "Men, you are the first Negro tankers ever to fight in the American Army. I would never have asked for you if you weren't good. I don't care what color you are, so long as you go up there and kill those Kraut sonsabitches!"[70]

Patton was not alone in being antiblack in World War II. The whole US military was organized that way, with segregated units and most blacks in noncombat roles such as truck drivers. More damaging to Patton as a military leader was his stereotypical thinking and elitism—his opinion of the men he sent into battle as an ignorant rabble. Patton's style was a throwback to the autocratic style of previous centuries and certainly to his mentor, Black Jack Pershing, for whom officers were essentially a superior race to enlisted men. Upper-class, college-educated, white-collar officers in the past had always given orders to working-class, high school-or-less-educated, blue-collar soldiers to fight and die. For Patton, West Point–trained officers were a superior race to non-West Pointers. When his unit missed out on a battle in Mexico in 1916, Patton suspected that it was because his commanding officer was overweight. From that day forward, he distrusted all fat officers.[71]

On the question of racism biographer D'Este also gives Patton a free pass with the assertion that what today he acknowledges to be Patton's blatantly racist attitudes were more acceptable in his day, plus this artful hairsplitting: "That Patton expressed anti-Semitic and antiblack views is beyond question; that he was a racist is less certain."[72] Regardless—for purposes of this book it is the clear demonstration of Patton's arrogance or haughty attitudes—snobbishness—here and in chapter 3 that will suffice.

CRUELTY TO ANIMALS

Patton's lack of empathy for less fortunate beings was also reflected in wanton acts of cruelty to animals. His well-publicized shooting of a mule that had been blocking the movement of troops over a bridge in Sicily (and dumping the mule and cart over the bridge) helped to publicize his "tough guy" image, but it had a legitimate military function.[73]

For an alleged horse lover, however, Patton dished out some serious abuse. Nephew Fred Ayer Jr. recalls that Patton "did not tolerate disobedience from horses any more than he did from subordinates." Fred's mother, Hilda, had a stubborn horse called Gun Metal that had a habit of rearing up on its hind legs. Rejecting Patton's suggestion of breaking water balloons on the horse's head to make it think it was bleeding, Hilda allowed Patton to try a second method. Jumping into the saddle, he yanked on Gun Metal's reins till the horse reared up. Then he deliberately leaned backward, causing the horse to lose balance and fall to the ground. As the horse tried to get up, Patton sat on its head for a time as the animal thrashed around, saying, "I guess that'll teach the dirty son-of-a-bitch a lesson." The horse was dangerously nervous for some time thereafter, and Hilda was outraged.[74]

In the summer of 1937, at his Green Meadows estate in Hamilton, Massachusetts, Patton, while riding his horse admittedly too close to Beatrice's horse, got kicked in the leg, suffering a compound fracture, followed by phlebitis, which led to four months in the hospital and another six months recuperating at home. The first day home from the hospital, he limped out to the stable and proceeded to beat Beatrice's horse with one of his crutches and threatened to shoot it dead. Beatrice exploded, telling him to stop acting so childishly when the accident was his own fault. Patton relented but accused Beatrice of denying him one of the few pleasures he had left, killing the horse that had ruined his career.[75]

When a neighbor asked Patton to please feed her twenty-four pet cats while on vacation, he spent the next three weeks shooting them with a BB gun. When Beatrice asked him if it bothered his conscience, he replied that it did not.[76]

• 5 •

Maternal Love Lost

> I used to kiss Papa [good night] many times and Mama only once.[1]
>
> —Patton, from his letter titled "My Father," 1927

> When Ma [Beatrice] got sick, Georgie fell to pieces.[2]
>
> —Patton's daughter, Ruth Ellen, from her book *The Button Box*

> Daddy broke her spirit.[3]
>
> —Ruth Ellen on her sister Little Bee's death from alcoholism at age forty-one, from Robert Patton's *The Pattons*

In this chapter, I emphasize the importance of the maternal bond in child development and argue that at a critical point in toddler Georgie's life, there was a rupture in this bond, which he experienced as emotional abandonment. The evidence for this is his lack of intimacy with and affection for his mother, his lack of grief at her death, his lifelong search for mother substitutes, and his own ineptitude at parenting his three children.

IMPORTANCE OF A CHILD'S FIRST THREE YEARS

When Georgie was born, Sigmund Freud was a little-known medical doctor in Vienna, and the field of psychology was in its infancy. A newborn infant, however cute, was considered a more-or-less brainless blob of protoplasm that lived in order to suckle, sleep, and excrete. Parenting was governed by a set of traditional rules: "Children should be seen and not heard" and "Spare the rod and spoil the child." The fact that some kids turned out to be successful and well-adjusted while others turned out as quarrelsome alcoholics and ne'er-do-wells was attributed to insufficient punishment and perhaps the luck of the draw. If a child was found to be a masturbator, for example (as confirmed by a "slack jaw," bad complexion, and a "certain look" in the eyes), leading texts in the early 1900s declared the child to be essentially a lost soul. The parent could make sure that a child suffering from the sin of "onanism" slept with his or her hands on top of the blankets, but except for lots of prayer, there was really nothing else that could be done for the child. For the majority of families, the goal was to have enough babies that some would survive the plagues of childhood disease, not to mention childbirth itself. Back then, there was little evidence that the *nature* and *quality* of *parenting* had much to do with the happiness, well-being, and success of the future adult.

Through the first half of the twentieth century, "experts" taught parents that babies needed to learn to sleep on a regular schedule and that picking them up and holding them whenever they cried would only teach them to cry more. Parents were told to feed their children on a schedule and not to kiss or hug them, which would leave them weaker and less prepared for a harsh world. In 1946, Dr. Benjamin Spock's best-selling book alerted parents how wrong the previous parenting rules had been and encouraged treating each child as an individual with emotional needs.[4] But what are the emotional needs of children? Around this time, child psychological development became the subject of intense laboratory investigations. "Attachment theory," regarding the quality of the mother-child bond in the first years of life, was in full flower by the late 1960s, owing to the pioneering work of the British psychoanalyst, John Bowlby, and his protégé, the American psychologist Mary Ainsworth.[5] Meanwhile, Margaret Mahler originated a parallel school of thought called "separation-individuation," focusing on four stages by which infants separate from their mothers and, normally, by thirty-six months of age become individuals.[6]

More recent research on infants only a few weeks old has demonstrated that they have more sense of self and capabilities for nonverbal communication than previously realized.[7] It is now clear that the infant receives clues at a very early age (even words and music in the womb[8]) to the all-important questions:[9] "Am I safe? Am I wanted? Will I be loved?" The answers hinge largely on the emotional availability of the principal caregiver.[10] The twentieth century ended with a strong consensus among psychologists that, with some variability due to genetics and disease, the personalities of children are mostly formed by the age of three, and a strong determinant is the nature and quality of the parenting they receive.

DEATHS OF PATTON'S PARENTS

The funerals of Patton's father, mother, and aunt Nannie reveal much about the nature of the emotional bonds between Patton and his three parental figures. In early 1927, Papa Patton's health was in decline. Major Patton traveled from Hawaii to California to be with his father during a successful operation on his tubercular kidney. His father said to him, "Son, you had more experiences and saw more of life in two years in France than I have in all my seventy years." Major Patton knew that his papa had played his life too safely, but he let him off easily, writing, "He had a romantic and venturesome spirit which had been curbed by circumstances and a sense of duty to those he loved." Yet, as Robert Patton pointed out, "It was an excuse that Georgie would have been ashamed to accept for himself."[11]

In subsequent months, Papa seemed to lose the will to live. On June 10, 1927, Patton received the news that Papa was dead. The cause of death was TB of the liver and cirrhosis from alcoholism.[12] Waiting for the ship to take him back to California, Patton wept bitterly throughout the week. He arrived too late for the funeral. The hysterical wailings of Aunt Nannie described in chapter 4 were finished, and she was moving out. Patton went alone in uniform to his father's grave and stood there weeping for an hour. Later, in Papa's office, he went through a tin strongbox containing personal treasures, many of which were from Papa's revered Civil War ancestors and his own beloved son. Patton wrote a letter titled "My Father" containing these sentences:

> I knelt and kissed the ground then put on my cap and saluted not Papa, but the last resting place of that beautiful body I had loved. . . . Oh! darling Papa. I never called you that in life as both of us were too self-contained but you were and are my darling. . . . I never did much for you and you did all for me.[13]

The death of his papa was the most traumatic event of Patton's life.[14] The health of Patton's mother, Ruth, had been failing steadily since the death of her husband the previous year. On October 6, 1928, she died of a heart attack in New Mexico on a train from California while traveling with her daughter Nita to visit the Pattons at Fort Myer, Virginia. The Pattons attended the funeral in California, but Major Patton left no record of his sorrow at his mother's death until three years later.[15]

When Aunt Nannie, a seventy-three-year-old alcoholic, died on November 26, 1931, Patton went to the funeral in California. Like Papa, Aunt Nannie had kept a shrine of letters, locks of hair, poems, and mementos of Georgie, her beloved nephew.[16] At last, Patton felt something about his mother's death and wrote her a letter that sounded more like an apology than an expression of grief or loss:

> Darling Mama . . . I never showed you in life the love I really felt nor my admiration for your courage and sporting acceptance of illness and losses. . . . Forgive me. I had always prayed to show my love by doing something famous for you, to justify what you called me when I got back from France, "My hero son." . . . Nothing you ever did to me was anything but loving. I have no other memories of you but love and devotion. . . . Your devoted son G.S. Patton Jr.[17]

Where are the tears, the grief at the loss of the maternal bond? Robert Patton referred to this as "the emotional remove between Georgie and his mother."[18] Where did Georgie learn the shame, the sense that he had to earn his mother's love by being a hero? A mother's love should be freely given to the helpless infant with no strings attached. As John Bradshaw said, "How my mothering person feels about me in these earliest years is how I will feel about myself."[19]

IMPORTANCE OF BONDING TO PRIMARY CAREGIVER

It is now known that a healthy child, like the development of the fetus, starting with the combining of egg and sperm, cell division, and many changes that mimic all of human evolution, must receive proper nurturing from parents or parent surrogates at each of a number of critical stages in order to be prepared for the next stage. Development of human language, speech, and comprehension, for example, must take place within a certain optimal window when the neurons in the brain are prepared for it (the same phenomenon that may well have contributed to Patton's struggle to learn reading and writing, having been postponed until age eleven).

A healthy infant needs to form a trusting emotional bond with a primary caregiver, or he or she could spend the rest of his or her life trying to find it.[20] Of key importance: What is the mother's state of mind, and how well was she parented? Is she secure and comfortable in her life, happily married or involved with a significant other? Was the baby planned and welcome? When the baby cries because it is cold or hungry, does she respond to its needs or feed it later on a schedule? If the baby was unplanned, how resentful or bitter is she?

Mama, age ~61, and Papa, age ~66. Ruth Wilson Patton and George Smith Patton II.

SPLITTING

When children sense fear or danger, or feel that they are not being loved and protected, that their cries or needs for attention or stimulation are going unmet, that they are not good enough or lovable enough, they perceive it as a life-threatening situation. This is because they are totally dependent upon their parents for survival. Their best strategy involves adopting a role, becoming somebody that parents can love and admire. In the first months and years, the mother-infant bond consists largely of holding and fondling. It is not enough for the parent to tell a child that he or she is loved. The child must feel it. A child needs to be mirrored by its principal caregiver and to know that its feelings and needs are its own.[21]

In past generations, babies were fed on a schedule deemed most appropriate or convenient for the parents and often weaned prematurely, lest they be "spoiled." Now it is known that when an infant screams out because it is hungry, tired, wet, in pain, and is ignored, its feeling is the opposite of being loved.[22] This is where a split may take place. Instead of growing into his or her authentic self, the unloved child becomes his or her unreal self—the one that the parents wish and expect the child to be. The gap between the real and unreal selves fluctuates at various times in one's life. The greater the gap, the greater the distress it can bring in terms of substance abuse, overeating, overworking, and disrupted relationships at home and at work.

GEORGIE'S SEARCH FOR MATERNAL LOVE

"When I went to tell Papa and Mama good night I used to kiss Papa many times and Mama only once," Georgie recalled, adding contritely, "this was childish and thoughtless."[23] Writes Robert Patton, "He'd been reacting to what appeared compared with Papa's and Nannie's demonstrativeness, to be his mother's diffidence toward him."[24]

It is almost certain that Aunt Nannie's zealous attention to baby Georgie played an important role in disrupting the intimate dance between him and his mother. When Georgie was only twenty-one months old, his sister, Anne ("Nita"), was born. Out of frustration with Aunt Nannie's meddling, Ruth turned most of her attention to Nita.[25] Little has been written about the matter (except for the speculation by Martin Blumenson, Patton's official biographer: "Perhaps the birth of his sister hurt him"[26]). It would indeed be difficult to imagine that Georgie did not experience major envy of the attention bestowed upon Nita, particularly in view of his lifelong tendency to be envious of any and all rivals.[27] Instead of trying to soothe or mitigate these normal feelings in Georgie, Ruth evidently turned elsewhere. Maternal abandonment shames the child and teaches him or her that he or she is bad.[28] As opposed to guilt ("I made a mistake"), toxic shame says, "I am a mistake."[29] This probably happened at the time when Georgie needed his principal caretaker to discipline him gently, teaching him the limits of his behavior—in other words, "healthy shame."[30]

With the supposed withdrawal of his mother's love, Georgie appears to have embarked on a lifelong search for mother substitutes. During the critical early years when he should have received unconditional love from Ruth, he settled for attention from Papa and Aunt Nannie. Later on, he would seek unconditional love from his sexual conquests, his military promotions, excess drinking, his millions of fans worldwide, and, most of all, his wife, Beatrice. He once wrote to her, "If you were not around to admire what I did, what the rest thought would make little difference to me."[31] One can become addicted to fame, adulation, ego inflation—to receiving the same kind of motherly warmth that alcoholics receive from the bottle and junkies from the needle. As Blumenson stated, "What he wanted, above all, was applause."[32]

But most of the substitute love Patton found was conditional, and the price would be steep—that he become a military hero and, ideally, die a hero's death in battle. In the early stages of his career, it had little to do with patriotism or love of America.[33] It was purely a quest for personal military glory. Whenever he was in command of troops in battle, he felt good about himself. At such times, he had literally become his unreal self—the one that he thought would make his parents proud.

A consummate actor, he invented the flamboyant, pistol-packing, foul-mouthed Cowboy General and then proceeded to inhabit that character until it ultimately became his prison. The emotional cost of playing the character, wearing the mask, was especially high for a man who was essentially an introvert and recharged his batteries by reading. In peacetime or between commands, he was a very depressed, miserable human being. At the end of World War II, General Patton seemed tired of playing the hero. He was unstable, listless—totally spent.[34] As Blumenson remarked, "Toward the end of his life, even he could barely distinguish his real self from the portrait he had deliberately faked."[35] Like other American icons who became their own caricatures and died by suicide—Elvis Presley, Marilyn Monroe, Judy Garland, Michael Jackson, Ernest Hemingway—Patton might well have succumbed to the pressure of being completely unreal if death had not come when it did.

ENVY OF HIS OWN CHILDREN

Nowhere was the fact that Beatrice had become a mother substitute more evident than in the envy Patton exhibited for the time and attention she devoted to his own children. The first child, "little Beatrice," was conceived on the Pattons' honeymoon in 1911. Patton didn't like the sight of blood, and witnessing the difficult birth of his first child caused him to vomit.[36] He wrote, "The accursed infant is very ugly . . . brownish blue . . . a hideous specimen."[37] He was immediately envious of the baby.[38] Beatrice wanted to give him a son and, reluctantly, Patton in 1915 became father to another girl, Ruth Ellen. From France during World War I, Patton objected to Bea's talking too much in her letters about the children.[39] In a few years, Beatrice lobbied again for another child. He wrote, "Your childish procilivites [*sic*] of which you boast do not interest me at all. I love you too much and am jealous or something of children."[40]

INEPTITUDE AS A FATHER

Most people act out as parents whatever treatment they themselves received as children. For parents who never got their primary needs fulfilled as children, as Alice Miller states,

> A person with this unsatisfied and unconscious (because repressed) need will nevertheless be compelled to attempt its gratification through substitute means, as long as she ignores her repressed life history. The most

> efficacious objects for substitute gratification are a parent's own children. The newborn baby or small child is completely dependent on his parents, and since their caring is essential for his existence, he does all he can to avoid losing them.[41]

Parents are supposed to let their children become whoever they are, not to live through them vicariously as a means of resolving their own frustrated needs. What if Georgie had really wanted to become an architect, teacher, or musician instead of military hero? Similarly, none of his three children was allowed to live his or her own life. This denial is a process Bradshaw calls "soul murder."[42] It reflects what was done to Georgie by Papa acting out his career disappointments and by Aunt Nannie acting out her rage at Papa for marrying Ruth instead of her.

Few men were less prepared emotionally for fatherhood than Patton, so raw was the pain of his own unfulfilled needs. "A stern and uncompromising father," wrote D'Este, "Patton found it difficult to relate to his two daughters, both of whom he perpetually resented for not having been born male."[43] Ruth Ellen was taught to swim at age four by being thrown into the ocean by her father, who theorized that all animals are born with the instinct to swim. When she went down for the third time, Patton had to dive in to save her, and ruined a new pair of white flannel trousers, which he begrudged her for years.[44]

Ruth Ellen had a rebellious nature and learned to keep her distance from her father. All the children suffered from Patton's insensitive authoritarianism and military-like domination. Ruth Ellen was whipped as a twelve-year-old by Patton for not eating[45] and slapped for doing her algebra homework too slowly.[46] At the dinner table in 1919, there was a sign on one wall that read CHEW for Ruth Ellen and a sign on another wall that read SWALLOW for Little Bee. Especially as an adolescent, Ruth Ellen disliked her father while struggling to understand him.[47] The girls were given tennis lessons by their father in a manner so dictatorial that it put them off the sport for life.[48]

Little Bee's husband, John K. Waters, was handpicked by Patton like a piece of horseflesh for her first date in 1929 because he was the "best cadet" in his class at West Point.[49] Ruth Ellen found her own husband, James Totten, at West Point but had to fight to overcome Patton's opposition because Totten was a Catholic and supposedly too short. All of Patton's children were steered into activities prized by their father—sailing, fox hunting, horsemanship, horse jumping, horse shows, and military life, with few chances at being different.

Patton's son, George Smith Patton IV, went to West Point and became a major general who distinguished himself by fighting in Korea and Vietnam. His awards include two DSCs, two Silver Stars, two Bronze Stars, a Purple Heart, and the Distinguished Flying Cross (DFC). His father's advice upon entering West Point was harsh: "We are real proud of you for the first time. See to it that we stay that way."[50] George IV, like his father, failed math at West Point, having to repeat a year. He became a superb staff officer and battlefield commander of the "obtrusive" kind like his father.[51] But from the genuine compassion he showed for his troops, he was a better leader and more humane than his father.[52] George IV exhibited great balance and wisdom[53] and was a caring father to five children.[54]

From the time George IV entered West Point onward, his father was totally immersed in World War II, and they met only twice during that period. Although he idolized his father and learned from his writings[55] and letters,[56] George IV admitted frankly that he barely knew him.[57] In Vietnam, George IV became personal friends with the man who had served in Patton's Third Army and became arguably World War II's best tanker, Gen. Creighton W. Abrams.[58] Abrams was usually photographed with a smile. His colleagues knew he was tough enough, and he didn't need to wear a "war face" like Patton. It is ironic that George IV preferred as top man on his totem pole not his father but Creighton Abrams, whose character, compassion, and leadership qualities he could study firsthand and truly emulate. Being named after and following in the same career path as an American icon undoubtedly created problems as well as opportunities for George Patton IV. In his retirement years, he suffered from Parkinsonism and died in 2004, believing that he had let his father down.

His sister, Little Bee, died from alcoholism at the tender age of forty-one. Little Bee was never comfortable around Patton, fearing to make a misstep.[59] The bottle was evidently her relief from her father's inflated expectations. "Daddy broke her spirit," was the conclusion of her sister, Ruth Ellen. "Her brother doesn't disagree," added Robert Patton.[60]

THE BIRTH OF PATTON'S UNREAL SELF

The trauma Georgie suffered by the loss of maternal love as an infant was exacerbated by his humiliation at the hands of his teachers and classmates in his early teens. Both traumas led to a common solution: splitting. You must become somebody else. You are dumb and inherently unlovable. Why not become a military hero? You can continue the family military tradition, compensate for your papa's lack of spine, save the family's dreams of glory, and anyway, who is going to mess around with the next Frederick the Great? When coupled with a firm belief in reincarnation, you have in George S. Patton Jr. a soldier who is ready to risk everything for military glory and unafraid—even eager—to die in battle.

As cogently stated by D'Este: "It is hardly surprising that by the age of perhaps seven he was hopelessly seduced into the conviction that his life and destiny lay in perpetuating the Patton family name and its even more valorous achievement."[61] Robert Patton agreed: "From the age of seven until his death, his focus never wavered."[62] Fred Ayer Jr., wrote of his uncle, "He suffered a torment caused by the constant conflict between the educated, sensitive and romantic aspects of his nature, and his own image of what he was destined to be and towards which, perforce, he drove himself. He was most mature in professional learning and experience; and yet in certain ways he never quite grew up."[63]

Robert Patton on his grandfather's arrested development:

> Georgie never stopped developing as a soldier. . . . As a person, however, he scarcely seemed to develop at all after the age of twelve, when the dream of military greatness he'd so confidently adopted received the soul-shaking jolt of insecurity about his intellect . . . like a child, he was willful and selfish, small-minded, narcissistic, and spiteful. He had to have the last word in every argument, had to be the most captivating guy at the party and the toughest guy in the locker room.[64]

• *6* •

Personality Disorders

Narcissists are very often the most charismatic person in the room, the funniest person in the room, the most [seemingly] engaged and energetic person in the room.[1]

—Jeffrey Kluger, author of *The Narcissist Next Door*

There are only two kinds of people of use to Narcissists: those who can pump them up and those whom they can put down.[2]

—Dr. Sandy Hotchkiss, author of *Why Is It Always about You?*

In this chapter, I show that personality disorders are a subclass of mental disorders, and how the *Diagnostic and Statistical Manual of Mental Disorders*, fifth edition (DSM-5) is used to differentiate among them. I argue that the DSM-5 yields a diagnosis of General Patton suffering from pathological, overt, narcissistic personality disorder (NPD). I discuss ordinary narcissism, its increased incidence in modern society, how "healthy narcissism" can be useful, and why NPD is so destructive. I mention the history and prevalence of NPD. Finally, I propose how the parenting received by Georgie may have developed into NPD, both from separation-individuation theory and, briefly, from a family dynamics perspective.

According to the DSM-5, a mental disorder is disturbed perception, feelings, or behavior that is abnormal, and causes problems in one's ability to function in one's employment or personal relationships. Mental disorders range from stuttering to schizophrenia. A mental disorder such as schizophrenia or dissociative identity disorder involves a loss of touch with reality, is typically associated with a biochemical imbalance, and often responds to treatment; otherwise, the sufferer may require institutionalization. Other mental disorders include bipolar disorder, clinical depression, obsessive-compulsive disorder, and PTSD. Dyslexia is a mental disorder categorized under specific learning disorders. General Patton as an adult was always able to read and write very capably in his career and personal life, albeit with extra effort at times, and thus any childhood reading problems do not appear to have risen to the seriousness (i.e., in terms of personal impairment) of a mental disorder.

A personality disorder is a lasting pattern of deviant (depending on the culture)[3] feelings and behavior starting in teen years or early adulthood that leads to impairment or distress. There are ten personality disorders listed in the DSM-5:

1. paranoid personality disorder (suspicion, mistrust)
2. schizoid personality disorder (apathy, emotionlessness)
3. schizotypal personality disorder (social discomfort, distorted perceptions)
4. antisocial personality disorder (violates rights of others, big ego, manipulative, impulsive)
5. borderline personality disorder (unstable self-image, relationships, self-harm, impulsive)
6. histrionic personality disorder (attention-seeking, excessively emotional)
7. narcissistic personality disorder (grandiosity, need for admiration, lack of empathy)
8. avoidant personality disorder (feels socially inadequate, oversensitive to criticism)
9. dependent personality disorder (needs caring by others)
10. obsessive-compulsive personality disorder (perfectionism, control, rigid rules)

Personality disorders do not normally require institutionalization unless the patient is suicidal, and are difficult to treat either with drugs or psychoanalysis. But in no sense should personality disorders be considered less serious or less dangerous to society than mental disorders. The names of serial killers Charles Manson, Ted Bundy, Jeffrey Dahmer, and John Wayne Gacy might come to mind when thinking of antisocial personality disorder (APD). APD shares several characteristics with NPD, including grandiosity and lack of empathy.

When talking about seriousness, note the distinction that certain mental disorders, for example, stuttering (now called "childhood-onset fluency disorder"), can make life hell for the one afflicted without greatly disrupting those around him or her. A disorder such as NPD, on the other hand, can make life hell for those who come into contact with the narcissist without greatly disrupting the well-being of the narcissist.[4]

Most mental disorders such as problem gambling are experienced as "ego dystonic"—that is, they don't seem to sufferers as part of "who they are"—rather, they seem to the sufferers like an external problem. By contrast, disorders such as anorexia nervosa or NPD are perceived by sufferers as "ego syntonic"—part of who they are and typically not perceived to be problems at all, which makes them especially difficult to treat. The NPD sufferer is like a polio victim entombed in an iron lung, unable to obtain his own oxygen. His self-esteem must be supplied from external sources—either people he idealizes or people he looks down upon.

NARCISSISM

Have you ever known a selfish egomaniac? You may also have described him as cocky, arrogant, conceited, self-centered, egocentric, overconfident, flamboyant, aloof, overbearing, imperious, pretentious, smug, snooty, stuck up, high and mighty, vain, big headed, full of himself/herself, power happy, a megalomaniac, prima donna, blowhard, braggart, dandy, showboat, or big shot. Harvard-educated philosopher Dr. Aaron James has added the term "asshole" to the repertoire.[5] The abundance of descriptors for this person suggests that he or she is not uncommon. Such a person is often labeled a "narcissist" after the Greco-Roman fable of the handsome young man, Narcissus, who fell in love with his own reflection in the water, and stared at it until his death without ever knowing the love of another person.[6]

Some of those personal descriptors by themselves are not all bad. They describe some of our most successful leaders in business, education, sports, entertainment, politics—virtually every human endeavor. We all begin our lives as children, who have been labeled "self-absorbed, egocentric, parasitic, mean-spirited narcissists."[7] This is a necessary part of child development to ensure survival of the first months of life. Prior to the age of eight, most children think they're good at everything.[8] During adolescence, a boost in narcissistic self-esteem is often a useful and normal temporary mechanism for easing the transition from childhood to adulthood.[9] Self-confident, extroverted people often work harder and exhibit more creativity than others in the workplace—for some indicative of "healthy narcissism."[10]

CULTURAL NARCISSISM

In today's society, one reason we have a high tolerance for narcissists is that we tend to glorify them.[11] In fact, America is in the midst of a narcissism epidemic, as pointed out by Twenge and Campbell.[12] Testing of college students showed a 30 percent increase in narcissism during the period from 1979 to 2006, with the slope ever increasing toward the end.[13] After making a big first impression, the narcissist usually disappoints, and his or her efforts backfire. Among the root causes of the epidemic are shown to be parenting (my kids are *special* despite their lack of accomplishments), the educational system (no child must fail), the media (Kardashian who?), social media (*like* me on Facebook), and easy credit (what's in your wallet?).

Individualism is one of America's greatest strengths. But when too many individuals think of themselves as more important than their neighbors and too smart to learn anything from professional experts, the result can be people living inside their own information bubbles, students who are unteachable, and ultimately a society that is ungovernable and a planet that is uninhabitable.

NARCISSISTIC PERSONALITY DISORDER

Twenge and Campbell primarily discuss the ordinary narcissists that we all find annoying. However, they also point out that there is a more severe form of narcissistic behavior that is toxic and destructive to everyone it touches, qualifying as NPD. Henceforth in this book I will use the terms Narcissism and Narcissist (with capital "N"s, following the lead of Sandy Hotchkiss) when describing NPD and the person suffering from it. Exceptions to this usage will be direct quotations and beginnings of sentences.

"I'm fucking smart," said Jeffrey Skilling, former Enron CEO (now in prison), when interviewed for admission to Harvard Business School, as reported by Foster and Brennan. This brash approach demonstrates Skilling's orientation to the reward of being admitted due to self-confidence without due consideration that he might be rejected due to unprofessionalism.[14] In their research, these authors found that narcissists invested more and performed better in bull market conditions, but their behavior did not correlate with bear markets. The authors write,

> Much of the blame for the recent economic collapse has been placed on risk-tolerant and overconfident corporate executives who were willing and eager to let their companies' fortunes ride on the backs of terribly risky business and investment strategies. This seems to be a fair description of Jeffrey Skilling.[15]

Hogan and Fico agree[16] that "the same characteristics that facilitate an individual's emergence as a leader can also make this person a potentially destructive leader."[17] They add that,

> Technically competent leaders who are described as arrogant, vindictive, untrustworthy, selfish, overly emotional, compulsive, overcontrolling, insensitive, abrasive, aloof, too ambitious, or unable to delegate are at risk for derailing.[18]

According to Sandy Hotchkiss,

> The narcissistic leader is typically single-minded in the pursuit of power and recognition for specialness and feels entitled to these rewards. . . . [A] subordinate can expect to be used mercilessly, criticized liberally for whatever disappoints or deflates the leader, and summarily dismissed when no longer needed. . . . The real danger is the insidious way that remaining in such a brutal situation erodes the self-worth of the exploited.[19]

NPD is defined by the DSM-5 as comprising a pervasive pattern of grandiosity (in fantasy or behavior), a constant need for admiration, and a lack of empathy, beginning by early adulthood and present in a variety of contexts, as indicated by at least five of the nine criteria listed in table 6.1.

APPLICATION OF NPD CRITERIA TO PATTON'S BEHAVIORS

In chapters 1 through 5, we have already seen examples of Patton's behavior that fit into all nine criteria for a diagnosis of NPD. In chapters 7 through 14, I will supply more examples. I believe that Patton scores a perfect nine in the NPD diagnosis (where five are sufficient). The scoring admittedly depends somewhat on how the criteria are applied to real-life situations and behaviors. To show the kinds of behaviors I have applied to each criterion, a list of examples is provided in column 2. There is room for some variability.[20] However, there are enough examples of Patton's misbehaviors in all categories to easily meet the nine criteria.

Table 6.1. *DSM-5* Criteria for Diagnosis of Clinical Narcissistic Personality Disorder

DSM-5 Criteria	*Examples*
1. A grandiose sense of self-importance (e.g., the individual exaggerates achievements and talents and expects to be recognized as superior without commensurate achievements)	Braggart; "big shot"; "the best"; "the most"; addicted to self-promoting, self-enhancing; ego self-inflating; thinks he or she is far brighter, stronger than he or she actually is; overconfidence impairs judgment; repeats stories of his or her "heroic achievements"
2. A preoccupation with fantasies of unlimited success, power, brilliance, beauty, or ideal love	Vanity; appearance is everything; spends excessively on clothes, grooming; feelings of invincibility, destiny; identifies with past heroes; believes in sixth sense, reincarnation, paranormal
3. A belief that he or she is special and unique and can only be understood by or should associate with other special or high-status people (or institutions)	Social climber; goes for prestigious labels, homes, autos, organizations, restaurants, social clubs, vacation destinations; loves schmoozing with celebrities or royalty; name dropper
4. A need for excessive admiration	"Life of the party"; center of attention; exhibitionist; creates image; turns conversation to himself/herself; addicted to headlines, fame, publicity, being on camera; sensitive to criticism; rages when accolades, money, honors, promotions not forthcoming
5. A sense of entitlement (i.e., unreasonable expectations of especially favorable treatment or automatic compliance with his or her expectations)	Exceptionalism; doesn't have to obey the same rules as others; shameless; rude; immoral and illegal behavior; insubordination; sexual infidelity; expects to be lucky; excess risk taking; never apologizes
6. Interpersonally exploitative (i.e., takes advantage of others to achieve his or her own ends)	Manipulative, brown-nosing; opportunistic; other people exist for his or her advancement; obsequious to people more powerful; likable (at first), charming, witty, flattering, sexy; often leaves a trail of wreckage
7. A lack of empathy (is unwilling to recognize or identify with the feelings and needs of others)	Humiliates, dominates others; takes credit for others' successes, blames them for his or her mistakes, so doesn't learn from past experience; friends, colleagues dropped when no longer useful; blind to how others see him or her; cruel to animals; poor parent
8. Envy of others or a belief that others are envious of him or her	Always comparing himself or herself with peers; bad mouths or is contemptuous of any rival, even his or her own children
9. A demonstration of arrogant and haughty behaviors or attitudes	Snobbishness; racism; xenophobia; flaunts rank, status, wealth, or privilege

Note: Examples in the right column are supplied by the author.

HISTORY

The British sexologist and physician Havelock Ellis first referred in 1898 to the Narcissus myth in connection with an autoerotic condition. Otto Rank helped to show that narcissism has a role in normal human development.[21] Sigmund Freud's ideas on narcissism, starting in 1914, were quite varied, including that it was in part a sexual perversion. The idea that narcissism might be a personality type emerged gradually over the next five decades.[22] Otto Kernberg in 1967 presented what he called "narcissistic personality structure," but it was Heinz Kohut who later introduced the term "narcissistic personality disorder." Kernberg and Kohut dominated the discussion of NPD for several decades and continued to develop and refine the diagnosis while differing on the causes of the disorder and the best treatments. Pathological narcissists are very satisfied with themselves, and very few are amenable to or would ever seek treatment unless they happened to be in a very depressed frame of mind.[23]

PREVALENCE

Researchers at the National Institutes of Health found that 6.2 percent of the Americans sampled had suffered from NPD at some time during their lives. This disorder tends to abate as we get older, dropping from 9.4 percent in the age twenty to twenty-nine bracket, down to 3.2 percent for those sixty-five and older.[24] The prevalence of narcissistic personality traits in the military population is shown to be much higher than in civilian populations.[25] In part this is probably because men have been proven to be more narcissistic than women.[26] Perhaps narcissists are also more likely to choose the highly structured military life because much of their outrageous behavior, such as dumping on subordinates and lack of empathy, instead of being discouraged, may actually lead to success. Any profession that offers a high degree of power and authority over many people (e.g., policeman, politician, or professor) should be highly attractive to the narcissist.

PARENTING AS A CAUSE OF NPD

There have been wide differences among psychologists as to what kind of parenting tends to produce NPD. Emotionally cold with high expectations, said Kernberg.[27] Spoiling the children with too much attention and too few boundaries, said Theodore Millon.[28] Kohut[29] and Arnold Rothstein[30] had more complex theories. The work of Lorna Otway and Vivian Vignoles indicates that a mixture of parental coldness and overindulgence is the best predictor of narcissism in adults.[31] As I have shown, Georgie's childhood combined elements of emotional abandonment, rejection, and ridicule, together with lavish attention, doting, and pampering. Thus the Otway/Vignoles theory seems to fit best, at least for General Patton.

SEPARATION-INDIVIDUATION THEORY

Margaret Mahler's research, starting around 1959, into the multistage process by which children separate from their mothers and become individuals was given full expression in her 1975 book.[32] Like a child that fails to graduate from elementary school, a child that fails to leap the hurdles of any of the stages of emotional development will be damaged goods—handicapped—and stuck in the past. The newborn baby is readily shaped by and shapes himself or herself to the environment.[33] He or she primarily wants comfort: seeking pleasure and avoiding pain.[34]

By the second or third month, the baby becomes more aware of the world outside and recognizes the principal caregiver as the special person that soothes and feeds him or her. This is the beginning of a state in which the identities of the baby and the all-powerful mommy are fused—namely, the "symbiotic" phase. The first subphase, called "differentiation," occurs from ages about four through ten months. The infant explores Mommy's face and body. He or she understands that there are additional people in the world and grasps the concept of "other" but is still fused with Mommy. It will take longer for him or her to realize that Mommy is actually one of the "other."[35] The infant discovers his or her own arms and legs, fingers and toes. During the latter part of this period, the infant is able to crawl, to climb, and to move away from its mother. This often consists of "peek-a-boo" games, crawling away, and visual checking back. It is important that Mommy keeps watch over these early explorations and makes herself available when the child returns to the "home base."[36]

The second subphase begins when the infant starts to walk, normally about ten to twelve months, lasting through about eighteen months. This phase is called "practicing" because the child is working hard to perfect the motor skills necessary for upright ambulation. It is the most glorious, exuberant time in the child's life so far, sometimes described as a "love affair with the world." The toddler feels empowered to explore the world around him or her, feeling as if he or she can almost do it alone, though the toddler's identity is still fused with the mother's, and he or she always returns to her for "refueling." Narcissism is in full bloom. As expressed by James Masterson,

> The child is able to search for toys, pick things up by himself, feel them, taste them, and bring them to adults. He is omnipotent, almost drunk with power, oblivious to his own limitations, busy and elated by his discoveries and his release from the confining world of the mother. Not even falls and bumps or other frustrations can stop him.[37]

The child loves to run away, knowing that his or her mother will sweep the child up and protect him or her from mistakes. All this is practice for greater independence down the road while still enjoying maternal security. "None of us really wanted to leave that heady state," writes Masterson of the practicing phase. "We never had it so good since. The narcissist, on the other hand, never gave it up."[38]

The third subphase, called "rapprochement," normally runs from about the eighteenth through twenty-fourth months. "The child and mother can no longer function as a symbiotic US."[39] The great egotism that facilitated the child's exploration has taken a hit. This is a time of limitations and disequilibrium for the child. He or she no longer feels omnipotent and is no longer fused with his or her mother. The child suffers separation anxiety when Mom is unavailable. Part of the child would like the comfort of being one with Mommy, but another part fears engulfment. He or she alternates between clinging to Mommy and pushing her away. Toilet training often starts during this period, causing further problems with control and autonomy. The "terrible twos" (which actually continue closer to age three)[40] are frustrating for the parents, constantly being told, "No," by the child. The inevitable result is a period of conflict and tantrums, requiring great understanding and skill by the parents in order to navigate these tricky waters so essential to the child's development.

The fourth subphase, sometimes called "consolidation of individuality," normally runs from the twenty-fourth through the thirty-sixth month.[41] At the end of this period, the child has developed an enduring image of its parents and itself—a person psychologically born, having completed its separation and individuation.[42]

"Failure to complete the separation-individuation process is what leads to a Narcissistic personality," according to Sandy Hotchkiss.[43] Masterson writes, "It appears that the narcissist suffers a developmental arrest prior to the emergence of the real self, between 18 and 36 months."[44] This is consistent with my hypothesis that Georgie's maternal bond was disrupted by the persistent interventions of Aunt Nannie, especially around the time of sister

Nita's birth at Georgie's twenty-first month of life. This caused Ruth in effect to surrender a significant part of her maternal nurturing. As stated by Robert Patton, "Ruth would not deign to compete with her husband and sister for her son's affection."[45]

THE ROLE OF PATTON'S FATHER IN PERSONALITY DEVELOPMENT

My hypothesis on the development of Patton's NPD is also consistent with the increasing role of Papa about this time. Papa had several narcissistic qualities. He was vain, snobbish, and racist, and sought admiration partly by running for public office, even if his narcissism did not rise to the level of NPD. Masterson writes the following about the role of the father in the origin of the narcissistic personality:

> When a child experiences the emotional unavailability of a mother who is particularly emotionally empty and unresponsive, he can use his experiences with the father as a corrective to rescue him from the resultant depression and the mother. The child transfers his fused, symbiotic image of the mother and himself, together with all the associated feelings and yearning, onto the father in order to deal with his abandonment depression and preserve his sense of omnipotence, which he doesn't want to lose. If the father is a narcissistic personality himself and the transfer occurs while the child still believes himself to be part of the omnipotent parents, the child's grandiose self will be preserved and reinforced through identification with the narcissistic father.[46]

FAMILY DYNAMICS

The family itself is a system that can get sick when various relationships are unhealthy. As Bradshaw has written, in dysfunctional families (like the Pattons), the father often bonds with one child (i.e., Georgie) and the mother bonds with the other (i.e., Nita). Each family member adopts a rigidly defined role in order to make a difference. The family is like a mobile that stays in balance only when each member plays his or her assigned role.[47] Likely roles are Papa as Victim and Alcoholic, Ruth as Victim and Enabler, Nita as Caretaker, Georgie as Super Hero, and Aunt Nannie as Control Freak, Alcoholic, and Martyr.

FURTHER ARRESTED DEVELOPMENT

The development of a conscience is normally well under way at least by the age of eight.[48] The healthy toddler needs to be gradually taught about limits and "healthy shame," his or her ego deflated by "a wound that must be inflicted gently"[49] and in a soothing way. Georgie's maternal abandonment seems to have happened before such limits were established. In addition, the homeschooling, with the lack of teachers and scarcity of children his own age to play with, could have enabled Georgie to bypass many of the normal mechanisms for developing a conscience.

One of the most significant events during this period was the severe "narcissistic wound" suffered as a result of Georgie's humiliation upon going off to school at age eleven, being unable to read, write, or do simple math. This traumatic experience simply increased his resolve to become a military hero and threw him deeper into the beginnings of NPD—a diagnosis not normally applied until the subject is in his or her twenties. It is interesting that Georgie did not undergo any kind of teenage rebellion, which might have saved him from his unreal self.[50] From the time he enrolled in Stephen Clark's school in Pasadena, he marched in lockstep to VMI, West Point, and a career in the US Army. Although he learned many things, traveled the world, and became an excellent soldier, he fits the criteria for having pathological, overt NPD.

Writes Sandy Hotchkiss, "The Narcissist may be intimidating, mesmerizing, even larger-than-life, but beneath the bombast or the charm is an emotional cripple with the moral development of a toddler."[51] In the remaining chapters, I will show how General Patton's conduct made him sometimes dangerous to friend as well as foe, both on and off the battlefield, and how it derives from his NPD in predictable fashion.

• 7 •

Dumping on Subordinates

> Determined and energetic, he [Patton] could also be boorish and abusive, incapable of distinguishing between the demands of a disciplinarian and the caprices of a bully.[1]
>
> —Rick Atkinson, author of *An Army at Dawn*

> He [Patton] was colorful but he was impetuous, full of temper, bluster, inclined to treat the troops and subordinates as morons. . . . He was primarily a showman. The show always seemed to come first.[2]
>
> —Gen. Omar N. Bradley

Many narcissists appear to have a "superiority complex." But under the mask lies a fragile ego that is never satisfied because it is aware that there might be someone better. "If they [Narcissists] are feeling deflated, they can reinflate themselves by diminishing, debasing, or degrading someone else."[3] In this chapter, I will give five examples of General Patton's dumping on American soldiers for ego self-inflation. The higher the reputation of the abused, the greater the potential reward for Patton. However, he was not above "skinning" the lowest buck private. When it comes to dumping on subordinates, I see some elements of most of the nine NPD criteria from the DSM-5: grandiosity, feeling invincible, need for excessive admiration, entitlement, exploitation, arrogance, sometimes envy, and most of all, lack of empathy.

Maj. Gen. Terry Allen.
US Army Signal Corps.

Maj. Gen. Orlando Ward. US Army
Center of Military History.

Maj. Gen. Ernest Harmon.
Norwich University Archives.

HUMILIATION OF TERRY ALLEN

The following incident, which happened in the Tunisian Desert in March 1943, records Patton's treatment of the popular, colorful, brash Maj. Gen. Terry de la Mesa Allen, commander of the renowned First Infantry "Big Red One" Division. Seriously wounded in the face in World War I, Allen had been a friendly rival of Patton's for many years as they debated cavalry tactics. Allen's assistant commander and sidekick, the diminutive Brig. Gen. Teddy Roosevelt Jr., was also present when Patton noticed some slit trenches near the command post. "What the hell are they for?" Patton yelled.

Allen replied they were for protection from German air attacks. (At this stage in World War II, the Allies did not possess air superiority, and German fighters and bombers were a serious, daily threat.)

"Which one is yours?" When Allen pointed it out to him, Patton walked over, unzipped his fly, and urinated into it. "There," he said. "Now try to use it."

This animalistic stunt was supposed to say, "You must be a coward, hiding from German aircraft in a slit trench. Look at me; I'm not afraid of anything." The atmosphere instantly froze. Generals Allen and Roosevelt's bodyguards were armed with Thompson submachine guns. The loud *clicks* of safeties being released on the "Tommy guns" gave Patton something to think about, and he departed without delay. This was not leadership, but precisely the kind of counterproductive behavior that made Gen. Omar Bradley despise Patton.[4]

THE DEBASING OF "PINKY" WARD

The First Armored Division ("Old Ironsides"), led by Maj. Gen. Orlando Ward, had made no progress in the previous forty-eight hours, March 23–24, 1943, against German infantry augmented by eight Tiger tanks dug into the rocky hills near Maknassy, Tunisia. In a phone call several days earlier, Patton had told Ward that getting officers killed was good for morale among the enlisted men.

> Patton: "I want you to get more officers killed."
>
> Ward: "Are you serious?"
>
> Patton: "Yes, goddammit, I'm serious. I want you to put some officers out as observers well up front and keep them there until a couple get killed."[5]

The mess Ward found himself in was primarily through the bungling of his II Corps commander, Maj. Gen. Lloyd Fredendall. The imperious and opinionated Fredendall had spent a lot of time and resources tunneling under the hills to fortify his headquarters, nicknamed "Speedy Valley," some seventy miles from the front. His orders were generally couched in a confusing code, he did not read maps carefully, and his forces had become seriously demoralized. He had summarily rejected Ward's recommendations and then blamed Ward for the fix he was in.[6] After the United States' disaster at Kasserine Pass,[7] Gen. Dwight D. Eisenhower sacked Fredendall, replacing him with Patton.

A West Pointer from Missouri, the fifty-one-year-old Ward had fought in Mexico in 1916 and in five battles in France during World War I. Thus, he had far more combat experience than Patton. The nickname "Pinky" came from his formerly red hair, now graying. He was an ambitious officer who had made a name for himself by legendary improvements in field artillery tactics.[8] His professionalism, penetrating intelligence, and decency were insufficient to impress Patton, who wrote, "No drive," and "tell him to 'get up off his ass.'"

Patton called Ward on the phone the evening of March 24:

> Pink, you got that hill yet? . . . [interrupting his reply] I don't want any goddam excuses. I want you to get out there and get that hill. You lead the attack personally. Don't come back until you've got it.[9]

Patton slammed down the phone. Shortly after midnight, two thousand infantrymen were astonished at the unprecedented sight of a major general leading an attack carrying a carbine. Ward urged his men forward, and they made it across the first two of three knolls. Ward's carbine jammed, but he kept moving forward. On the third knoll, he ran into blistering machine gun and mortar fire. Shrapnel hit near Ward's eye and nose, and blood streamed down his face. He and his men kept fighting until dawn and brought some tanks into action, but with hundreds of casualties, they finally had to give up the attack.

Gen. Omar Bradley was shocked at Ward's appearance when he arrived at the command post that morning. Ward's face was caked with blood and sulfa powder. He had purple bruises and scratches on his hands and legs, and his jacket had been creased by a red-hot machine gun bullet.[10] Patton wrote to his wife, "I think I have made a man of Ward."[11] Although Patton awarded Ward the Silver Star for bravery, within two weeks he removed him from command and sent him packing to the United States. Back in the United States, Ward distinguished himself by his training of new artillery troops, and then he returned to Europe as commander of the 20th Armored Division, which liberated Munich.

ROUGH TREATMENT FOR ERNIE HARMON

Nobody in World War II was tougher or more respected than the stocky, gravel-voiced, Maj. Gen. Ernest N. Harmon. He was a West Point–educated cavalryman from Vermont, once described as "a cobra without the snake charmer."[12] As commander of the 2nd Armored "Hell on Wheels" Division, he showed great personal courage during the invasion of North Africa in November 1942, and Patton held him in high regard. After Kasserine Pass, Harmon was appointed commander of the US 1st Armored Division.

According to Harmon, he arrived at Patton's command post at Gafsa, Tunisia, on April 5, 1943. Harmon had just survived a strafing attack by a Messerschmitt by diving into a roadside ditch while his jeep rolled down the road into a rock. Patton told him to go right away to Maknassy, forty miles east, to replace Maj. Gen. Orlando Ward. Harmon asked Patton whether he wanted him to attack or defend. "What have you come here for, asking me a lot of goddamned stupid questions?" Patton roared.

"I don't think it was stupid," answered Harmon. "I simply asked a very fundamental question, whether I am to attack or defend."

Said Patton, "Get the hell out of here and get on with what I told you to do, or I'll send you back to Morocco."

Harmon got a belated apology from Patton's chief of staff for the pointless, counterproductive abuse.[13]

THE "SLAPPING INCIDENT"

Many people have learned, if only from the movie Patton (1970), about the slapping incident in Sicily in 1943 that cost Patton his command of the Seventh Army and almost ended his career. The flagrant abuse of Patton's soldiers being treated for combat fatigue in evacuation hospitals is yet another example of how Patton inflated his ego by broadcasting to everyone, including himself, in effect, "These guys are cowards, *but I am brave*!"

Actually, there were two incidents. On August 3, Patton confronted Pvt. Charles Kuhl from the 1st Infantry Division, who had no visible wounds. Patton cursed him, slapped him with his folded gloves, pushed him out of the tent, and kicked him in the rear. Later it turned out that Kuhl was suffering from malaria and chronic diarrhea. On August 10, Patton met Pvt. Paul Bennett, an artilleryman, who was shivering on a cot. To Patton's inquiry about what was wrong, he replied, "It's my nerves, I can't stand the shelling anymore." Patton, trembling with anger, cursed Bennett, threatened him with his pistol, and slapped his face, leaving him weeping. Then he came back and hit him hard enough to knock off his helmet. Bennett, a veteran of six months of combat, had been upset and nervous about the wounding of a comrade. He resisted going to the hospital until he was ordered to go by his unit surgeon.

Patton shocked the hospital staff by telling them that these cowards were not to be treated in this hospital, leaving the staff extremely agitated. Patton bragged about the incident to Omar Bradley, saying he had "made a man" out of a soldier that day. Bradley, although realizing the seriousness of the incident, failed to report it out of loyalty to Patton, not out of any friendship. Eventually the story leaked out in the press.[14] For an officer to physically abuse a soldier is a court-martial offense.[15] Only with the help of influential friends, such as General Eisenhower and Chief of Staff General George C. Marshall, did Patton escape more severe punishment.

It is a measure of Patton's profound lack of empathy for his own combat soldiers, particularly the enlisted men, or "dogfaces," that he could not comprehend the limits of human endurance, which are well established today and were also obvious to most of his fellow officers in 1943. General Ernie Harmon wrote in his 1970 autobiography:

> It is my opinion that Patton's airy dismissal of the phenomenon [combat fatigue] as nonexistent was dead wrong. The time comes for every man when his nervous system has been taxed to its capacity, and he must rest. . . . Others, including a few men I had under my command during the war, can never return to combat at all. . . . No matter how brave he is, a man can stand only so much grief; then he breaks like a spring that has been flexed once too many times.[16]

Army psychiatrists already knew in 1943 from lessons in Tunisia that "the average soldier reached his peak effectiveness in the first 90 days of combat and was so worn out after 180 days that he was rendered useless and unable to return to military service."[17]

Today, PTSD, known in World War I as "shell shock" and in World War II as "combat fatigue" or "battle fatigue," is listed in the DSM-5 as a trauma- and stress-related disorder and is certainly not the same as "cowardice." Audie Murphy, the most decorated US combat soldier in World War II, suffered from PTSD.[18] It was even more prevalent in the Pacific, where 40 percent of evacuations in 1943 were "mental."[19] Between 11 and 20 percent of Iraq and Afghanistan veterans suffered from PTSD, according to the Department of Veterans Affairs.[20]

Patton was required by General Eisenhower to apologize to all military units under his command for the slapping, which he did. His references to his wrongdoing were oblique. Some units cheered him off the stage, not

The Thousand Yard Stare, painting by Tom Lea of infantryman in Pelelieu, 1945.
US Army Center of Military History.

allowing any contrition. Others were not so friendly. On August 27, an assembly of the fifteen thousand men of the entire 1st Infantry Division, who were still angry about the sacking of Terry Allen, received a typical twenty-minute Patton speech. He ended with the line, "Your fame shall never die," and then saluted the colors and exited. You could have heard a pin drop. "That's got to be the weirdest speech ever made by an American general," said one captain. One officer complained that Patton "used so much profanity that it wasn't clear to me what he was talking about." Another comment was, "That fucking fucker of a general swears too fucking much." An artillery sergeant said, "We despise him."[21] "These utterances of Patton's are *atrocities of the mind*," wrote Dwight MacDonald regarding the typical stump speech Patton made to his troops.[22]

Eisenhower also required Patton to apologize to all soldiers and staff who received or witnessed the abuse. After treatment for malaria, Private Kuhl was part of the force invading Omaha Beach on D-Day just eleven months later, and survived the war.[23] After Patton's apology to him, the private commented, "I think he was suffering a little battle fatigue himself." Considering the timing of the two slapping incidents, it is clear that Patton was indeed under severe stress, mostly self-imposed. He was in hot pursuit of the enemy to Messina—an all-out competition against his British rival Gen. Bernard Law Montgomery. This round was won by Patton when his troops entered Messina about two hours ahead of the Brits on August 16, 1943,[24] but the race toward Berlin would continue well into 1945. As I will show, it was basically envy and/or publicity seeking that prompted some of Patton's greatest risk-taking and consequent mistakes, sometimes causing loss of property and injury or death to scores of GIs.

The slapping incident in Sicily brought Patton's long-cultivated friendship with General Pershing to an end. The last thing Patton did before leaving for North Africa in 1942 was to pay a visit to Pershing in Walter Reed Hospital, where he knelt before Pershing to receive his blessings.[25] They exchanged letters during the North African campaign. After the slapping incident, Pershing denounced Patton and never returned his letters. This stung Patton, but as a three-star general, he had little further need for Pershing.[26] By the end of the war, in his memoir, Patton rationalized the "slapping incident" as proper and beneficial treatment for soldiers under stress. He was completely unrepentant.[27]

WHAT ABOUT PATTON'S EMPATHY IN MOURNING FOR DICK JENSON?

The death of Patton's principal aide, Capt. Richard N. Jenson, on April 1, 1943, in Tunisia due to German bombing was well publicized in the movie *Patton*. A number of officers with Jenson, including Gen. Omar Bradley, were assembled at a forward command post, when German aircraft dropped a dozen five-hundred-pound bombs on the men, who ran for cover to their slit trenches.[28] Bradley, several yards away, escaped injury, while Jenson was killed instantly due to the concussion, with hardly a scratch. When he saw Jenson's body, Patton wept inconsolably, kissed Jenson's forehead, cut a lock of his hair, and for days afterward wrote grieving letters home. It may be asked, "Is this the same Patton who showed so little empathy for the officers he belittled and the soldiers he slapped for 'cowardice'?"

1. First of all, one has to distinguish between empathy and grief. Empathy is walking in someone else's shoes, trying to imagine, "How would I feel if something like that happened to me?" Grief is suffering or distress over your own loss.
2. This loss for Patton was personal, similar to the death of his father, which caused him no end of grief. Dick Jenson was a hometown boy

from a good family in Pasadena, good looking and clean cut, a young man with no evident vices, and an officer. As a teenager, Patton had briefly dated Jenson's mother, Echo, and the Jensons and Pattons, especially Nita, remained close. Although Patton claimed not to fear death, this young man was someone he could identify with, perhaps reminding him of his own mortality.

3. Patton's tears, like his anger, were always close to the surface, needing very little to trigger either one.
4. Patton felt personally responsible for the incident. In a letter to Beatrice on March 30, he wrote, "I attatched [*sic*] Dick [Jenson] to Chauncy [Col. Chauncy Benson, leader of Task Force Benson] for the operation to get him blooded. There will probably be a big tank battle in the morning."[29] On April 1, after Jenson's death, he changed the story in a letter to Beatrice. "It was my fault in a way but this I did not tell Nita or Echo. . . . We were putting on a tank attack under Chauncy and were short staff officers so I sent Dick."[30]

The "blooding," or exposure to danger, of a young officer might be a good move for a career officer, but it is not clear whether it was Jenson's wish as well as Patton's.

MANTON EDDY, PATTON'S UNHERALDED RIGHT-HAND MAN

> In all my career I've never been talked to as Patton talked to me this morning. I may be relieved of my command.[31]
>
> —Maj. Gen. Manton S. Eddy,
> 9th Infantry Division Commander

Patton's favorite whipping boy was Manton "Matt" Eddy, a scholarly looking, burly Chicago native who, says Rick Atkinson, "was in fact energetic and imaginative."[32] General Eddy spent more time under Patton in World War II, commanded more of Patton's troops, and was mentioned by name in Patton's memoir seventy times, more often than any other subordinate.[33] Eddy earned a commission in the army as second lieutenant by graduating in 1913 as the top cadet at Shattuck School, a military academy in Faribault, Minnesota. He worked his way up through the ranks, starting as a machine gunner in World War I, where he was wounded in the leg, and after two months returned to combat as a major in command of a machine gun battalion. Between the world wars, Eddy taught strategy and tactics at Fort Leavenworth,

Generals Eddy and Patton, February 1945. Library of Congress.

and in 1942 was sent to North Africa in command of the untried 9th Infantry Division.[34]

The dressing down of Eddy by Patton quoted above occurred at El Guettar in Tunisia on the morning of March 29, 1943. What had Eddy done wrong? He had obeyed Patton's orders to attack Hill 369 at dawn with two of his three regiments, but Patton's plan was badly flawed.[35] Patton had inadequate intelligence and worse maps. He believed Hill 369 to be lightly defended, when in fact it had been turned into a well-manned fortress dug out of solid rock by the Germans and Italians. Eddy's troops ran into a "hornet's nest," and some companies took 90 percent casualties. The Americans lost 219 men and 12 officers in the first fifteen minutes.[36] Many of the rocky hills and convoluted valleys did not appear on the old, large-scale maps. One battalion got lost for thirty-six hours. Worst of all, without telling Eddy, Patton had allowed the famous Darby's Rangers to withdraw two days earlier from the highest point of land, Djebel Berda (Hill 926), conceding to the enemy the perfect artillery spotting position of the entire battlefield.[37] Instead of accepting responsibility for his blizzard of blunders, Patton found it convenient to blame the hapless Eddy.

The respected army historian Brig. Gen. S. L. A. Marshall said this about failure in one's first battle:

> The darkest hour for the novice in war comes with the recoil after the unit has been badly hit. It is then that the young commander has greatest need of the friendship and steadiness of his superior or of any other officer whose judgment he respects. Criticism or tactical counsel are of no value at that time. They can be given later if necessary, but in the wrong hour they add to the hurt.[38]

General Eddy and the 9th Infantry, like the rest of the fledgling US Army, soon gained experience and confidence, playing a vital role in defeating the Wehrmacht in North Africa and taking some 250,000 Axis prisoners. A seasoned Eddy and his 9th Infantry Division were next engaged under Patton's Seventh Army command in the successful battle for Troina, Sicily, at the time called "the toughest battle Americans have fought since World War I."[39]

NINTH DIVISION CAPTURE OF CHERBOURG

The capture of this deep-water port was the highest priority of the Normandy campaign. Following the D-Day invasion, Eddy's 9th Infantry Division was operating not under Patton, but under VII Corps Commander "Lightnin' Joe" Collins and US First Army Commander Omar Bradley. Eddy's 9th captured the port of Cherbourg on June 26, 1944, and sealed off the Cotentin peninsula right on schedule. "After the capture of Cherbourg the enemy confessed that Eddy's swift change in direction had robbed him [the enemy] of the respite he had counted upon to organize that port city's defenses."[40] General Eddy was awarded the DSC. Wrote Lt. Col. George Dyer, "The citation for this award speaks of his repeated acts of extraordinary heroism from 14 Jun to 26 Jun 44, of almost continuous presence in the forward elements of his division. His activities were exposed to enemy machine gun fire only fifty yards away, and to heavy artillery fire. This combination of audacity and expertness in the art of war contributed immensely to the fall of the well-fortified and stoutly-defended port."[41]

The now-veteran 9th Division was awarded several Distinguished Unit Citations. Ernie Pyle wrote, "The Ninth was good. In the Cherbourg campaign, it performed like a beautiful machine. . . . It kept tenaciously on the enemy's neck. When the Germans would withdraw a little the Ninth was right on top of them."[42] Thomas R. Henry, reporting for the *Saturday Evening Post*, wrote that Gen. Manton Eddy was the "most brilliant division commander" and that Eddy believed that "victories should be won by sweat and surprise, not by blood and death."[43]

EDDY AS XII CORPS COMMANDER UNDER PATTON

Shortly after his breakout from Normandy, Patton had an opening due to the illness of one of his three corps commanders. He immediately called for General Eddy to come to the Third Army and lead his XII Corps, normally consisting of two armored and three infantry divisions. This promotion, becoming the right-hand man of General Patton, would cause Eddy a lot more personal stress than just a many-fold increase in the number of troops commanded.

It didn't take long before the abuse from Patton continued. Why was Eddy such a convenient target for Patton? He was trained as an infantryman, wore glasses, and was slightly overweight—not like Patton. He was not a West Pointer like Patton, not a millionaire like Patton, and not an elite cavalryman like Patton. Eddy was emotionally grounded, well balanced, the voice of reason, and a humanitarian—not like Patton.

Patton characterized Eddy as being nervous and afraid in order to inflate his own narcissistic ego and to make himself look like the cool and courageous one. It started the first day, August 20, 1944, with Eddy as the new corps commander. The story is told here by D'Este:

> When Maj. Gen. Manton S. Eddy took command of XII Corps, his 9th Division had been slugging it out in the bocage [hedgerow country], where gains had been measured in yards. Within an hour of becoming a corps commander, he was ordered to capture the town of Sens, fifty miles away, which was off his map. When he telephoned his new boss that night, he reminded Patton that XII Corps had only four divisions, and that there were an estimated 90,000 Germans to his north and another 80,000 to his south: "How much should I worry about my [right] flank?" Patton replied that it all depended on how nervous he was. "He had been thinking a mile a day good going. I told him to go fifty and he turned pale."[44]

The first question is how Patton could have judged the color of Eddy's face over the telephone. Second, Eddy said nothing in his diary about the exchange. Who could blame Eddy, a man who had taught military tactics for four years at Fort Leavenworth and had been burned previously by a half-baked Patton plan (e.g., at El Guettar) for being skeptical?

The real answer to Eddy's legitimate question, had Patton chosen to answer him like an adult, was that Patton's new alliance with the XIX Tactical Air Command (TAC),[45] led by the renowned Brig. Gen. Otto P. Weyland, would be there in close support, protecting the Third Army's southern and rear flanks in its dash across France. Patton might have said, "Manton, your concern is legitimate, but suddenly, thanks to Ike,[46] we've virtually got our own air force to perform aerial reconnaissance and close tactical air support. We're putting air liaison officers right in our tanks to keep radio contact with the pilots. Not only that, we've cracked the German ENIGMA code, and I'm starting to receive ULTRA intercepts on a regular basis.[47] The Germans are on the run. We're going to keep after them, leaving our right and rear flanks exposed. This is a calculated risk, but we're keeping a watchful eye on it."

Despite Patton's insulting manner, it took little time for Eddy to adapt to and enjoy the American Blitzkrieg, Patton-style. The day after taking command, Eddy phoned Patton to proclaim, "General, I had a lovely drive. I'm in Sens. What's next?" Patton replied: "Hang up and keep going."[48] Omar Bradley wrote, "Eddy went 72 miles on his first day as a corps commander. The next time I saw him he grimaced, 'Hell's bells, Brad, you guys have been holding out on me—this business of running a corps is a cinch. I've been wasting my time with a division.'"[49]

The XII Corps under Eddy's leadership became the "Spearhead of the Third Army." They got out in front and stayed there for the next six weeks, reaching the Moselle River, some 250 miles east, where they outran their gasoline supplies. Eddy's XII Corps was credited with a classic double-envelopment of Nancy. Some of the war's most spectacular US tank victories took place in Lorraine, battles with names such as Arracourt and Juvelize. Here the XII Corps' vaunted 4th Armored Division, led by the dashing, popular Maj. Gen. John "P" Wood (P for the former professor of chemistry) and inspired by the cigar-chomping, baby-faced Lt. Col. Creighton Abrams, continued to beat superior German tanks by improvising a whole new playbook in tank warfare. Patton once said, "I'm supposed to be the best tank commander in the Army, but I have one peer—Abe Abrams. He's the world champion."[50]

THE NOVEMBER 8, 1944, LORRAINE OFFENSIVE

After the "October lull," during which most of the Allied forces marked time while waiting for gasoline, Patton was itching to get on the attack again. Patton's forces as shown in map 7.1 were lined up west of the Moselle River some forty miles north of Nancy behind the fortress city of Metz (Maj. Gen. Walton H. Walker's XX Corps) and east of the Moselle near Nancy (Eddy's XII Corps). Now Patton was ready to beat his archrival Montgomery by driving directly for Berlin. Monty's forces, some 250 miles north of Nancy, were already closer to the Rhine River.

Patton had promised his superiors (and his press corps[51]) an attack on November 8, 1944, and it was "high noon." Mother Nature was the only force that could have gotten in Patton's way. Eddy's XII Corps was lined up on the west side of the Seille River, normally a minor stream. However, weeks

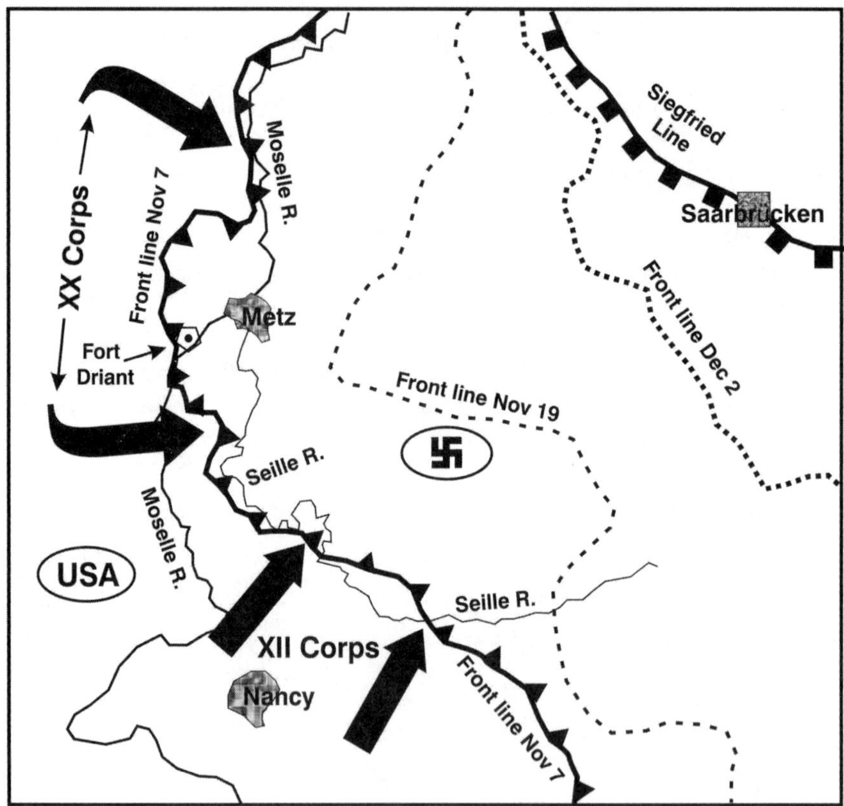

Map 7.1. Third Army's Lorraine Offensive, November 8, 1944. Adapted from Atkinson (2013), 344.

of rainy weather in Lorraine had turned the earth into a sea of mud, and the Seille River on the night of November 7 was at a one-hundred-year flood stage. With air support impossible and all rivers too wide to bridge, Generals Eddy and Grow (commander of the 6th Armored) came to see Patton in the pouring rain, seeking a twenty-four-hour postponement. Patton, who was praying and too nervous to sleep, wrote in his diary:

> At 1900, Eddy and Grow came to the house to beg me to call off the attack due to the bad weather, heavy rains, and swollen rivers. I told them the attack would go on. I am sure it will succeed.[52]

Eddy's diary confirmed this rather benign exchange, saying, "The General was very nice and said I was well justified."[53]

In his memoir written in late 1945, Patton embellished the story at Eddy and Grow's expense: "Generals Eddy and Grow came to the house and argued with me to hold off the attack. . . . I asked them whom they wished to name as their successors. . . . They immediately assented and, as usual, did great work."[54] Patton sometimes used the *name your successor* treatment as the ultimate threat on subordinates—for example, the formidable Maj. Gen. Lucian Truscott in Sicily—(more in chapter 10)—but probably not on Eddy or Grow on this occasion.

The attack went off on schedule, but the rains continued, and it bogged down into a month-long slugfest against seasoned German units, making the "Lorraine campaign" one of Patton's most dismal offensives.[55] Largely due to minefields and muddy ground, where tanks were primarily confined to the highways and thus lost all maneuverability and surprise (*the very conditions Generals Eddy and Grow had argued to forestall*), by November 18, the 4th Armored alone had suffered 1,063 battle casualties, including 202 KIA, and the loss of dozens of tanks.[56] Trench foot incapacitated more soldiers than battle wounds did.[57] To advance about fifty miles took over three months, causing the Third Army fifty thousand casualties—one-third of their total for World War II.[58] The 4th Armored commander, former artilleryman Gen. John S. "P" Wood, suffered from the battering of his beloved division, couldn't sleep, and became insubordinate. Patton regrettably had to send him home to the United States.[59] Under new leadership and improved weather, however, the 4th Armored soon sprang back to life. By December 19, the XII Corps had breached the Maginot Line and was knocking on Germany's door in the Saar Basin.

What was so damaging to General Eddy, having worked for so long directly under General Patton and his NPD, was being characterized by Patton as "slow" and "nervous." Compared to the often brash and impetuous Patton, Eddy might well have seemed cautious and tedious. Patton's oft-repeated exaggerations about Eddy "turning pale" and cowed by alleged threatened firings were picked up as fact by subsequent authors. For example:

1. The only mention of General Eddy in Stephen Ambrose's book, *Citizen Soldiers*, is as follows: "The CO of XII Corps, Maj. Gen. Manton Eddy, was scheduled to send his divisions into Metz on November 8. But the downpours . . . lack of air support . . . the mud . . . swollen rivers combined to demand postponement of the offensive. Eddy so informed Patton, who invited him to name his successor. The attack went off on schedule."[60] (Note Ambrose's lack of knowledge in stating that Eddy's attack was *into Metz*, when it was actually *from Nancy*.)
2. Russell Weigley writes that: "Late on November 7, General Eddy urged that the downpours, the mud, and the swollen rivers demanded postponement of the offensive. Patton invited him to name his successor."[61]
3. The military historian John Nelson Rickard, author of *Patton at Bay*: The Lorraine Campaign, September to December 1944, is very critical of Patton's generalship during this time, but he also finds opportunities to scapegoat General Eddy. He writes, "He could not be considered aggressive or opportunistic. Working at the pace of the infantry, he rarely understood what Patton was trying to accomplish in Lorraine."[62]

Rickard recites the worn and old tongue-lashing at El Guettar and the turned pale lines,[63] stating that "he and Patton had widely different concepts of what constituted 'speed' of operations." Incredibly, Rickard seems to blame Eddy for the high casualties during the first week of the Lorraine campaign and labels Eddy "an ill-fitted cog in the Patton fighting machine."[64]

THE REMAINDER OF EDDY'S WAR

After joining Patton, how did Eddy's reputation fall from America's "most brilliant"[65] to "stolid and humorless"?[66] Here are some highlights of his remaining career:

1. Siegfried Line (January 18–February 21, 1945). Crossing into Germany, the XII Corps met stiffening resistance. A landscape full of hidden concrete pillboxes and furrowed with deep river valleys and freezing weather made advancing here extremely tough and logistically complex. Combat engineers worked tirelessly under enemy fire to make multiple bridges across the rivers Our, Sauer, Nims, Prum, and Kyll. Patton was full of praise, writing on February 6: "General Eddy came in, brimming with confidence as to the success of his

opening attack."[67] "The XII Corps forced a crossing of the Our and Sauer Rivers. In my opinion the audacity of the operation was its chief virtue, because, to look at it, no human being could possibly have envisaged a successful crossing."[68]

2. Palatinate Campaign (March 1–21). On March 1, the ancient city of Trier fell to the Third Army. Starting with XII Corps' southward crossing of the Moselle on March 14, the reduction of the Moselle-Rhine-Saar triangle by the Third Army was considered by many the most brilliant campaign of World War II, bagging some five hundred thousand German prisoners. Eisenhower wrote, "The Germans were completely surprised when the XII Corps leaped straight southward in one of the war's most dramatic advances, to strike deeply into the heart of the Saar defenses."[69]
3. Sneak across the Rhine (March 22). While British Field Marshal Montgomery put the finishing touches on Operation PLUNDER, his typical set piece to cross the Rhine with twenty-six divisions, hundreds of bombers, and massive artillery, General Patton sneaked a division of the XII Corps across the Rhine near Oppenheim on the night of March 22 in rowboats. The next day, Patton called General Bradley to announce that his troops had crossed the Rhine.[70] Said Patton in his memoir of the first assault crossing of the Rhine since Napoleon, "The execution of this *coup* was magnificently planned by General Eddy."[71] Patton wrote, "As a matter of fact, Eddy got across 24 hours earlier than I thought he could,"[72] and further that "Eddy had selected this point [for the river crossing] many months before."[73]

EDDY RESIGNS DUE TO HYPERTENSION

No doubt aggravated by Patton's unauthorized raid on the Hammelburg POW camp, of which he disapproved (more in chapter 13), General Eddy had been feeling increasingly tired, which he tried to conceal. On April 17, he suffered an unusually severe headache and consulted a doctor, who found his blood pressure at an alarming 200/150,[74] putting him at risk of a stroke. After an array of doctors recommended treatment back in the United States, the fifty-two-year-old General Eddy reluctantly packed his bags. German resistance was fading, Hitler would be dead by suicide within ten days, and World War II would be over in three weeks. In his final efficiency report on Eddy, Patton ranked Eddy as fifth-best out of all other (eighty-nine) corps commanders he had observed.[75]

In his memoir, Patton wrote: "He [Eddy] had been a very fine Corps Commander and I hated to see him go. Also, he had been with me almost since the initial landing in Africa and had probably commanded larger units of combat troops longer than any general."[76] Thoughtlessly, Patton wrote in a letter to a friend that Eddy had "cracked up."[77] Historian Dr. Stanley P. Hirshson then falsely indexed Eddy's departure under "nervous breakdown."[78]

General Eddy had given his all in a most stressful situation. What he needed more than anything was a divorce from General Patton. After a few months' rest in the United States and some surgery, he made a complete recovery and retired as lieutenant general (three-stars) after serving in several positions, including commander in chief of the US Army in Europe (1952–1953). Being the right-hand man to a narcissist who sucks all the oxygen out of the tent invariably takes its toll. In the workplace, writes Sandy Hotchkiss, "The practice of stretching employees until they break and then getting rid of them has become so common that it even has a name: 'rubber band management.'"[79]

As Third Army commander, Patton had certain license to dream and think big. As XII Corps commander, General Eddy had to deal with reality—the nuts and bolts of making Patton's dreams into workable military operations. Therefore, Eddy played a major role in winning World War II. But due to the movie *Patton*, the life-size Patton statues at West Point, Boston, and Ettelbruck, the museums, the celebrations around the world, and the largely favorable press, the name "Patton" stands for prestige, excitement, and glamour. But serving under Patton the narcissist has relegated General Eddy to the also-rans of history, and to virtual anonymity.

Lt. Gen. Manton S. Eddy's grave at Arlington National Cemetery.

• 8 •

Patton versus Eisenhower and Everybody Else

> Whether on the playing field, the drill field, or the battlefield, Patton viewed as an adversary anyone who posed a threat to his aspirations, be he another athlete or a fellow army officer.[1]
>
> —Carlo D'Este, from his *Genius for War*

Criterion 8 of a Narcissist from the DSM-5 is envy of others or belief that others are envious of him or her. In chapter 5, I showed Patton's envy toward his children for the time and attention they received from his wife, Beatrice. In this chapter, I will show Patton's envy of and contempt for rival officers and how those feelings motivated his behavior.

THE BALLOON MODEL OF NPD

The narcissist is not always on top of the world. His or her ego fluctuates like a balloon inflating or deflating as circumstances change with time and as "narcissistic supplies" (the fuel that feeds the ego) fluctuate. See appendix A for Patton's career mood swings, 1920–1945, and why they are different from those of bipolar disorder. Inflated by hubristic pride and deflated by shame—this is the model of Tracy et al.[2] Patton's shaming during World War II was usually administered by General Eisenhower.

Inside the Narcissist, says Sandy Hotchkiss,

> [I]s a fragile internal balloon of self-esteem that is never satisfied with being good or even very good—if they are not better than, then they are worthless . . . if someone else's stock goes up, theirs automatically goes down.[3]

Patton was supremely sensitive to his status and military rank, and constantly compared himself to other officers of the same age or West Point graduating class. When he was promoted to colonel just after his wounding in World War I, he wrote to his wife, Beatrice:

> What do you think of me. I just got my colonelcy over the wire and am not yet 33. That is not so bad is it. Of course I have class mates in the engineers who are colonels but none others. So I feel quite elated.[4]

A few days later, he wrote Beatrice, "My dear classmates are reported as being very jealous of me. I don't blame them."[5]

When World War II broke out, Patton was up against a group of army officers for career advancement, some with World War I combat experience and some highly decorated, as shown in table 8.1.

Table 8.1. Patton's Rivals in World War II

Rival	*West Point?*	*World War I*	*DSC?*	*World War II Commands*
Douglas MacArthur	1903 infantry	yes	1917 1918 1945	US Army Forces, Far East; Supreme Commander, Southwest Pacific
George S. Patton Jr.	1909 cavalry	yes	1918	II Corps, Tunisia; Seventh Army, Sicily; Third Army, Europe
Courtney H. Hodges	1909* infantry	yes	1918	First Army, Europe
Jacob L. Devers	1909 artillery	no	no	Commander, European Theatre, US Army (ETOUSA)**; 6th Army Group, Europe
Dwight D. Eisenhower	1915 infantry	no	no	Commander in Chief, (AFHQ),*** Tunisia, Sicily; Supreme Commander, Allied Expeditionary Force, Europe (SHAEF)****
Omar N. Bradley	1915 infantry	no	no	II Corps, Tunisia, Sicily; First Army; 12th Army Group
Mark W. Clark	1917 infantry	yes	1943	Fifth Army, North Africa, Italy; 15th Army Group, Italy

* Failed out of West Point
** European Theater of Operations, US Army
*** Allied Force Headquarters
**** Supreme Headquarters, Allied Expeditionary Force

Some of Patton's rivals were promoted more rapidly than he was, as shown in table 8.2—fertile ground for envy. Dates in bold type indicate they outranked Patton (Patton's dates in italics).

Table 8.2. Patton's Rivals in World War II and Their Promotions

Name	*Brigadier General (Assistant Division)*	*Major General (Division)*	*Lieutenant General (Corps)*	*General (Army)*	*General of the Army (Army Group)*
Stars	*	**	***	****	*****
Douglas MacArthur	**6/28/18**	**1/1925**† 7/26/41	**7/27/41**	**12/20/41**	**12/18/45**
George S. Patton Jr.	*10/2/40*	*4/4/41*	*3/12/43*	*4/14/45*	
Courtney H. Hodges	**4/1/40**	5/1/41	**2/16/43**	4/15/45	
Jacob L. Devers	**5/1/40**	**10/1/40**	**9/6/42**	**3/8/45**	
Dwight D. Eisenhower	9/29/41	3/27/42	**7/7/42**	**2/11/43**	**12/20/45**
Omar N. Bradley	2/20/41	2/15/42	6/2/43	**3/12/45**	
Mark W. Clark	8/4/41	4/17/42	**11/11/42**	**3/10/45**	

† Retired from US Army December 31, 1937, and reenlisted as major general, July 26, 1941

Note: Dates of Patton's promotions from MB2, 863 and 864. MacArthur's promotions from Perret, 1996. Other promotions from *Official Army Register* (1946). Most of these ranks during World War II were temporary. The number of stars on the general officer's insignia is shown by asterisks as part of the top row, plus the size of unit (in parentheses) a person of that rank would normally command if promotions were always timely. The brigadier general in earlier years would have commanded a large part of a division called a "brigade," but in World War II he acted as "assistant division commander." A World War II infantry division contained about fifteen thousand men. A corps typically contained from three to six divisions. An army typically contained three corps. An army group typically contained three armies.

Every officer in this table ranked high in Army Chief of Staff General George C. Marshall's opinion. Devers had extra strong support from Marshall and was on the fast track, promoted over 474 other colonels to become the army's youngest serving brigadier general at age fifty-two. Clark was a protégé of General Eisenhower and had a meteoric rise as World War II approached, jumping two grades directly from lieutenant colonel to brigadier general. Note that on April 4, 1941, before World War II, Patton outranked everybody but his West Point classmate Devers. By March 12, 1943, near the end of the Tunisian battle, everybody except Bradley outranked Patton. By April 14, 1945, near the end of World War II, everybody except Hodges outranked Patton.

What really exasperated Patton was the fact that rising stars Eisenhower, Bradley, and Clark from the West Point classes of 1915 and 1917 were five to ten years younger than him. For example, when Lieutenant General Eisenhower became Major General Patton's superior in 1942, Patton could well remember the time in September 1940 when Lieutenant Colonel Eisenhower was asking Colonel Patton for a job in his new 2nd Armored Division.[6]

PATTON DISPARAGING MARK CLARK

Mark Clark was half Jewish, taller (six feet, three inches) than Patton (six feet, one inch), and Eisenhower's "fair-haired boy"—three strikes against him in Patton's mind. Patton did not react well to the sudden rise of the young upstart ten years his junior. After a dinner where Generals Marshall and Clark were present, Patton praised Clark's helpfulness but later wrote in his diary, "If you treat a skunk nicely he will not piss on you—as often."[7]

When Clark became the youngest lieutenant general in the US Army (and on Patton's birthday in 1942), "Patton was bitter, frankly jealous."[8] Still, Patton could not resist sucking up to his now superior and sent Clark the message, "Please accept my sincere congratulations on your promotion and also on the magnificent work you have been doing in connection with this operation [North African invasion]."

In his diary on December 10, 1942, Patton wrote, "[Eisenhower and Clark] have no knowledge of men or war. Too damned slick, especially Clark." On December 20, he wrote,

> I am certain when and if Wayne [Clark's middle name] tries to run this country, it will be very differant [*sic*]. . . . I have a feeling that he has no idea of ever assuming command. I cant [*sic*] quite fathom his game, he is very clever and very indirect.[9]

Lt. Gen. Mark W. Clark.
US Army Signal Corps.

Lt. Gen. Jake Devers.
US Army Signal Corps.

When Clark visited Patton in Morocco on January 10, 1943, Patton wrote in his diary,

> Clark arrived . . . I met him and had a guard of honor . . . took him on inspection of all local troops and installations. He was not the least interested. His whole mind was on Clark. . . . Clark is an s.o.b.[10]

When Clark was promoted to four-star general a month ahead of him, Patton wrote in his diary, on April 18, 1945,

> While I am glad to be a full General, I would have appreciated it more had I been in the initial group [Bradley, Devers, and Clark], as I have never had an ambition to be an also-ran.[11]

PATTON DISPARAGING JAKE DEVERS

Devers came from a strict, religious, hard-working background in the Pennsylvania Dutch country. He did not go overseas during World War I, and he had a reputation for being dependable, persistent, and a teetotaler who did not seek headlines. Early in the North African campaign, Devers was asked by General Marshall to make an inspection tour of North Africa and the British Isles. When Lieutenant General Devers came to visit Major General Patton in January 1943, Patton wrote this in his diary:

> Jake, who has at last heard a gun go off in anger, talked in a big way till [late]. . . . He has now become a great strategical expert, but he believes everything he is told until someone tells him different.[12]

Patton also wrote to his wife, "Jake has been with both the First and Eighth British Armies and is much impressed with them. It amuses me how our country boys fall for tea and titles." Nevertheless, on April 13, 1943, Patton wrote to Devers, "You may smile when I tell you that the confidence you expressed in me in your last letter was a constant source of comfort and inspiration to me."[13]

After the Normandy invasion, the Allies planned Operation DRAGOON, commanded by Devers, in order to invade France on a second front in the south near Marseilles starting August 15, 1944. To strengthen Devers's Sixth Army Group, Eisenhower proposed to take the XV Corps from Patton's Third Army and give it to Devers. In a letter to Beatrice, Patton wrote, "If Jake Devers gets the XV Corps, I hope his plan goes sour."[14] When the plan was confirmed, Patton wrote in his diary, "May God rot his guts."[15] Patton tried to get drunk [the "balloon model" of Narcissism at work] but when that failed, he took a green pill, probably for digestion or sleep.[16] The next day, he wrote, "As usual, Devers is a liar and, by his glibness, talked Eisenhower into giving him the [XV] Corps."[17] When Devers's Sixth Army Group approached the Rhine near Strasbourg on November 23, 1944, prior to the Third Army, Patton was depressed. As reported by John Rickard, "Two days earlier Patton lamented, 'I wish things would move faster in this Army,' but this sentiment was partly the product of professional jealousy."[18]

PATTON DISPARAGING OMAR BRADLEY

Eisenhower dispatched Bradley to keep an eye on Patton, the newly appointed replacement commander of the II Corps in Tunisia. On March 13, 1943, Lieutenant General Patton made Major General Bradley his deputy corps commander, arguing that he "didn't want any goddamn spies running around in his HQ."[19] A few months later, during the invasion of Sicily, Major General Bradley, as II Corps commander, served under Lieutenant General Patton as Seventh Army commander. Thus, it was a bitter pill when Lieutenant General Patton learned that during the D-Day invasion of Normandy, he, as Third Army commander, would be serving under Lieutenant General Bradley as 12th Army Group Commander. Of course, Patton had nobody to blame except himself for the "slapping incident" and "Knutsford incident,"[20] which ruined his chances for the 12th Army Group command. Nevertheless, the vitriol came pouring out in his diary and letters, as described by Blumenson,

> In his bitterness, he characterized Bradley as a man of great mediocrity. "At Benning . . . he failed to get discipline. At Gafsa . . . he suggested that we withdraw. . . . In Sicily . . . he bolted . . . in fear. . . . He tried to stop the landing operation [near Messina]. . . . The news about Omar was most disconcerting," he wrote Beatrice. "I felt so low that I just stayed in bed."[21] [The "balloon model" of Narcissism demonstrated once again.]

Throughout the war in Europe, there was great tension between Bradley and Patton because of Bradley's allegedly cautious nature and incompatibility with his subordinate's fighting style.[22] The personal and professional differences between this "odd couple" have been written about in detail by Martin Blumenson.[23] Although the relationship improved somewhat as the war went on, Patton frequently criticized Bradley for what he believed to be excess caution. As Bolger wrote,

Lt. Gen. Omar N. Bradley.
US Army Signal Corps.

Lt. Gen. Courtney Hodges.
US Army Signal Corps.

> Intelligent, if unimaginative, Bradley possessed a genial nature. . . . Bradley certainly knew how to get along with most people, superior or subordinate. . . . He never had to develop. . . . For Bradley, success in combat meant applying doctrine and picking the right subordinates, defined as those who knew their tactics. In Patton's sarcastic opinion, Bradley thought "that all human virtue depends on knowing infantry tactics."[24]

PATTON DISPARAGING COURTNEY HODGES

Hodges failed out of West Point due to a deficiency in math; otherwise, he would have graduated in Patton's class of 1909. Enlisting in the army as a private, Hodges earned a commission within three years. Wounded in World War I, he earned the DSC. Later, he became an instructor at West Point. Distinguishing himself at the Infantry School at Fort Benning, Hodges became a favorite of Generals Marshall and Bradley. At the end of the war, Bradley praised Hodges for being "a military technician whose faultless techniques and tactical knowledge made him one of the most skilled craftsmen of my entire command . . . [i.e., better than Patton] rivaled only by Simpson [Ninth Army commander]."[25] Bradley seems to have overlooked the fact that Hodges came emotionally unglued during the first days of the Ardennes offensive and was virtually incapacitated for several days.[26]

Patton's criticisms were often fired at the two of them. For example, in his diary on July 14, 1944, he wrote: "Sometimes I get desperate over the future. Bradley and Hodges are such nothings." In a letter to Beatrice on January 16, 1945, Patton wrote, "Even the tent maker [Bradley] admits that Courtney is dumb. He is also very jealous of me."

PATTON DISPARAGING DWIGHT EISENHOWER

Patton saved most of his envy and contempt for a man five years his junior, a man who never personally led troops into battle, and a man who routinely chewed him out, disciplined him, and kept him on a short leash. At Camp Meade, starting in 1919, the Eisenhowers and the Pattons were next-door neighbors. While their wives socialized, Ike and Patton spent hours at night playing poker and discussing military history, politics, and tactics. They both favored greater utilization of tanks—an armored force separate from the infantry, which, contrary to dogma at that time, would have introduced greater flexibility and offensive power. When Ike circulated some of these ideas in writing, they were quickly stifled by top brass, and he had to stop upon pain of court-martial.[27] This long personal friendship with Ike, in which Patton had been the ranking officer, made the situation during World War II especially painful for Patton. During the planning for Torch, the North African invasion, Patton wrote in a letter to Beatrice, "Ike is not as rugged mentally as I thought; he vacillates and is not a realist."[28]

In Morocco in early 1943, Patton increasingly lost respect for Eisenhower:

> Eisenhower lacked decision and a sense of reality. . . . Their headquarters was "a mess and gets out contradictory orders almost daily." . . . Eisenhower was pro-British in outlook and "spoke of lunch as 'tiffin,' of gasoline as 'petrol,' and of antiaircraft as 'flack [*sic*].'" . . . Permitting political and economic problems to divert his attention from the battlefield, "Ike is not commanding."[29]

As Patton chomped at the bit after D-Day, waiting for his Third Army to enter the fray, he wrote in his diary on July 12, 1944:

> Neither Ike or Brad has the stuff. Ike is bound hand and foot by the British and does not know it. Poor fool. We actually have no Supreme Commander—no one who can take hold and say that this shall be done and that shall not be done.[30]

Gen. Dwight D. Eisenhower.
US Army Signal Corps.

Gen. Bernard L. Montgomery.
Patton Museum.

Gen. Douglas MacArthur. US Army Signal Corps.

Because his future depended so strongly on Eisenhower, Patton was careful not to publicize these criticisms, often using the code "D.D." or "Divine Destiny" to refer to Ike in his letters. What Patton disclosed to his personal physician, Col. Charles B. Odom, however, came out uncensored after the war.

> Patton resented Eisenhower's vindictive manner and hubristic conduct as Supreme Allied Commander. General Patton was uncomfortable when Eisenhower was around and he felt that Ike treated him unfairly. . . . Although General Patton felt obligated to publicly display loyalty toward Ike, he privately detested the "Supreme Commander" and his sycophant Chief of Staff Bedell Smith. . . . He [Ike] never fired a shot in battle and he lacked combat command experience. Patton was understandably convinced that Ike was incredibly naive in the arena of international politics. Patton felt that Ike surrounded himself with people who gave him very poor advice, that he was heavily prejudiced in favor of the British, and that he was a purely political officer. . . . Eisenhower was almost always vindictive toward Patton because he disliked the way Patton made headlines. He viewed Patton's loyalty as a weakness and took advantage of it.[31]

Dr. Odom gave Patton's view of Eisenhower's British driver and companion, Kay Summersby, which bordered on paranoia:

> Churchill . . . had been able to get a woman named Kay Summersby to be assigned as Ike's driver. Ike became so infatuated with Ms. Summersby that he set up a private cottage outside of London where they both lived.[32] Patton firmly believed that she was nothing more than a British agent put in place purposely by Churchill. He told me once that, "Through Kay, Churchill always knew when Ike talked in his sleep."[33]

> Eisenhower's lack of backbone kept him from standing up to Montgomery. He very simply failed in his duty and let Montgomery do whatever he pleased. . . . It was Patton's belief that Churchill (through Kay) had a large part in this decision [to carry out Monty's airborne operation "MARKET GARDEN" in September 1944]. As a result of the plan, Holland was decimated, thousands lost their lives, supplies were wasted, and nothing was accomplished. . . . Kay's close connection to Churchill is well documented and toward the close of the war, he decorated her with the British Empire Medal.[34]

The reality is that Churchill and Eisenhower had an open, trusting relationship, which grew stronger as World War II progressed; thus it seems unlikely that Churchill would have anything to gain by spying on Ike.[35]

Toward the end of World War II, Patton sensed the possibility of Eisenhower's running for president, which filled him with the greatest envy.

On March 17, 1945, just after a visit from Ike in which they stayed up late drinking, Patton told his staff, "'Before long, Ike will be running for President.' When those present began to smile, Patton continued: 'You think I'm joking? I'm not. Just wait and see.'"[36] Dr. Odom wrote,

> It has been reported that Ike once answered a question about which party he would represent as President with the comment, "Which ever party nominates me." In other words, he had no political stand other than wanting to be President. Patton once told me, "I hope he makes a better President than he was a General . . . the Allies won the war in spite of the numerous blunders made by Eisenhower. Unfortunately, we are still wrestling with the problems created because of his incompetence and naive [*sic*]."[37]

Patton in his diary also unfairly[38] blamed Eisenhower personally for the failure to take Berlin and Prague. As described by D'Este,

> Until the day he died Patton believed Eisenhower's failure to take Berlin to be a monumental blunder, once writing: "I believe historians will consider [it] a horrid crime, and a great loss of prestige in letting the Russians take the two leading capitals of Europe [Berlin and Prague]."[39]

In support of Eisenhower, Trevor Royle wrote,

> He [Patton] could never have exemplified the kind of corporate command exercised by Eisenhower at SHAEF, where politics were as important as military strategy. Patton would never have had the patience to deal with allies or acquired the understanding to grasp the bigger picture.[40]

PATTON DISPARAGING BERNARD MONTGOMERY

General Montgomery was a graduate of Sandhurst Military Academy in 1908. In hand-to-hand combat at the battle of the Somme, he was shot in the lung and knee and barely survived, for which he was awarded the Distinguished Service Order. "Monty" was promoted to lieutenant general in July 1940 and general in February 1943. He was Patton's greatest rival for military glory in the North African, Mediterranean, and European theaters. They went head-to-head in the races across Tunisia to Bizerte, across Sicily to Messina, across France to the German border, and across the Rhine to the German heartland. This also involved fierce competition for military priority, gasoline, and headlines.

In his memoir, Patton wrote that August 29, 1944, was one of the most critical days in the blitz across France.

> Everything seemed rosy, when suddenly it was reported to me that the 140,000 gallons of gas we were to get that day had not arrived. . . . I later found that . . . the delay was due to a change of plan by the High Command, implemented, in my opinion, by General Montgomery.[41]

On September 1, 1944, Patton wrote in his diary, "We heard on the radio that Ike said Monty was the greatest living soldier and is now a Field Marshal [equivalent to five-star general]."[42] Later that day he wrote to Beatrice, "The Field Marshal thing made us sick, that is Bradley and me."[43] "Monty is a tired little fart," wrote Patton in his diary, December 27, 1944, during the Battle of the Bulge. "War requires the taking of risks and he won't take them."[44]

PATTON DISPARAGING DOUGLAS MACARTHUR

General MacArthur was five years Patton's senior. Considering that the highly decorated MacArthur had been a brigadier general in World War I, that he had served as army chief of staff from 1930–1935, that he had been a four-star general since December 20, 1941, and that during World War II he served in the Pacific theater, you would think that MacArthur was in a class by himself. This did not stop Patton from competing with MacArthur for something he valued as much as anything—headlines.[45]

Some five hundred American soldiers, mostly survivors of the Bataan Death March, were held in a Japanese POW camp near Cabanatuan City in the Philippines. On January 30, 1945, MacArthur launched a nighttime raid some thirty miles behind enemy lines to rescue the prisoners, using several hundred rangers, scouts, and guerrillas. Several hundred Japanese guards were killed, and the prisoners were liberated with minimal American casualties.[46] MacArthur got front-page headlines when news of this daring act was released. There was another great celebration on March 8, 1945, when the ship carrying the liberated prisoners sailed into San Francisco Bay.[47] As I will show in chapter 13, envy of this event triggered in Patton's mind a copycat raid on the German POW camp at Hammelburg that ended in disaster.

On the final day of the war, May 8, 1945, Patton gave a press conference, about which Carlo D'Este wrote, "Although he expressed a desire to help finish the war in the Pacific, Patton already understood that Marshall would never send him where there was already a prima donna in command. Patton told the III Corps commander, Maj. General James Van Fleet, 'Jim, the war is all over. The S[O]Bs won't fight any more. I would like to go to the Pacific theater but they won't let me. There is already a star [MacArthur] in that theater and you can only have one star in a show.'"[48]

NARCISSIST VERSUS NARCISSIST

There are additional facts about the personalities of Generals Clark, Montgomery, and MacArthur that probably intensified their mutual animosities with Patton.

Clark

Robert Citino wrote, in reference to Clark's negative qualities:

> Clark was a blatant careerist and glory hog, his legion of attackers claim, whose ambition exceeded all bounds. He cared more about public relations and cultivating a heroic image than he did about fighting wars. He only let photographers shoot his "good side" (his left, for the record). He was cocky to the point of arrogant, dubbed Marcus Aurelius Clarkus by some cynical subordinates. He was peremptory with his subordinates. He was inexperienced, and was jumped up over more experienced and deserving officers. He was a hard-core Anglophobe, distrusting his British allies while commanding a campaign in which cooperation was essential.[49]

This looks like narcissism with at least a small "n." Like two con artists competing for the same quarry, it is not difficult to see how two pompous men, Patton and Clark, distrusted each other from the beginning. D'Este writes that at the end of World War II, when Patton was looking for a new job, "Mark Clark, now the American occupation commander in Austria, had written to Eisenhower that he did not want that 'sonofabitch' near him."[50]

Montgomery

"British General Bernard L. Montgomery's narcissism is too well known to need elucidation," writes Edwin Hoyt.[51] Monty was a highly self-assured, arrogant, abrasive, tactless, glory-seeking megalomaniac, once described by Air Chief Marshal Sir Arthur Tedder as "a little fellow of average ability who has such a build-up that he thinks of himself as Napoleon."[52] Historians Murray and Millett described Monty as, "Not a nice person; dogged, conceited, vain, completely sure of his own abilities, and incapable of understanding other human beings."[53]

MacArthur

D'Este writes:

> "The first among peacocks." Those who knew or served under MacArthur either admired his genius or despised his narcissism . . . an officer whose extraordinary brilliance was matched only by his towering ego. . . . All genius has its price, and for MacArthur it was an inviolate belief in his own infallibility.[54]

Eisenhower worked as a staff officer for MacArthur in both Washington and Manila from 1932 to 1938.

> Although impressed by his genius, charm, and especially his flattery toward a junior officer, he deplored MacArthur's posturing and unwillingness to accept advice. . . . MacArthur "spoke and wrote in purple splendor." . . . Whereas Patton and MacArthur believed themselves to be men of destiny, Eisenhower had no such illusions or aspirations. . . . When it came to melodrama, complete with exhortations to duty and invocations to the Almighty, punctuated by exaggerated body language, MacArthur had no equal. . . . MacArthur's most polished performance was to parade back and forth in front of a large mirror across from his desk, dressed in a Japanese silk dressing gown, an ivory cigarette holder clamped in his mouth, admiring his profile while orating.[55]

Writing about the necessity of a narcissist to build an airtight cocoon to reinforce his or her self-admiration, psychiatrist Dr. James Masterson states,

> There was a widespread notion among General Douglas MacArthur's top staff that his role in post-war Japan was the equivalent of the Second Coming of Christ. The fact that very few people outside his staff thought so suggests the real possibility that MacArthur carefully hand-picked his staff to mirror his own grandiose image of himself and his role in history.[56]

MacArthur clearly believed himself to be more important than any US president. Prior to his problems with Truman over the Korean War, MacArthur made the following remark upon hearing of the death of Roosevelt in April 1945: "Well, the old man is gone—a man who never told the truth if a lie would suffice."[57] Whether Clark's, Monty's or MacArthur's narcissism should be written with a small or capital "N" are subjects for other investigators. It is also clear that Ike had great problems dealing with Patton, Monty, and Mac-Arthur, although he did get along well with Clark.

PATTON FELT THAT HE WAS BETTER THAN ALL THE REST

Martin Blumenson described Patton's feelings toward the end of World War II:

> He was fettered by the system, and he wished to be free to achieve the glory for which he ached so desperately. Yet he was bound by the men above him—and to a certain extent by those beneath. No wonder he reached for his diary to unburden himself of the unpleasant facts of life. For he saw himself—most of the time—as greater than any of them.[58]

As we will see, Patton's feelings of supremacy manifested themselves in disregarding the spirit of orders if not the letter of them (e.g., "reconnaissance in force" or the "rock soup"[59] method in Lorraine). He wasted lives and resources in mindless competition against impregnable fortresses (e.g., Fort Driant) or rival generals (e.g., Montgomery in the Battle of Brolo), and in the instigation of his own, unauthorized military operations (e.g., the Hammelburg raid). In some cases, Patton's "loose cannon" behavior produced beneficial results. But a senior general officer who feels superior to all his commanders and enacts his own personal agenda should not be allowed to wear the uniform.

• 9 •

Poet, Inventor, Mechanical Genius, Designer, Hero

> Narcissists display unreasonable self-confidence regarding their future performance prospects and overly optimistic views of their past achievements.[1]
>
> —Dr. Harry Wallace, "Narcissistic Self-Enhancement," *Handbook of Narcissism*

> From Brest to various towns in southern Germany and Austria, whose names I can't pronounce, but whose places I have removed, the trail of the Third Army . . . is marked by more than 40,000 white crosses.[2]
>
> —Patton, Los Angeles Coliseum, June 9, 1945

In his official writings and letters of commendation, Patton usually gave due credit to the men who earned it. In fact, he often praised them lavishly, using heroic prose, knowing full well that he himself would be a principal recipient of the praise. But in his spoken words, especially in front of an audience, he could seldom resist taking the credit, as if he had fought the battles single-handedly. This tendency of Patton to feel that "I am the Third Army" was his equivalent of King Louis XIV's "L'etat c'est moi" ("I am France").

TAKING PERSONAL CREDIT FOR THE ACTIONS OF OTHERS

On the night of March 22, 1945, after lead elements of the Third Army sneaked across the Rhine River, Patton phoned Bradley, "Brad, don't tell anyone, but *I'm across*" [italics mine].[3] Patton was not across. What he meant was that Maj. Gen. Stafford L. "Red" Irwin's 5th Infantry Division courageously fought its way across the river in the dead of night in rowboats, taking twenty-eight casualties.[4]

In a conversation on March 6, 1945, with his nephew, Fred Ayer, Patton described the difficulty of fighting in the bocage country of Normandy. The five-hundred-year-old hedgerows, consisting of shrub and tree roots, could not be crossed by American tanks without exposing their soft underbellies to the Germans. Then Patton said,

> I fixed this by having my armorer weld razor-sharp steel rails in a V out front of the tanks like a plow. Nobody else thought of this, but I did and it worked. Hell, it could cut through those hedgerows like a bullet through cheese.[5]

Unfortunately, Patton had nothing to do with the invention of the "rhino tank." Its development was begun on a large scale about two weeks before Patton's Third Army invaded the continent. The original suggestion came while Patton was still in England from a Private Roberts of rural Tennessee and was put into practice by twenty-nine-year-old Sgt. Curtis Culin of New Jersey, both members of the 2nd Armored Division.[6] Yet somehow this blatant lie served the purpose of Patton's ego self-inflation, if only for the moment.

Criterion 1 of a Narcissist from the DSM-5 is the tendency to boast, to self-inflate, to exaggerate achievements, and then to tell the world about them at every opportunity. In this chapter, I will show how Patton's NPD led to constant inflation of his own ego. His achievements, no matter how modest, rose to legendary proportions in his mind, and he bragged about them often. Overvaluing of past achievements led quite naturally to overestimating the results of his future performances. In both examples, we also see criterion 7 at work, a lack of empathy for others, including taking credit for their accomplishments. I will give more examples of Patton's overinflated achievements here, and in chapter 10 I will deflate several myths.

NARCISSISTIC SELF-ENHANCEMENT

Narcissists take the opportunity to self-enhance by "overclaiming"—even claiming knowledge of bogus information set up by researchers.[7] Harry Wallace has written eloquently about the paradoxical behavior of the sufferers of NPD, which is essentially a disruption in self-esteem regulation. "Many individuals with high self-esteem conduct themselves with modesty and humility. . . . Why are narcissists so compelled to shove their self-perceived greatness down other people's throats? Their somewhat reckless approach to self-enhancement is reminiscent of junkies desperate for a fix."[8] Narcissists are less willing or able to delay gratification and are prone to risk-taking. This is because they overestimate their ability and are motivated by the imagined rewards (i.e., loving the carrot and not adequately fearing the stick). They deflect criticism by blaming others for their mistakes and thus are less likely to learn from any negative outcome.[9] Wallace writes that "Narcissists want to be the star in domains where being the star offers prestige, and they would rather not share the spotlight."[10] He summarizes by stating that "the narcissism literature as a whole suggests that narcissists self-enhance either to fight feelings of low self-worth (i.e., to self-protect), or to revel in the experience of displaying their self-perceived special status."

CREATING FLATTERING PRESS

In a 1942 *Life* article by John Field titled "Patton of the Armored Force: Old 'Blood and Guts' Leads US Troops in Morocco and Pines to Challenge Rommel to Personal Tank Combat," Patton lays it on thick.[11] The ten-page "puff piece," filled with distortions and some outright lies, has all the makings of Patton's homemade legend right from the beginning of World War II. Much of the content came from an interview with Patton, probably with Beatrice present, and he demanded final approval.[12]

The article included these points:

1. Patton had brought the war's largest convoy safely through the nests of German submarines. (Patton was a guest of the US Navy on the flagship of the task force commander, Admiral Hewitt.)
2. Tomorrow he may be chasing Rommel out of Africa. (Rommel left Africa due to health problems. Over the next five months, it would take the combined force of two British armies, one French corps, and one American corps to defeat the Germans in North Africa.)
3. Patton has been sure of the fact that he is destiny's child. Someday, he knew, his army and his country would call on him. (This is pure DSM-5 criterion 2: fantasies of unlimited success or power.)
4. When, as a young lieutenant in Mexico, he captured a dangerous bandit single-handed, he was looking forward to something bigger. (The single-handed capture never happened.)
5. He looks ten years younger than his fifty-seven years. He stands more than six feet tall, with broad shoulders, narrow hips and strong

arms and legs. With his piercing eyes, he is capable of defeating any of his junior officers at sharpshooting. He can still play polo and handball better, or run the one hundred yards faster than most Army graduates fresh out of West Point. (This is pure vanity, also DSM-5 criterion 2.)[13]

Nephew Fred Ayer, who practically worshiped Patton, made this critique of his polo playing,

> Uncle George was never one of the great, or even of the highly skilled polo players. He did, however, make up for most of his deficiencies by the drive and energy he put into its every minute. I have watched him play many times and think it possible that he overdid this and so lost some of the coolness and concentration necessary for true effectiveness.[14]

John Field writes that during the Louisiana maneuvers in 1941,

1. "One of Patton's tanks got stalled in a stream. Down into the deepest water jumped Patton, hauled away at the tank, meanwhile screaming epithets." (Did Patton really think he could move a tank in deep water by "hauling away" at it or by screaming epithets?)
2. "He expects to be killed in battle, not bombed out of headquarters somewhere to the rear, but blown up, bit by bit, in a tank advancing at the head of a victorious attack through the enemy's strongest lines." (More delusions of glory, a la criterion 2.)
3. "Both Patton and his wife are inclined to believe that the possession of wealth by an Army officer, provided it is used, as they have used it, to live comfortably but not spectacularly, to entertain moderately but in good taste, is a help rather than a hindrance to a military career." (Probably no army officer and his wife have ever lived more spectacularly or entertained more lavishly than the Pattons, all to the benefit of his career.)

Field writes that, at West Point, Patton's ambition was "to be a football hero," at which he admittedly failed. (To be a contributing team member would never satisfy a narcissist. He would have to be a football hero.) Field continues that Patton, however, "did succeed at becoming a class adjutant—one of the two highest honors. Actually he worked so hard becoming an adjutant that he took five years instead of four to graduate." (No. What took five years was his failing mathematics.)

Then, unbelievably, Field recites one of Patton's favorite "Negro stories."

> [A Negro soldier] came to him one day when he was commanding officer at Fort Riley, Kan. The Negro had been charged with shooting another soldier. Said he, "You see, suh, it was this way. This friend of mine, he got misery in his foot." He asks eve'body how in hell he gonna cure dat misery. So I says, "Son, I'se gonna cure your misery." So I tells him to close his eyes and den I shoots his toe off. (While it would be outrageous to ridicule the supposed poor speech and low intelligence of a black soldier today, I wonder if many readers even in 1942 didn't find it objectionable.)

POET

Regarding Patton's literary output, Field writes that during peacetime,

> Patton composed much of two volumes of poetry which, he says, will be published posthumously. These verses have the same vividness that stamps his stories. They tell about soldiers in no-man's land, of suffering and bitterness, and final historical glory. Today, in wartime, Patton has had to curb his literary output.[15]

Patton's first poem was spoken at the age of seven and transcribed by Aunt Nannie.

> Forward Knight! Forward Knight! Go and do your best, Knight,
> In the Tournament.
> Forward Knight! Forward Knight! Don't lose the prize, Knight,
> On jousting day.
> Forward Knight! Forward Knight! Knock down the champion,
> Knight, Of the lot, lot, lot.[16]

At age nineteen Patton wrote the following verses in his notebook:

> Oh! here's to the snarl of the striving steel
> When eye met eye on the foughten fiel'
> And the life went out with the entering steel
> In the days when war was war.
>
> Oh here's to the men who fought and strove
> Who parried and hacked and thrust and clove
> Who fought for honor and fought for love
> In the days etc.[17]

At least two of Patton's poems, all of the same heroic battle genre, were published in women's magazines, such as *Cosmopolitan* ("Fear")[18] and *Woman's Home Companion* ("God of Battles").[19] Another poem, called "A Soldier's Burial," was published in the *Chicago Sun* on August 1, 1943. According to war correspondent James Wellard, in this poem Patton "tries to express, with considerable poetic feeling but inadequate skill, the quintessence of his faith." Wellard felt that "the general feeling and form of the poem have both been subconsciously borrowed from Gray's *Elegy*."[20]

Author Trevor Royle commented on the "general artlessness of the verses" in a poem about the World War I armistice.[21] Patton's daughter, Ruth Ellen, wrote that her father sent his wife a poem called "To Beatrice," which, she said "was as bad as the rest of his poetry, but Ma treasured it always."[22] His nephew, Fred Ayer, wrote about Patton's poems "most of which were obviously very bad."[23] Patton's grandson Robert said, "Though he could compose a striking phrase now and then, Georgie's poetry was simplistic and frequently awful. He took it seriously, however."[24] "Don't lose my poems. They may be priceless some day," he wrote to Beatrice in 1917.[25]

INVENTOR: THE "PATTON SABER"

The idea of being run through or hacked apart by a sharpened steel blade has been a primal fear to soldiers for centuries. Thus, for example, the bayonet charge has been used as recently as the Iraq War. The mounted cavalry in the US Civil War continued to exploit this fear by means of the Model 1860 Light Cavalry Saber, which they carried in scabbards around their belts. As shown in the photo on page 100, it had a curved blade whose edge was sharpened for its primary use—cutting and slashing the enemy.

After his summer of 1912 studying swordsmanship in Saumur, France, with M. Cléry, the "Master of Arms," Patton wrote an article espousing the idea that it was more effective to use the *point* of the saber for stabbing rather than the *blade* for cutting. Thus, argued Patton, a better design would be a straight blade (sword) rather than a curved one.[26] He advised the Ordnance Department how to make the changes in the sword (see top of the photo on page 100), which would always be mounted to the cavalryman's saddle. Then he returned to France for more fencing lessons during the summer of 1913. Back at Fort Riley, Kansas, Second Lieutenant Patton, Master of the Sword, wrote a pocket-sized training book titled *Saber Exercise*, published in 1914 by the Office of the Chief of Staff for the US War Department.[27] The sixteen pages had many line drawings to illustrate the various lunges.

Top: Model 1913 Cavalry "Patton Saber" and scabbard. Bottom: Model 1872 Light Cavalry Saber and Scabbard. Varnum Memorial Armory Museum.

Reviews on the saber were mixed. After Patton had become close to General Pershing in Mexico, he told Pershing about his invention. Patton wrote in his diary: "Discussed the saber with Pershing. He does not think much of it."[28] K. J. Parker, author of "Cutting Edge Technology," said that it was light, slim, ergonomic, and well-balanced—"the best sword ever issued to an army."[29] J. C. Amberger, author of *The Secret History of the Sword*, was afraid that the saber could not be withdrawn quickly enough from the stabbed enemy and called it "Patton's Folly."[30] At the high speed of a cavalry charge, said Amberger, the attacker would either have to abandon his blade, break his wrist, dislocate his arm by holding on to it, or risk something worse: "His dead opponent would drag him off his own horse—making him an unarmed foot soldier in an ocean of falling saber blades and trampling hooves." In any case, when issued, the saber was already obsolete because modern warfare did not include cavalry charges. K. J. Parker could find no record that the Patton saber had ever been used in anger.[31]

Patton deserves credit for diligence and following through on his idea, none of which would have been possible without his money and connections. The amount of notoriety he reaped was large compared to the modest creativity involved in changing a saber blade from curved to straight.

MECHANICAL GENIUS

When Patton took over America's first Tank Center in France in 1917, he worked very hard to understand the inner workings of the Renault Light Tank FT-17 and to make sure the US version of it would be the best possible. He was fortunate to have the assistance of Lt. Elgin Braine, an introverted, slightly deaf officer from New Jersey, a trained technician, perhaps even a mechanical engineer. Together they spoke to experts, visited the French tank training school, and toured the Renault tank factories, where they came up with suggested improvements. The list of improvements included a self-starter[32] and raising the eye slits by 1½ inches to take account of the Americans' greater height compared to Frenchmen. They worked together[33] on a fifty-eight-page report titled "Light Tanks," summarizing what they had learned about the mechanical aspects of tanks, lists of tools, spare parts, and so on. Patton considered Braine so valuable that he dispatched him to America to oversee the procurement and delivery of the U.S.–made Renault light tanks.[34]

In a letter to Beatrice on January 31, 1918, Patton wrote,

> You ask how I know so much [about] machinery I think I am more or less of a mechanical genius for I simply know by looking at an engine all about it. In fact the French adopted some of my ideas of change on their Tanks.

How quickly the contributions of Lieutenant Braine were overlooked. Other soldiers would contribute improvements to the tank, such as an extended tail for crossing wider trenches.[35] A compass-like device to improve tank navigation was offered by Col. Sereno Brett.[36] In July 1918, Patton wrote that his suggested changes on the tanks "will give me prestige as an inventor."[37] Later that month, he envisioned the use of tanks working together with infantry in a variation of the "rolling barrage" with tanks substituted for artillery. He wrote to Beatrice, "I am going to G.H.Q. Tomorrow [*sic*] and expand this revolutionary theory of mine. For truly it is just that, you may have a genius for a husband yet."[38] When a British officer seemed to endorse this tactic in a lecture, Patton wrote, "Hence I have a swelled head for which I ask no pardon."[39]

When ordinary progress becomes viewed as a revolution or product of genius, it often arises from a narcissist's impaired ability to regulate his or her self-esteem (DSM-5 criterion 1, exaggerated achievements). When Patton took credit for Lieutenant Braine's share of the contributions, which he could easily get away with because of Braine's lower rank, Patton exhibited narcissistic exploitation of others (criterion 6) and lack of empathy (criterion 7).

UNIFORM DESIGNER

Patton's intentions were laudable enough. Starting in World War I, he had tried various ways of building *esprit de corps* in his tankers, who dressed like a bunch of grease monkeys in coveralls. Patton worked hard to make them better conditioned, better trained, and better disciplined than the regular army.

But there was still the problem of the uniform. In June 1918, he assigned several of his officers the task of designing a shoulder patch for his tankers. The red-yellow-and-blue triangular shoulder patch and crest was a very successful design and is still used by all US armored divisions today.[40]

By World War II, the requirements for a tanker's uniform were clear. There was no need for steel helmets or camouflage. Tankers needed protection for their heads from noise and concussion. They needed streamlining so they could get in and out of narrow hatches in seconds, and yes, they needed concealment of grease stains. Patton's answer was described by Blumenson:

Patton modeling his design for tankers' uniform, 1942. Patton Museum.

> He designed a new uniform for his elite tankers—of dark green gabardine to conceal grease spots. The double-breasted jacket had a row of white buttons down the side. Padded trousers cushioned the bruising jolts of tank travel. Pockets on the legs held first-aid packets, map, and ammunition clips. The headgear was a football helmet of light plastic, furnished according to rumor by the Washington Redskins. Patton had a suit tailored, then modeled it for photographers. He looked ridiculous. He seemed to be clowning, but he was deadly serious.[41]

"He resembled a football player dressed as a bellboy," wrote D'Este.[42] Behind his back, he was jeered as "the Green Hornet," "Buck Rogers," "the Man from Mars," and "Flash Gordon."[43] He dropped the uniform. Patton deserved high marks for initiative, completion of his concept, and willingness to take chances, even fail. What made him different, however, was his supreme, narcissistic self-confidence, sense of infallibility, and ability to deflect failure by distorted reasoning.[44] Being a rank amateur was no impediment to Patton.

HERO

There was a sailing incident involving Beatrice and (then Major) Patton in September 1923, off the Massachusetts coast, described by Blumenson:

> They were sailing off Little Mission rocks near Salem in a twelve-foot catboat when a sudden squall almost swamped them. As they turned and headed for shore, they heard cries and saw three boys—two were sixteen years old, the other was ten—whose boat had capsized, struggling in the water. The youngsters had managed to turn their dory over and, about three-quarters of a mile from land, were standing in the boat in water to their waists, waving their oars and shouting. The Pattons went to their aid. The wind was so uneven and uncertain that they had to go past the boys, then tack back. They took the youngsters aboard with great difficulty and at some personal danger, then brought them and their boat to land. "Their deed, especially Mr. Patton's," one of the boys later stated, "was one of fine skill in handling the boat in such weather and also one of courage and of almost self-sacrifice."[45]

Beatrice got from the boys signed affidavits and personal accounts of the rescue. She sent the documents, along with her own version of the event, to the secretary of the treasury, who was responsible for bestowing Life Saving Medals. In February 1926, the Treasury Department sent to Patton in Hawaii a silver Life Saving Medal of Honor. In the presence of a military band and a host of friends, the decoration was pinned on Patton with great ceremony by Major General Lewis, commander of the Hawaiian Division.

Compare Patton's self-promotion with that of Seth W. Moulton, who ran successfully in 2014 for Congress in Massachusetts's Sixth District. The Harvard graduate was awarded the Bronze Star for valor as a Marine Corps lieutenant in 2003 and 2004 but did not disclose it even to his family until pressed by the news media. In an interview with the *Boston Globe*, Moulton asked that the paper not describe him as a hero. "Look," he said, "we served our country, and we served the guys next to us. And it's not something to brag about." The greatest honor, he said, his voice choked with emotion, had nothing to do with the medals. "The greatest honor of my life was to lead these men in my platoon, even though it was a war that I and they disagreed with."[46]

• 10 •

Brilliant Strategist? Led from the Front?

> Fellow officers have either worshipped him or hated him. But all of them have admitted that he is a brilliant strategist. . . . Patton believes that no general can command from the rear. . . . He will be up near the front.[1]
>
> —John Field, *Life* magazine, 1942

> On contentious ground [possession of which imports great advantage to either side], attack not.[2]
>
> —Sun Tzu, *The Art of War*, 6th century BC

> I'll go through the Siegfried line like shit through a goose.[3]
>
> —Patton, September 1944

In this chapter, I will examine two characteristics commonly attributed to General Patton: (1) That he was a brilliant strategist, and (2) that he led from the front.

First, let me try to define some terms. Strategy is the "what" a person or organization intends to achieve, and tactics are the "how." For the military, the distinction depends on both the time scale and level of the decision-making—thus there can be gray areas. Military strategy is "what" a military organization intends to accomplish, generally over an extended period of time during peace or war, and is generally planned at the national, army group, or army level. Military tactics are "how" a military organization achieves its strategy, through deployment of military power, generally on a shorter time scale and generally at the division level or below (and comparable units for air force and navy). The term "grand tactics" was used by Rickard to describe what General Patton exercised at the army level because of the greater latitude afforded him by his commanders.[4]

Patton emphasized the lower levels when he said, "I know that no general officer and practically no colonel needs to know any tactics. The tactics belong to battalion commanders. If Generals knew less tactics, they would interfere less."[5] However, a strategy is useless unless there are tactics for its implementation, so a great strategist must be at least a capable tactician.

WAS PATTON A BRILLIANT STRATEGIST?

Clearly, he thought of himself as one. When he ordered men into battle, he never showed the slightest doubt that his decisions and plans were the best. He did not always trust the military intelligence, weather reports, or casualty reports he received. But he had total faith in his own instincts, his knowledge of history, and his "sixth sense." Patton said, "You can have doubts about your good looks, about your intelligence, or about your self-control, but to win a war, you must have no doubt about your ability as a soldier."[6] One of Patton's frequent incitements to the troops was, "Attack, attack, and when you can't go forward any longer, attack again."[7] This hardly qualifies as a strategy.

His favorite maneuver was the oft-repeated "grab the enemy by the nose and kick him in the ass."[8] One engages and distracts the enemy in the front while sweeping around him and hitting him from behind, causing panic and destroying his supply and communication lines. The concept was credited to a Greek general called Epaminondas, who used a special formation of troops called the "oblique order" to defeat the Spartans in 371 BC while outnumbered two to one.[9] The principle has been used ever since, from the cavalry charges in the American Civil War to the tank maneuvers in the 1991 Gulf War. But what else did Patton have in his "bag of tricks"?

During the Third Army blitzkrieg across France, from August 1 until about September 23, 1944, when it ran out of gasoline, the Germans were in disarray. They were a demoralized, disorganized rabble, unable to muster a serious defense. The same is true of the Third Army rout of the Germans in the Palatinate area during the first two weeks of March 1945. Patton's greatest innovation was probably the use of close air support by getting the XIX TAC officers to ride up front in the lead tanks with dedicated radios. He orchestrated the combination of armor, mobile infantry, artillery, and air power, "the American Blitzkrieg," better than any other World War II American general. I will discuss three battles, however, for which Patton's generalship has been brought into question.

THE AMPHIBIOUS "END RUN" AT BROLO, SICILY

The Seventh Army had taken Palermo, on the north coast of Sicily, on July 22, 1943. Palermo was not a high-priority target, but it opened a path to Messina, which sits on the northeast corner of Sicily. Being the exit route of the Germans, Messina was certainly the prize of the Sicilian campaign. To capture Messina before General Montgomery, who had gotten bogged down on Sicily's east side near Mount Etna, became Patton's obsession because he felt it would finally prove the combat worthiness of the American soldier and himself as an American commander. The stress caused by this "Messina-mania" was partly responsible for the "slapping incident" discussed in chapter 7. No doubt the same stress contributed to Patton's haste and impaired judgment at the battle of Brolo.

It took only four days for Patton's Seventh Army to go the final fifty miles north to Palermo and Sicily's north shore. It would take twenty-six days to cover the one hundred odd miles along Highway 113 from Palermo east to Messina. The reason was that the coastal Nebrodi mountain range running east and west just south of the highway, with peaks averaging four to five thousand feet, made perfect defensive terrain for the Germans. In some places, the coastal plain was only a few hundred yards wide. In other places, Highway 113 clung to the seaside cliffs. Deep north–south ravines carved over centuries by raging rivers covered the mountain range. The highway and its bridges were destroyed by the retreating Germans, and the surrounding areas were mined or booby-trapped. To bypass Highway 113 through rugged terrain too steep for vehicles required hundreds of mules and horses to carry ammunition, food, and water.

The 3rd Infantry Division headed by Maj. Gen. Lucian Truscott was assigned the job of getting along this route to Messina. Fortunately, no American division was better trained and conditioned for this demanding assignment. The Texas-born Truscott, one of the army's toughest polo players,[10] the architect of the First American Ranger Battalion ("Darby's Rangers"),[11] required his 3rd Infantry troops to do the "Truscott Trot." This meant marching with full packs at five miles per hour for the first mile and four miles per hour thereafter. Working in the dusty heat of the Sicilian August, fighting mostly at night, and covering many trails too steep for even the pack animals required extraordinary stamina. The 3rd Infantry and its highly respected General Truscott were as qualified for this assignment as anyone in the US Army could have been.

General Patton requested that the US Navy provide a dozen or so amphibious landing vessels to be used for an "end run" around defensive strongholds if necessary. Just east of the Furiano River, the Germans were dug in all around the flat-topped, 2,200-foot Monte Fratello—the most formidable defensive position the 3rd Infantry had ever encountered. Truscott was given full control to plan and execute the amphibious operation.

In order to disarm and take all the Germans prisoner, Truscott required a well-coordinated double pincer movement. His land forces would work around the enemy stronghold from behind, arriving at exactly the same time as the amphibious battalion. Army engineers had to build a three-mile road up a mountainside southward just to get their artillery into position. The amphibious landing took the Germans by surprise and was spectacularly successful, bagging 1,600 German POWs on August 8. However, the 3rd Infantry suffered heavy losses in the four-day battle, the bloodiest they'd ever fought.[12]

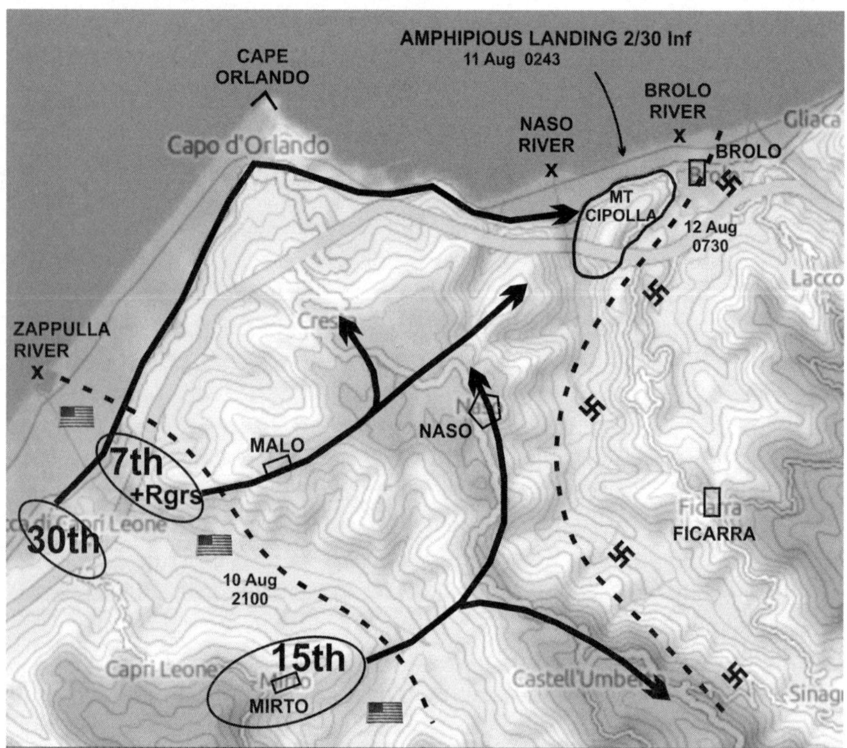

Map 10.1. Battle of Brolo (upper right) and Naso Ridge, Sicily, attacked by the 3rd Infantry Division plus attached rangers. Adapted from Map 8 in Garland et al. (1965), 395. Highway 113 is closest to the sea. The wider inland highway is a postwar superhighway with many tunnels and bridges.

Advancing about twelve miles along coastal Highway 113, the 3rd Infantry ran into another German stronghold in a range of hills northeast of the Zappulla River (map 10.1). By the evening of August 10, after being knocked back once, the 3rd Division's 7th Infantry Regiment had gained a foothold across the river, and the 15th Infantry Regiment had started across with mule transport. Emboldened by the success of the first amphibious attack, "Patton called me to his advanced CP," wrote Bradley, "and ordered another north-coast landing on August 11."[13] "Patton had wanted to launch the operation [a landing at Brolo] on the morning of the 10th in conjunction with the 15th Infantry's turning movement, but a Luftwaffe attack the evening before had sunk one of the LSTs earmarked to lift the task force. This setback, together with the 7th Infantry's trouble at the Zappulla, induced Patton, the Seventh Army commander, to call off the operation for twenty-four hours. Now Patton was in no mood for another postponement, about which he left no doubt in Bradley's mind."[14]

After struggling all day to get his artillery in position to support the attack on Naso Ridge, Truscott decided to postpone the amphibious landing another day so that his infantrymen would definitely arrive in Brolo in time to close the pincer and provide mutual support to the landing battalion, called Task Force Bernard. In the early evening, he called Bradley, who was in complete agreement. At 7:45 p.m., Truscott explained his reasons for the delay to Patton on the phone.[15] But Patton had arranged for a number of war correspondents to accompany the raid, and Patton would not listen. "Dammit, that operation will go on," Patton sputtered and slammed down the receiver.[16] This was the same day Patton's high state of agitation had led him to curse, slap, and punch the shivering Pvt. Paul Bennett (chapter 7). Patton then went in person to make sure the task force set sail, complete with several war correspondents.

An hour later, Patton arrived at Truscott's command post in an olive oil factory. As described by author Rick Atkinson,

> "What's the matter with you, Lucian?" Patton said. "Are you afraid to fight?"
> "General," Truscott said . . . "you know that's ridiculous and insulting."
> "General Truscott, if your conscience will not let you conduct this operation, I will relieve you and put someone in command who will."
> "General, it is your privilege to reduce me whenever you want to."
> "I don't want to," Patton said. "You are too old an athlete to believe it is possible to postpone a match."
> "You are an old enough athlete to know that sometimes they are postponed."
> "This one won't be," Patton said. "Remember Frederick the Great: L'audace, toujours l'audace! I know you will win."

> Patton looped an arm around Truscott's shoulder. "Let's have a drink—of your liquor." . . . Patton confessed to his diary, "I may have been a bit bull-headed."[17]

"That day of August 11th I will never forget," wrote Truscott.[18] Task Force Bernard's 650 men included a platoon of five Sherman tanks, two field artillery batteries, an engineer battalion, and fifteen mules as ammunition carriers. They came ashore just west of Brolo in nine landing craft and several DUKWs (amphibious trucks) starting at 2:43 a.m. and were all ashore by 4:00 a.m. without loss.[19] Their objective was to occupy Monte Cipolla, an eight-hundred-foot-high hill that sits just west of Brolo and just south of Highway 113 and the sea, thus trapping any Germans trying to retreat eastward. This, however, depended on the arrival of the US infantry over Naso Ridge, without which the landing party could be readily destroyed on Monte Cipolla. The operation was aided by sporadic air support and naval gunfire from the light cruiser Philadelphia and six destroyers, but the ships kept returning to the safety of Palermo harbor unless recalled.

The landing party was discovered by chance encounters with a German half-track[20] and staff car, which they destroyed with rifles and a bazooka. So much for surprise. The tanks were unable to cross the thirteen-foot-high railroad embankment, and three became disabled trying to cross the Naso River bed and the other two were damaged ramming into stone walls so that none were unable to aid in the attack. Seven of the eight artillery pieces were lost. Most of the mules and about fifteen communications personnel and ammunition bearers were killed by German gunfire, especially crippling Bernard's mortars.[21] The Germans counterattacked repeatedly with infantry and tanks from every direction. Throughout the day, Truscott received increasingly alarming radio messages such as this sampling:

> TIME: 0945. WHERE IS DOC AND HARRY? [Commanders of the 15th and 7th inf. regiments]
>
> TIME: 1140. ENEMY COUNTERATTACK MASSING EAST BROLO 1000 YARDS. REQUEST AIR MISSION ON THAT POSITION AND 753513 AND 729511. URGENT. ALSO NAVY.
>
> TIME: 1340. ENEMY COUNTERATTACKING FIERCELY. DO SOMETHING.
>
> TIME: 1725. BEING COUNTERATTACKED BY BATTALION FROM WEST. MUST HAVE NAVY AND AIR ON 702504 IMMEDIATELY OR WE ARE LOST.[22]

At 1850 the radio went silent in mid-transmission. There was no information about the fate of Task Force Bernard until 0730 of August 12, when the rescuing infantry arrived at Monte Cipolla. The Germans had executed a stealthy withdrawal during the night and, except for leaving a handful of POWs, they escaped the trap intended for them. They would live to fight another day, delaying the Allied march to Messina which ultimately enabled the full escape of some forty thousand Germans, sixty thousand Italians, and their equipment. Patton offered no apology for the bungled Brolo operation; in fact, on the morning of August 12, he came to Brolo to claim victory. As recounted by Rick Atkinson,

> An open command car flying three-star pennants pulled up on the highway. Patton stood in the rear, his helmet gleaming in the sun. "The American soldier is the greatest soldier in the world," he proclaimed. He pointed to Monte Cipolla with his swagger stick. Men and mules lay like stepping stones up the blackened slope. L'audace had cost Bernard's battalion 177 casualties [99 killed, 78 wounded]. . . . Listening near the road, [Don] Whitehead [a news reporter who had spent the night on Monte Cipolla with Task Force Bernard] jotted in his diary, "The whole little tableau sickened me."[23]

It is ironic that Patton's efforts to impress the war correspondents backfired so badly. The race to Messina, and especially the Brolo fiasco, caused irreparable damage to Patton's relationship with Truscott and Bradley.[24] Both were frustrated that they had to carry out an order they knew would fail. No time was saved, because the infantry required until August 12, just as Truscott predicted. Instead of closing the trap on the Germans, Task Force Bernard became their target for the next twenty-four hours. Lives and equipment were squandered, and the goal of trapping prisoners failed. Patton's behavior during the North African and Sicilian battles was described by Bradley:

> Canny a showman though George was, he failed to grasp the psychology of the combat soldier. For a man who lives each day with death tagging him at the elbow lives in a world of dread and fear. . . . To his troops an army commander is little more than a distant figure who occasionally shows himself on the front. . . . George irritated them by flaunting the pageantry of his command. He traveled in an entourage of command cars followed by a string of nattily uniformed staff officers. . . . These exhibitions did not awe the troops as perhaps Patton believed. Instead, they offended the men as they trudged through the clouds of dust left in the wake of that procession.[25]

British Field Marshal Alan Brooke met Patton early in the Sicilian campaign and recorded this first impression (which was unchanged thereafter): "A dashing, courageous, wild and unbalanced leader, good for operations requiring thrust and punch but at a loss in any operation requiring skill and judgment."[26] Patton's skill and judgment as a strategist were certainly lacking in the Brolo affair.

PATTON VERSUS IMMOVABLE OBJECT (FORT DRIANT)

What happened when General Patton came up against an enemy well dug in and heavily fortified? Did he have any special strategies? This is one of the main themes of the book by John Nelson Rickard called *Patton at Bay: The Lorraine Campaign, September to December, 1944*. Rickard points out that since the attacker should have at least a three-to-one numerical superiority, Patton's attack on the Moselle line in early September, where he only had rough parity with the Germans, was problematical.[27] Some of Patton's statements at that time "bordered on feelings of invincibility" (NPD criterion 2). Writes Rickard, "He had great faith in his own deductive abilities, and as Captain Harry C. Butcher, Eisenhower's naval aide, noted, Patton felt that he possessed a sixth sense and could 'guess the intentions of the enemy better than a staff of G-2's.'" Patton often ignored the advice of his own G-2 (intelligence officer), Brig. Gen. Oscar W. Koch,[28] the leading voice that later warned of the Ardennes offensive.

During the "October lull," when the Third Army was virtually out of gas, Rickard calls Patton's attack of Metz "certainly his single most questionable decision of the entire campaign."[29] Metz in 1944 was the most strongly fortified city in the world, the centerpiece of the Maginot Line.[30] There was an inner ring of about twelve forts dating from the Franco-Prussian war of 1870 and earlier. An outer ring of eight forts was built prior to World War I. They had interlocking fields of artillery fire and could defend each other from attack from any direction. Probably the most formidable was Fort Driant, one of the outer ring of forts, and located on a flat-topped hill of 360 meters elevation southwest of Metz, where it could protect against attack from the west or from the Moselle river valley to the south.

Fort Driant, modernized and strengthened by both French and Germans since built by Germans in 1902, had a pentagonal inner fort surrounded by ditches sixty feet wide and up to thirty feet deep in places. The inner fort was protected from all directions by machine gun fire from casements with reinforced concrete walls up to seven feet thick. Numerous concrete blockhouses and four concrete bunkers were each capable of holding two hundred to five hundred soldiers with provisions for a month. Five batteries containing triple 100 mm or 150 mm guns sitting inside hydraulic retractable rotating steel turrets could pop up, fire, and then disappear into the ground. The roofs of many of the concrete buildings were flush with the ground, so that very little was visible from the outside. Some of the underground chambers were big enough (and had been used) for aircraft factories. The outer perimeter was protected by a barrier of barbed wire sixty feet wide. And contrary to the Americans' expectations, Fort Driant was defended by hundreds of fanatical Nazi officer candidates. With very little information, "Red" Irwin's Fifth Infantry Division from Walker's XX Corps, after a bombardment by P-47 ("Thunderbolt") fighter-bombers and some heavy (155 mm, eight-inch, and 240 mm) artillery, attacked in mid-afternoon on September 27. The bombardment did little damage, and almost every tactic by the 5th Infantry failed to penetrate the fort. After taking heavy casualties they withdrew.

When the 5th Infantry came back on October 3, they had obtained detailed maps from the French showing the construction of Fort Driant. This time they were prepared with a "tankdozer" for filling up ditches, bangalore torpedoes, TNT satchel charges, flamethrowers, acetylene torches, and twelve Sherman tanks. They gained entrance into the fort and would spend the next nine days sitting atop it, almost as prisoners, being picked off by German snipers from unseen portholes. This was a game of what war correspondent James Wellard described as a deadly version of "Whack-a-mole."[31] The tankdozer broke down, and almost every other tactic failed. The Americans threw explosives into ventilation shafts and fought the Germans heroically in a deafening, asphyxiating game of "tunnel warfare" inside the underground labyrinths.[32] Soon, the Germans called artillery fire on top of Fort Driant from the surrounding sister forts.

Wrote John Rickard,

> So grueling was the fighting around the [Metz] perimeter that Irwin's [5th Infantry] division alone sustained 380 men killed, 2,097 wounded, and 569 missing since early September. . . . This represented . . . the division's entire strength of riflemen. . . . Yet even the best and most highly motivated infantry would have had an extremely difficult time dealing with the Metz forts if they had had no previous training whatsoever in fortress warfare.[33]

The attacks worried Bradley, who appealed to Patton: "For God's sake, George, lay off."[34] Why did Patton choose to attack the Metz forts? Prestige. "To assault a famous and legendarily impregnable fortified city was a challenge scarcely to be resisted by a soldier with Patton's sense of his military destiny."[35] Yet he seemed strangely disengaged from the attacks on the forts by Walker's XX Corps, whom he did not visit once during the ten-day span of September 6–16.[36] Once again, it seems that Patton's oversized ego, like that of the narcissist General Custer at Little Big Horn,[37] destroyed his ability to make sound strategic decisions.[38]

From September 22 through October 13, Patton's XIX TAC bombed the legendary Fort Driant with dozens of napalm, five-hundred and one-thousand-pound bombs, which did little damage.[39] On October 13, Patton gave up the attack, his 5th Infantry having fought valiantly and suffered 64 men killed, 547 wounded, and 187 missing in the attempt on Fort Driant alone.[40] Then he finally did the smart thing—he bypassed Metz. Fort Driant, Fort Jeanne d'Arc, and others would capitulate within a month or two, their defenders facing starvation. Patton's oft-repeated contempt for any kind of defensive warfare[41] probably contributed to his compulsion to conquer the massive fortifications. A narcissist always needs to be right.

PATTON'S 94TH INFANTRY DIVISION AGAINST THE "SIEGFRIED SWITCH"

During the Battle of the Bulge, Maj. Gen. Walton H. Walker's XX Corps remained in a defensive posture near the Moselle River, protecting the gains made by the Third Army in mid-December, 1944. Walker was considered "a little martinet who patterned his life after Patton's," and would "fight anytime, anyplace, with anything that the army commander desires to give him." He was described by peers as "a fine, gallant field commander—approachable, but it seems he was never really liked."[42]

The XX Corps was nicknamed the "Ghost Corps" by the Germans because they moved so fast and so often. With the Allies having stopped the German advance in the Ardennes after the first week in January 1945, Patton was ready to resume the assault on Hitler's West Wall, also known as the "Siegfried Line." The West Wall was an elaborate series of defensive fortifications running north and south the entire length of the western German boundary of about four hundred miles from the Netherlands, Belgium, Luxembourg, and France down to Switzerland. Built between 1938 and 1940, it consisted of some eighteen thousand concrete pillboxes with interlocking fields of fire, tunnels, barbed wire, tank ditches, and obstacles (e.g., "dragon's teeth"). Generally two miles deep, it was built in double depth around certain cities (e.g., Aachen, Saarbrücken).

At one place just east of Luxembourg, a special section of the West Wall ran east to west, called the Orscholz Switch by the Germans and the "Siegfried Switch" by the Americans. Its purpose was primarily to defend

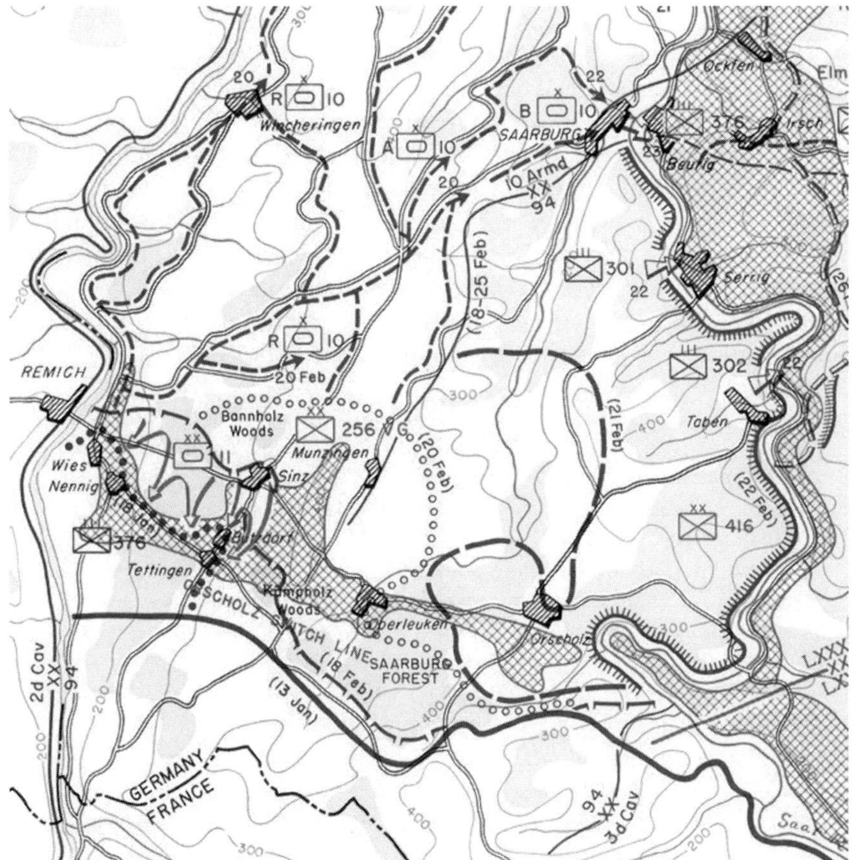

Map 10.2. Moselle-Saar triangle and the east–west "Siegfried Switch" (cross-hatched), January 13–February 25, 1945. Arrows show German counter-offensives. Cropped from Map V of MacDonald (1993).

the important crossroad city of Trier, which lay near the northern apex of a sixteen-mile-high, thirteen-mile-wide triangle formed by the Moselle River on the west and the Saar River on the east. Along the thirteen-mile-wide base of the Moselle-Saar triangle, facing the formidable Siegfried Switch (see map 10.2), Patton brought in the green 94th Infantry Division as replacements. Led by Maj. Gen. Harry J. Malony, the 94th had been in Europe for six months, primarily doing garrison duty in Brittany, where the Germans were holding out in a few ports that held U-boat pens.[43]

Starting January 13 and for the next five weeks, the 94th Division would take heavy casualties, attacking valiantly and repeatedly with one hand tied behind its back, gaining less than three miles. Facing three German divisions (the 416th Infantry, the 256th Volksgrenadier, and the first-class 11th Panzer Division),[44] intense German artillery, and extensive minefields combined with the natural hazards of cold, snow, ice, rain, and mud gave the Americans very slim odds of success. The 94th had no tanks of its own and got little air support, mostly because of bad weather. Its soldiers had no winter boots, clothes, or camouflage until weeks later. The olive-drab uniforms made the Americans excellent targets on snow-covered fields. Many soldiers took sheets and linens from abandoned homes and made them into camouflage snowsuits. Because of a very high water table (about four inches below the surface), trench foot became a major source of incapacitation. Dr. Nathan N. Prefer writes of GIs living like animals in the ground, and that even during "quiet" periods,

> Artillery, rocket, and mortar fire fell at regular intervals on the American front-line positions. The cold continued to be intense and made the defensive positions especially uncomfortable. The American infantry lived in holes dug in muddy ground, usually with water up to their ankles. The use of blankets taken from dead or captured Germans to line the holes did little to make conditions more bearable. While under fire or during hours of darkness a man could only relieve himself inside the same hole, further aggravating the miserable conditions.[45]

Why did Patton think that with a single US division, he could attack three enemy divisions protected by heavy fortifications, when every rule of thumb would say the attacker needs at least a three-to-one advantage to succeed? The reason is that in southern Germany, the Germans started what would be their final advance of the war on January 31, 1945, pushing Devers's Sixth Army Group westward, away from the Rhine, producing the "Colmar Pocket." Patton was under pressure to lend his troops to his rival, Gen. Jake Devers, and feared that there was a conspiracy to exclude him from the final push to Germany unless he could demonstrate progress himself.[46] Thus, his reasoning in attacking the Siegfried Switch with inadequate forces was based not on sound strategy but on narcissistic envy.

With his main forces still reducing the "Bulge" up north in the Ardennes, Patton was not willing to allow the 94th to fight in strength. Instead, he ordered them through Walker to make "limited objective attacks in battalion strength [roughly one-ninth of the division] to shorten and straighten the front lines."[47] He hoped such "nibbling" or "stabbing" attacks would elicit counterattacks from the Germans, which the Americans might be able to crush.[48]

The 376th Regiment took the first bite. Its 1st Battalion plowed through a foot of snow at dawn on January 14 and captured Tettingen from the surprised Germans. By noon, they had fought their way into Butzdorf.

The next day, 3rd Battalion captured Wies and Nennig, aided by chemical smoke, which also confused a platoon of Americans who were surrounded and forced to surrender.[49] Subsequently, the 2nd Battalion forced its way into the Siegfried Switch between the 1st and 3rd Battalions. When the expected counterattack came on January 18, it was the veteran 11th Panzer Division, preceded by German mortars and artillery, that roared out of the woods to take back Butzdorf and Tettingen. American bazooka teams knocked out five of the first fifteen Mark IV tanks. Attack followed counterattack through the day with hand-to-hand combat and heavy casualties on both sides. US tank destroyers came forward, some model M36s carrying the big 90 mm cannons. But with their open cockpits, they had to retreat from the withering fire of snipers and mortars.

Three mail clerks who volunteered to bring supplies forward spotted four German tanks. They found a box full of bazookas and, having no prior experience with the weapon, knocked out three of the tanks and hit the fourth at 150 yards as it tried to escape. Later in the afternoon, twelve to eighteen German tanks came at Butzdorf from all sides. The corridor between Tettingen and Butzdorf was so hot that the Americans could bring neither supplies nor reinforcements forward. General Malony had successfully caused the Germans to deplete some of their reserves, and he authorized a retreat. Carrying their wounded on doors from wrecked homes in pitch darkness, pelted by sleet and rain, the survivors of the 1st Battalion withdrew successfully. They brought a slew of German prisoners with them.

General Malony thought it was a waste of time to continue these battalion-sized attacks. He phoned General Walker to request permission to increase the size of his attacks to exploit what he had gained.[50] Walker said he would ask Patton. A few minutes later, the XX Corps chief of staff called Malony to complain that the 94th Division was expending more than its allotted share of ammunition.

The village of Orscholz, the eastern anchor of the Siegfried Switch, was the next target. Sitting atop a ridge with snow-covered fields sloping southward, Orscholz had to be attacked through a forest from the southwest. The 1st Battalion of the 301st Regiment, led by Lt. Col. George F. Miller, was chosen for a surprise attack before dawn on January 20. A swirling snowstorm and a bitterly cold night delayed the men from getting into position. Company B on the left moved silently forward. As Company A moved through the rows of dragon's teeth, the silence was shattered by the drumbeat of powerful mines they detonated. Company A tried to follow Company B, but it was too late. The Germans in surrounding pillboxes were awakened and laid down a crossfire of machine guns. The men of Company A hit the ground, but soon mortars and artillery swept the clearing with deadly fire. Colonel Miller was among those killed. Another company was sent to reinforce the attack, but that simply increased the death toll. Wrote military historian Charles MacDonald, "One company lost sixty men to antipersonnel mines alone."[51]

The next morning, Company B, led by Capt. Herman C. Straub, was under fire and had taken an all-round defensive position. Despite some help from the 301st Field Artillery, Company B had suffered serious losses aggravated by the extreme cold but was holding. Straub was ordered to fight his way out. He replied that he could not comply because of the many seriously wounded, one already frozen to death, and almost depleted ammunition. Every attempt to move brought heavy enemy fire that pinned them down. "Company B and attachments, a force of approximately 230 men, raised a white flag."[52] The 1st Battalion, 301st Regiment, which constituted nearly 1,000 men before the attack on Orscholz, then numbered only 19 officers and 415 enlisted men remaining.[53]

The restrictions on the size of operations from XX Corps were lifted. Eventually, the 94th Division, having been deemed to show sufficient progress, received help from detachments of various armored divisions, such as the Eighth Armored, whose Combat Command A (CCA)[54] they were allowed to use for three days, January 24–27, to very beneficial effect. The 11th Panzer Division became so beaten down by these battles that, a shadow of its former self, it gradually withdrew. Starting February 20, the awesome 10th Armored Division joined the fray. They drove ahead with all three combat commands and, together with the 94th, cleaned out the Moselle-Saar triangle in a matter of about two days. Next, the 94th crossed the Saar and by March 1 would participate in the conquest of Trier, the first time since the Romans. This shows the 94th to have been a very capable fighting machine when given proper support.

During these attacks, the 94th Division reported 1,087 men killed in action, 4,684 wounded in action, 113 missing in action, and 5,868 men evacuated for trench foot, frozen feet, or other nonbattle causes.[55] As Dr. Prefer writes,

> Yet much of the blame, as has been pointed out, for those casualties rests with Third Army headquarters, of which General Patton held personal responsibility. Inadequate footwear, inadequate rations, lack of sufficient warm clothing, and the general conditions under which the men fought all contributed to the nonbattle casualty rate.[56]

Patton was never afraid of taking high casualties. While starting across the Atlantic in October 1942 as commander of Operation TORCH, the invasion of North Africa, Patton made a remark that, even if typical Patton exaggeration, appalled both Rear Admiral Hewitt and Captain Ballantine: *he didn't care if he lost three-quarters of his men as long as he gained the victory.*[57] He envied the prestige that Mark Clark seemed to gain in Italy[58] and the Marine Corps in the Pacific[59] by boasting high casualties. However, Patton was skeptical about any report he received of high casualties among his troops. He said, "A casualty report of more than ten per cent is seldom true, unless people have run away or surrendered."[60] He believed that it was better to take high casualties in a brief, violent battle than to take an ordinary level of casualties in a protracted battle.[61] However, the battle of the Siegfried Switch was a protracted battle with high casualties for little reward, and certainly did not show any brilliance from Patton as a strategist. In fact, the battle should go down in World War II history, along with Kasserine Pass, Operation MARKET GARDEN, and the Huertgen Forest as a monument to poor generalship.

Regarding Patton's ability as a strategist, Blumenson stated, "No strategist or theorist, Patton had few equals in preparing, then directing men and units to fight in war."[62] Hogg wrote that Patton instinctively chose the correct course of action only when he had the enemy off balance and in motion.[63] But if the enemy was in "prepared defensive positions, Patton's touch was less sure and he was prone to reinforce his own weakness and persist in courses of action even when they had been demonstrated to be wrong or ineffective."[64]

DID PATTON LEAD FROM THE FRONT?

The phrase "led from the front" combined with "Patton" is so common it produces more than sixteen thousand hits in a Google search. Patton often used the analogy of an army and spaghetti. You can't push a piece of spaghetti; you've got to get in front and pull it.[65] But to what extent did Patton put this idea into practice?

Gen. William Westmoreland, former army chief of staff during the Vietnam War era, was a young West Pointer and artillery officer in March 1943, serving with the 9th Division under Patton's II Corps in Tunisia. Westmoreland noted that Patton "would head for the front, standing erect in his jeep, helmet and brass shining, a pistol on each hip, a siren blaring. For the return trip, either a light plane would pick him up or he would sit, huddled, unrecognizable, in the jeep in his raincoat."[66] His image, which was uppermost in his mind, meant always going forward, never backward. Patton had no shame about this deceptive practice. In his memoir, he said, "It is always best, where practicable, to drive to the front, so that the soldiers can see you going in that direction, and to save time, fly back by Cub so that you are never seen going to the rear."[67]

Patton also wrote, "The ideal situation would be for the Army Command Post [CP] to be within one half hour's drive in a C & R [command and reconnaissance] car of the Division Command Post."[68] At thirty miles per hour (perhaps a good average for unpaved roads in a combat zone), that would put Patton's CP fifteen miles away—beyond the range of conventional artillery, and he and his staff could normally get a good night's sleep. From October 11, 1944, through March 25, 1945, Patton's Third Army CP occupied only two locations. In Nancy, Patton occupied a walled three-story former chateau at 4 Rue d'Auxonne in a quiet residential area. In Luxembourg City, Patton occupied a large, four-story palace called Fondation Pescatore, built in 1892 and donated to the city by a wealthy businessman for housing of senior citizens.

Let us calculate Patton's actual distance from the front during this period. The direct distance (as the crow flies) was measured from Third Army CP in Nancy, France to the various 4th Armored CPs using Google Earth.[69] On October 11, 1944, the 4th Armored was in Remerville, a distance of 9.4 miles. The next move put the 4th Armored CP on November 12 in Chateau-Salins, 17.2 miles away; on November 20 in Haboudange, 24.0 miles; on November 25 in Loudrefing, 31.1 miles; on November 28 in Fenetrange, 39.8 miles, and finally on December 19 in Norry, 46.3 miles.

The distances from Third Army CP in Luxembourg City, Luxembourg, to the 4th Armored CPs were as follows: December 20, Arlon, Belgium, 15.4 miles; December 28, Bodange, Belgium, 25.8 miles; January 10, 1945, Asse-

Patton's Third Army forward CP from December 21, 1944, to March 27, 1945. Courtesy of Rina Sergeeva. Flickr, Creative Commons.

nois, Belgium, 32.1 miles; January 12, Rodemack, France, 11.4 miles; January 15, Dudelange, Luxembourg, 9.2 miles; February 23, Mersch, Luxembourg, 9.9 miles; February 26, Oberweis, Luxembourg, 27.8 miles; March 4, Bitburg, Germany, 30.3 miles; March 7, Darscheid, Germany, 53.7 miles; March 8, Polch, Germany, 71.1 miles; March 15, Gamlen, Germany, 64.7 miles; March 16, Simmern, Germany, 66.6 miles; March 20, Frei-Laubersheim, Germany, 80.3 miles; March 23, Kongernheim, Germany, 96.3 miles; March 24, Leeheim, Germany, 104.8 miles, and finally March 25, Rossdorf, Germany, 119.1 miles.

The average distance from Patton's CP and that of the 4th Armored Division was 44.8 miles. Taking account of the duration of each 4th Armored stay, the "weighted average" is still a comfortable 29.7 miles of separation. Distances by road are probably another 50 percent greater than the "as the crow flies" distances listed here. Thus, in practice, Patton kept himself about three times as far away from the front lines as the fifteen miles he recommended in his memoir.

This is not to say that Patton's CPs were always safe from attack. In Nancy, France, during the early morning hours of October 24, 1944, Patton's HQ had a close call from a German railway gun (Krupp K5 283 mm or 11.1 inches), which lobbed sixteen 550-pound shells into the Nancy area from the Landonsviller area, thirty-three miles north-northeast. One of them landed within thirty-five yards of Patton's house, blew out most of his windows, and completely destroyed the front of the house at number 5 Rue d'Auxonne across the street. As Patton went outside with a flashlight to help pull the residents out of the wreckage, another shell landed 160 yards away.[70] By extrapolating the paths of the shells northward, Third Army was able to determine the location of the railway gun. Within a few days, XIX TAC put it out of action.[71]

With that one night's exception, the security of Patton's command post was not seriously breached for the five and a half months described earlier. His CP in Nancy, the former chateau, sat on 1.5 acres surrounded by eight-foot-high stone walls, with MP guards and sentries always on duty, and a bomb-proof cellar.[72] The CP in Luxembourg City sat on seven acres, with barbed wire augmenting the iron picket fence.[73] Antiaircraft batteries were doubtless positioned close by. Patton's CP had a well-stocked wine cellar, was staffed with chefs, and equipped for lavish entertaining.

The average dogface struggled to find a few minutes of sleep during the winter months, his boots soaking wet in a muddy foxhole that smelled of excrement and death, with cold feet and toes sometimes turning black from trench foot and needing amputation. He was wrapped in as many army blankets as he could find and spent many nights cuddled up against other GIs to maintain bodily warmth. Most dogfaces didn't reliably get hot meals, hadn't showered for weeks, and hadn't had sex for months, if ever. Patton had a personal valet just to keep him looking and feeling like a million dollars. He could shower every day and, best of all, he could sleep in silk pajamas, cuddled up with his wife's half niece, Jean Gordon. Patton was not the only general to enjoy first-class billeting during World War II. In fact, many high-ranking officers prided themselves on "requisitioning" the best accommodations and consuming the best food and drink. Many of them also had sex with Red Cross donut girls and other women. However, not all of them postured to "lead from the front."

If a commander could spend time at the front consulting with his troops, he could grasp all the local variables—terrain, weather, logistics, equipment, and the nature and severity of the enemy threat. He could look into the eyes of his men and tell if they had any fight left in them. If he also had knowledge of the bigger picture, his military judgments and plans of attack could be based on cold, hard, facts—not theory, fantasy, or blind ambition. Spending much time at the front, unfortunately, was impractical during World War II for most regimental, division, corps, army, or army group commanders—nor should they have been excessively exposed to the danger of the front lines.

For Patton, the next best thing was to make frequent trips to as many of his units as possible. Just visiting the Third Army, scattered over hundreds of miles, was dangerous enough. Patton's day on March 26, 1945, flying in a Cub (L-4) airplane might have been typical:[74]

1. From Luxembourg City to the First Army area (Spa, Belgium) to meet Ike and Bradley as well as Hodges (63 miles)
2. To Eddy's XII Corps (Undenheim, Germany) to launch the Hammelburg raid (more in chapter 13, 114 miles)
3. To rear echelon of XII Corps (probably around Wörrstadt) to meet Walker of the XX Corps (5 miles)
4. To Bad Kreuznach to make a hospital visit to Colonel Hines of his 6th Armored, who had been hit the previous day by an 88 shell, removing his eyes, nose, upper jaw, and left hand (he survived) (11 miles)
5. Home to Luxembourg City (81 miles)

That's a total of 274 miles with five takeoffs and landings in one day.

Traveling to the front by jeep or light aircraft was fraught with danger, and Patton had many close calls. He escaped death when a shell whizzed inches away from his head[75] and when a defective one failed to detonate. He was strafed in the air[76] and strafed and bombed on the ground[77] and nearly smashed by a runaway bull cart.[78] Earlier in the war, the front was not so large, and in North Africa and Sicily, Patton visited it more frequently, though he was not always welcomed[79] by the troops he tried to impress.

In Tunisia on April 7, 1943, he found Colonel Benson's armored column on the road to Gabes, having encountered a minefield, stalled, the men eating lunch. Patton theorized that minefields are "mostly psychological" barriers. He showed up Benson by driving through the minefield, despite everyone fearing he would be killed. To be sure, there were two vehicles ahead of Patton's, which presumably took the greater risks.[80] On April 10, Patton, with Gen. Ernest Harmon in tow, walked conspicuously through a minefield near Faid (Kasserine) Pass,[81] despite Eisenhower's warnings about "personal recklessness."[82] Patton wrote in his diary that the troops were much impressed at seeing him in the minefield.

But "showing off," legend building, or conspicuous displays of pageantry at the front are not the same as leading from the front. Patton was fortunate, however, to have many officers in the Third Army who were excellent tacticians and performed spectacularly with great daring and imagination leading from the front. Two notable examples from the 4th Armored Division were Lt. Col. Creighton Abrams and Maj. Albin F. Irzyk, both later to become generals. Abrams gained fame in September 1944 during the encirclement of Nancy, the victorious Lorraine tank battles, and in December 1944 in the 150-mile march to rescue encircled Bastogne, Belgium. The Germans feared him and assumed that, like his sidekick, Lt. Col. Harold Cohen, he was Jewish, which he was not, and posted billboards calling them "Cohen and Abrams. Roosevelt's highest paid butchers. Jewish criminals."

Major Irzyk's 8th Tank Battalion (TB) did much of the heavy lifting, not always recognized, in preparation for the relief of Bastogne, as will be described in chapter 12. Both Abrams and Irzyk commanded from their tanks, slept like their crews on the ground or in the tanks, and were trusted and beloved by their men, whom they treated humanely, with fairness and respect. Abrams's commander's hatches were always open in his 37th TB, and he reminded his tankers that the infantry fighting alongside had only an olive-drab shirt for armor.[83] Irzyk's Sherman command tank was split open by a German 88 shell which he narrowly survived during the Bulge, and Abrams went through seven different tanks named "Thunderbolt."

Another outstanding example of a soldier who led from the front was Maj. Gen. Maurice Rose, commander of the 3rd Armored Division. At the time of his death on March 30, 1945, General Rose, riding in the second jeep of an armored task force near Paderborn, Germany, was the highest-ranking Jew (though a nonpractitioner of religion) in the US Army. He was described as "over six feet tall, erect, dark haired, and had finely chiseled features. He was firm and prompt of decision, brooking no interference by man, events or conditions in order to destroy the enemy. . . . He travelled with the forward elements of his command."[84] Rose was intensely private and seldom sought publicity. Andy Rooney, World War II war correspondent, wrote:

> Maj. General Maurice Rose . . . may have been the best tank commander of the war. He was a leader down where they fight. Not all great generals were recognized. Maurice Rose was a great one and had a good reputation among the people who knew what was going on, but his name was not in the headlines as Patton's so often was. Rose led from the front of his armored division.[85]

In conclusion, I give General Patton a good but not excellent rating on leading from the front. My reservations are not with the sufficiency of time he spent at the front or his unquestioned courage to be there but with the quality of his leadership while there, curbed by his NPD, as I will discuss further in chapter 14. Among those who truly led the Allies from the front in World War II were the squad and platoon leaders and the company commanders. They suffered a disproportionate percentage of casualties and deserve our undying gratitude and respect.

• 11 •

Vanity Case

> The [West Point] Commandant is such a fool that he will only let me have ten pair [of white duck pants] so I must get at least five more pair.[1]
>
> —Patton, from letter to Aunt Nannie, spring, 1907

> He [Patton] wears special uniforms, which, like Goering, he designs himself and which are calculated, like the ox horns worn by ancient Gothic chieftains, to strike terror into the enemy.[2]
>
> —Dwight MacDonald, from "My Favourite General," in *The Responsibility of Peoples*

The essence of the Narcissus legend was his fixation on his own image reflected in a pool of water. He loved the way he looked and could never get enough of it. A preoccupation with fantasies of perfect beauty are part of criterion 2 in the DSM-5 diagnosis of NPD. In this chapter, I will recount stories of Patton's personal vanity. Patton severely punished his subordinates for any violation of army dress codes or his own stricter rules, but he personally dressed as he pleased, showing both his need for excessive admiration (DSM-5 criterion 4) and his sense of entitlement (criterion 5).

YOU LOOK MAH-VELOUS!

The first and often the most lasting impression people had of meeting General Patton was how good he looked, described here by Edgar F. Puryear:

> As a general officer he wore a magnificently tailored, form-fitting battle jacket with brass buttons. Above the left pocket were four rows of campaign ribbons and decorations, and on each shoulder and shirt collar were pinned oversized general's stars. His trousers were whipcord riding breeches. He wore high-topped cavalry boots, shined to a mirrorlike finish, and spurs. Around his waist was a hand-carved leather belt with a gleaming brass buckle. On each hip rested an ivory-handled pistol ornamented with general's stars. In his hand he carried a riding crop. His helmet was polished to a lustrous finish. The impression you get the first time you see him is boom![3]

The tailor-made clothes and custom-made boots worn by Patton were the most expensive that money could buy. In 1918, from France, Captain Patton wrote to Beatrice, "I have just gotten a new pair of very nice boots at a very high cost but one must look well in order to hold peoples [*sic*] attention."[4] Later that year he wrote to Bea, "I wear silk khaki shirts made to order, Khaki [*sic*] socks also made to order. I change my boots at least once during the day and my belts are wonders to see they are so shiney [*sic*] and polished. I have the leather on my knees blancoed every time I ride and my spurs polished with silver polish. In fact I am a wonder to behold."[5] Starting in 1942 until his death, Patton had a personal valet, Sgt. William George Meeks, who did all the cleaning, pressing, and polishing. When Patton was a high-ranking officer in World War I, it is likely that he found underlings to do his spit and polish for him. Of course, he never had to dirty his boots by sleeping in muddy foxholes like the majority of his men.

As a small child, Patton was described by his Aunt Nannie as "almost painfully beautiful," with "curly golden hair, big blue eyes, a lovely nose and a sensitive, tender mouth."[6] "Occasionally [sister] Nita and I would wear each others [*sic*] clothes to dinner," Patton wrote. "One night when I was wearing Her [*sic*] clothes Papa began talking about [Robert E.] Lee and I got all excited and when he told me that since I was dressed as a girl I should not get so bloodthirsty I cried."[7] "Until the last year of his life when he was too ill," Patton wrote, "Papa always dressed for dinner and I have followed his example both here [in California] and in the Army."[8] At Fort Sheridan in 1915, the Pattons always dressed for dinner, meaning a tuxedo for George and a floor-length gown for Beatrice. They had between three and nine servants.[9] Daughter Ruth Ellen wrote in 1932 about her mother, "She always dressed for dinner in a long gown, and Georgie always wore a tux with a soft collar, and my sister Bee and I also dressed in long dresses."[10] Dressing up and looking great seems to have been an essential, daily component of Patton's ego self-inflation.

At West Point, Patton was spoiled to death by his mother or aunt, who lived in a hotel near the campus. In his letters, it was clear that he took their support for granted. As his grandson, Robert Patton, records,

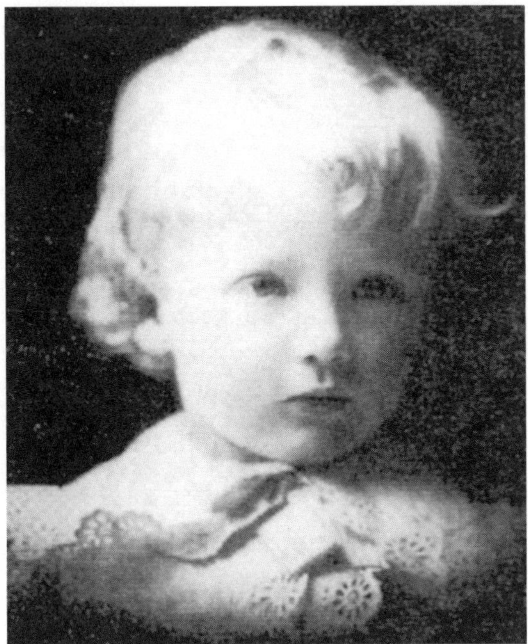

Baby Georgie, 28 months.

> [Patton wrote:] "Don't bring me any blue writing paper. It is not military and I don't like it. I like white." "Do not bring any more canday [*sic*] because I will eat it." (He had a major sweet tooth and fretted obsessively about his figure. He lifted weights hoping "to have a pair of very pretty arms to wear in a bathing suit" and worked out at a gym to build up "my confounded legs," which were long and stick thin.) Very fashion conscious, he directed Nita to "save all the old Vogues with articles about men's clothes in them and send them when I tell you to." . . . To stem the alarming retreat of his hairline, hair tonic became a frequent item on Georgie's shopping lists. He applied the stuff to his scalp religiously, though the results were not very encouraging. . . . He joked, "I shall need a wig."[11]

Patton knew he would not be able to earn high academic honors at West Point like his father, who was first captain at VMI, but he was determined to achieve the highest possible military honors. At the end of 1906, his plebe or freshman year, Patton was awarded the rank of second corporal, meaning that only one person in his class was judged more military in appearance and conduct.[12] Within ten weeks, he was demoted from second to sixth corporal, which upset him greatly.[13] He wrote to Aunt Nannie in the spring of 1907 that "he had bought a self-heating gas iron for pressing 'great creases in my trousers,' and he seemed to be spending a great deal of time ironing his clothes. . . .

He asked for five pairs of white duck pants exactly like the pair he would send her. 'You see,' he explained, 'I must get a high ranking corp [*sic*] and to do it I must have lots of white trousers.'"[14] Grandson Benjamin Patton added that he "actually had one uniform that he never sat down in."[15] Near the end of his sophomore year, Patton was promoted from sixth corporal back to second corporal.[16] In the middle of his junior year, Patton was promoted to adjutant of the cadet battalion with the rank of lieutenant. Wrote Blumenson, "What consumed much of his time was his habit of changing his uniform, he told Beatrice, fifteen times a day in order to be clean and neat always."[17]

Patton was aware of his vanity and even bragged about it. After a particularly successful attack into the German lines near Saint-Mihiel on September 14, 1918, Patton summarized the day's battle in his diary. Then he said, "This is a very egotistical letter but interesting it shows that vanity is stronger than fear."[18]

TURNING VIRTUE INTO A BLUDGEON

It's one thing to look good. It's another to use your good looks (or high status) to punish those who don't look as good as (or rank below) you. This practice has been institutionalized for centuries in the military and wherever hazing occurs. The reason that Patton was demoted to sixth corporal was because of his excessive punishment of the incoming class of plebes during the summer after his freshman year. As explained by Blumenson,

> He was a holy terror to the plebes that summer, a god of wrath who reported them without mercy for the slightest infraction of dress, discipline, or regulation. He even went so far as to record in his notebook some guides for "skinning"—that is, things to look for when inspecting the plebes. Many years later, Patton wrote beside these entries: "Such sentiments are unworthy of a man and a soldier. . . . They are left in this book to show what a fool a boy of twenty is."[19]

In other words, Patton the cadet had become "power mad"—a malady sometimes experienced by upperclassmen when they get their first stripes. The above apology in his notebook is disingenuous, however, because Patton continued skinning his troops for trivial infractions and continued to be power mad for the rest of his career. The newfound power of a narcissist when promoted to a higher military rank provides tremendous ego inflation that feeds his grandiosity (DSM-5 criterion 1), fantasies of power or beauty (criterion 2), belief in high status and uniqueness (criterion 3), need for excessive admiration (criterion 4), sense of entitlement (criterion 5), exploitation of and lack of empathy for others (criteria 6 and 7), belief that others are envious of him (criterion 8), and arrogance (criterion 9). Skinning troops for minor uniform or saluting violations became one of Patton's most famous attributes. These practices were another form of dumping on subordinates (see chapter 7).

DISCIPLINE, MORALE BUILDING, OR JUST "CHICKENSHIT"?

When Patton took over command of the 304th Tank Brigade in World War I, he had the problem of creating a new kind of military unit. The promised tanks were late in arriving, and he wanted to create some pride and a sense of elitism in a growing number of soldiers filtering in from other units. When Patton took over the II Corps in Tunisia in World War II, his troops had just taken a serious beating at Kasserine Pass. Not only were they demoralized, but they had gotten lazy through poor leadership from General Fredenhall.

In both cases, Patton came down hard on the troops, demanding tougher physical conditioning, harder work, and stricter enforcement of the most minute rules and regulations. This kind of "shock treatment" was probably beneficial in order to prepare the troops for combat in a short time, although not everybody agreed. For the II Corps and all succeeding troops under his command in World War II, Patton devised a series of his own rules enforceable by fines deducted from soldiers' paychecks. If a soldier was caught not wearing his helmet (even while sitting on a latrine), the fine would be $25. Also, there was a $25 fine if the soldier was not wearing a necktie. Twenty-five dollars was worth about $350 in 2015 dollars—a half month's salary for a buck private. Failure to wear leggings cost $20.[20]

General Westmoreland, who served under Patton in Tunisia, wrote the following,

> General Patton had two fetishes that to my mind did little for his image with the troops. First, he apparently loathed the olive-drab wool cap that the soldier wore under his helmet for warmth and insisted that it be covered; woe be the soldier whom the general caught wearing the cap without the helmet. Second, he insisted that every soldier under his command always wear a necktie with shirt collar buttoned, even in combat action.[21]

General Truscott had a better idea. Because of enforcement difficulties, he kept the number of rules down to the few most important. When he discovered men in his 3rd Infantry Division not wearing helmets in the combat zone, he fined the platoon leader $50 in the presence of his men and sent a memo to the regimental leader. The policy soon eliminated the offenses, because although soldiers were willing to accept punishment for their misdeeds, they were not willing to have their leaders punished for them.[22]

With his new tank force in World War I, Patton laid down the law, as described by Carlo D'Este:

> "I am getting a hell of a reputation for a skunk when officers don't salute me I stop them and make them do it. . . . I expect some of them would like to poison me." His first memorandum dealt with soldierly appearance and deportment. Shoes and brass would be highly polished and hair cut short, "so that they look like soldiers and not poets."[23]

Regarding Patton's command style, Gen. Omar Bradley wrote:

> While some men prefer to lead by suggestion and example and other methods, Patton chose to drive his subordinates by bombast and by threats. Those mannerisms achieved spectacular results. But they were not calculated to win affection among his officers or men.[24]

If Bradley believed the results of the shock treatment were "spectacular," as D'Este wrote, "one of Bradley's first acts after he assumed command of II Corps was to revoke Patton's edict that everyone wear neckties, and to permit shirtsleeves to be rolled up."[25]

How well did the shock treatment work? Brig. Gen. Paul M. Robinett of the 1st Armored Division had been a friend of Patton's for almost twenty years. As Stanley P. Hirshson wrote,

> He [Patton] also said that in six days he had restored discipline to the command. "While admiring Patton very much," Robinett related, "I consider these but the exaggerations of a man of unlimited ambition who had just come into a combat zone from a training area." Robinett saw "no change in myself or in those under me. Everyone continued on the job exactly as before." . . . Patton . . . did address an assembly of officers. "It was so fantastic that the best of us could not give a good report of just what was said," Robinett wrote. "In any case, it would be unprintable. . . . Intemperate and vile language, vanity, lack of judgment, and excessive ambition are not commendable in anyone."[26]

Patton's rationalization for his strict enforcement of uniform regulations was suspect. In Tunisia, April 19, 1943, he wrote in his diary:

> It is absurd to believe that soldiers who cannot be made to wear the proper uniform can be induced to move forward in battle. Officers who fail to

> perform their duty by correcting small violations and in enforcing proper conduct are incapable of leading.[27]

This is reminiscent of his absolutism in the belief that obedience must be automatic and instantaneous.[28]

Brig. Gen. S. L. A. Marshall fought in World War I and was a chief combat historian during World War II and the Korean War. He was a pioneer in the collection of hundreds of combat veterans' oral histories as soon after combat as possible, while impressions were still fresh. Marshall also authored some thirty books, and while some of his research and statements were controversial,[29] his knowledge on what made American GIs fight is still highly respected. When you try to determine which soldier will carry the fight and which will go along for the ride, one problem pointed out by Marshall is that,

> Discipline is not the key. Perfection in drill is not the key. The most perfectly drilled and disciplined soldier I saw in WWI was a sergeant who tried to crawl into the bushes his first time over the top. Some of the most gallant single-handed fighters I encountered in WWII had spent most of their time in the guardhouse . . . we found in our work that there were men who had been consistently bad actors in the training period, marked by the faults of laziness, unruliness, and disorderliness, who just as consistently became lions on the battlefield, with all the virtues of sustained aggressiveness, warm obedience, and thoughtfully planned action. When the battle was over and time came to coast, they almost invariably relapsed again. They could fight like hell but they could not soldier.[30]

S. L. A. Marshall also wrote,

> A salute from an unwilling soldier is as meaningless as the moving of a leaf on a tree. . . . But a salute from the man who takes pride in the gesture because he feels privileged to wear the uniform, having found the service good, is an act of the highest military virtue. . . . They prize a commander the more if he looks and acts the part of a soldier, but the characteristic of a fine appearance will but betray him the sooner if he has no real kinship with the men.[31]

Finally, S. L. A. Marshall's words on discipline and morale:

> One of the oldest myths in the military book—that morale comes from discipline. . . . The process is precisely the reverse: . . . true discipline is the product of morale. By "true discipline," however, I do not mean a mere muscular response to orders. . . . Beyond the basic physical requirement, the essential is that he [the soldier] be given freedom to think with a clear

> mind, which freedom can be his only when he becomes convinced that the Army—and particularly the Army as represented by his immediate superiors—is doing everything possible for his welfare.[32]

Beauty may be only skin deep, but for Patton there was nothing more important about a soldier than the *neatness of his appearance*. That meant the closeness of his haircut and shave, the fit and freshness of his uniform, the shine of his shoes and belts, the polish of his brass buttons, the cleanliness of his rifle and/or saber, and the correctness of his posture or "military bearing." His knowledge, competence, skill, expertise, courage, and character didn't matter for the time being—they all took a back seat to the superficial yardsticks. In his memoir, for example, Patton describes various troops that he reviewed:

> Just across from us was a battalion from one of the British Guard Regiments, who put up an exceedingly fine appearance. On my immediate left was a very large French ecclesiastic with a purple sash around his middle, which acted as a background for a tremendous cross with an amethyst in it. . . . The Foreign Legion was very resplendent, with enormous whiskers, many of which were red or blond. In fact it seems to me that the French Foreign Legion is largely composed of Germans and Swedes. They are very fine-looking troops.[33]

> [I met] General Anders, who commands the Polish II Corps. . . . We had a guard of honor of a very fine-looking group of soldiers. . . . His troops are the best-looking troops, including British and American, that I have ever seen.[34]

> The RAF in Malta is the best-dressed and best-disciplined Air Force that I have ever seen, whether it be American or English.[35]

"Chickenshit" was the word used by many GIs for a lot of rules, attitudes, and methods like Patton's. The historian and World War II veteran Paul Fussell had a precise definition:[36]

> Chickenshit refers to behavior that makes military life worse than it need be; petty harassment of the weak by the strong; open scrimmage for power and authority and prestige . . . insistence on the letter rather than the spirit of ordinances. Chickenshit is so called—instead of horse- or bull- or elephant shit—because it is small-minded and ignoble and takes the trivial seriously. Chickenshit can be recognized instantly because it never has anything to do with winning the war.[37]

Fussell compared Patton to Hitler when he argued that both men were "masters of chickenshit."[38] Stephen Ambrose minced few words: "Patton's

Sgt. Bill Mauldin cartoon, 1945. US Army Center of Military History.

spit-and-polish obsession sometimes cost dearly. It not only had nothing to do with winning the war, it hurt the war effort."[39]

PATTON VERSUS ANDY ROONEY AND BILL MAULDIN

Andy Rooney, the curmudgeonly gentleman who for decades hosted the closing minutes of CBS's *60 Minutes*, started out his journalistic career as a war correspondent for the *Stars and Stripes* GI newspaper. Private Rooney spent three of his four years in the army on or near the front lines. He flew on bombing missions over Germany and visited the Buchenwald death camp. Rooney was never a big fan of General Patton. Here are some quotes from his book, *My War*:

> Many of the soldiers in Patton's army hated him and hated that nickname, "blood and guts." Their line was "Yeah, his guts and our blood." . . . He was a loudmouthed boor who got too many American soldiers killed for the sake of enhancing his own reputation as a swashbuckling leader in the Napoleonic style. . . . Patton was not a frontline soldier—not that any general should be—but neither should he have the reputation for being one when he was not . . . a dangerous charlatan. . . . Patton never grew up. . . . Patton's disregard for the lives of men . . . and I have nothing but contempt for George Patton.[40]

Also on the staff of *Stars and Stripes* was a twenty-five-year-old baby-faced cartoonist named Bill Mauldin. Patton was extremely annoyed at Mauldin's cartoons because they pinpricked pomposity and glorified the slovenly, cynical pair of GIs, "Willie and Joe." Patton found the cartoons "damned unsoldierly"[41] and threatened to prohibit distribution of *Stars and Stripes* among the Third Army unless Mauldin was fired. Ike called his aide, Navy Capt. Harry Butcher, and said, "Get George out of this mess, Harry." As described by Rooney,

Sgt. Bill Mauldin, cartoonist.
USPS postage stamp, 2010.

With Mauldin listening in on an extension in his office, Butcher telephoned Patton and told him that the best thing to do was for him to get Mauldin up there and have a talk with him. It was not comforting to Bill when he heard Patton on the other end of the line yell, "All right. Send the little sonofabitch up here." When Mauldin got to Patton's headquarters, he was escorted to the general's office in a grand palace in Luxembourg [City]. Bill describes the scene as something out of a movie. As Bill came in the door of an ornately decorated, cavernous room, Patton was seated behind a huge desk at the far end and a visitor had to make the long, lonely walk to face him. It was an old belittling trick of kings.

Patton lectured Mauldin on the necessity for authority in the Army and said that Bill was undermining that authority with his drawings. Mauldin was finally dismissed by Patton but Patton was the clear loser. Bill never backed off. His cartoons continued as sharp as ever, and *The Stars and Stripes* was never barred from Third Army distribution.[42]

GENERAL PATTON, SIR. YOU ARE OUT OF UNIFORM!

Here is the utmost in hypocrisy. General Patton was almost always out of uniform. Yes, the stickler for rules and regulations, the martinet who demanded obedience from others, the officer who would fine a buck private half a month's salary for not wearing his necktie in combat often violated the rules himself. With his homemade collage of nonregulation pants, helmets, boots, belts, buckles, pistols, and insignias, Patton was often in flagrant violation of the dress code, Army Regulations No. 600-40. The forty-page document from the War Department, dated March 31, 1944, regarding the wearing of service uniform was signed by Gen. George C. Marshall. Why was Patton, not a cavalry officer, sometimes wearing jodhpurs, cavalry boots, and spurs (forbidden unless on "mounted duty" by Section III, items 32a1, 34 a1, and Section VI, item 78)? AR 600-40 specifically states under Section III, item 39b that: "Neckties will not be worn in the field or under simulated field conditions." So Patton's necktie rule in combat situations was apparently illegal.

Third Army historian Dr. Hugh M. Cole recalls, "The only GI bit of uniform I ever saw him wear was the service coat."[43] Fred Ayer, in reference to his uncle's profanity, wrote, "Patton did not conform in uniform any more than he did in language. He often appeared wearing nonregulation belt and pistol."[44] The only exceptions allowed under AR 600-40 is for five-star generals (Section I, item 1b). Evidently, the five-star general, a grade Patton never made, could wear whatever he pleased. Patton's narcissistic sense of entitlement (DSM-5 criterion 5) and exceptionalism made him feel that rules did not apply to him. Every day he got away with these uniform violations may well have inflated his self-esteem while he penalized lesser mortals (lack of empathy, criterion 7).

Patton was not the only general to take liberties with the dress code. Eisenhower developed what became known as the "Eisenhower jacket," a waist-cropped jacket incorporating the functionality of the British battle jacket. Soon, though, this jacket became standard issue and available to other officers. Truscott wore a russet-colored leather jacket as his trademark and a white silk scarf. Others in his 3rd Division began to wear the white scarves with Truscott's blessings, giving them a distinctive look.[45] Truscott and a number of other former cavalry officers sometimes continued to wear cavalry pants and boots. However, Patton was the one infamous for strict enforcement of dress codes, both official and self-styled.

DRESS CODE ENFORCEMENT OF OTHER GENERALS

If Patton was correct that "it is absurd to believe that soldiers who cannot be made to wear the proper uniform can be induced to move forward in battle,"[46] then how was the performance of soldiers under commanders more relaxed about spit and polish? Eisenhower was a perfectionist, with one exception, described by Carlo D'Este:

> Eisenhower was so immersed in the demands of his new job that he was habitually careless of his personal appearance, and once had to be reminded by General Joyce that brass polish and his belt buckle had never met. Eisenhower could not be bothered with what he deemed minutiae and promptly detailed an NCO to purchase eight new belts and replace them whenever one got dirty. Although Eisenhower's casual attitude toward his military dress was wholly inconsistent with his reputation as a strict disciplinarian, it did accurately reflect his disinterest in the spit and polish imposed by Patton and other officers who insisted that it was part and parcel of good morale and discipline.[47]

Many other great generals cared little about their own appearance. Ulysses Grant always looked like he'd just slept in his uniform. The neat but scruffy and slightly pudgy Creighton Abrams never looked very good in a uniform.[48] MacArthur was notorious for his indifference to uniforms and saluting.[49] General Terry Allen of the First Infantry Division was described as follows by Omar Bradley:

> Terry sat with his black hair disheveled, a squinty grin on his face. He wore the same dark green shirt and trousers he had worn through the Gafsa campaign. His orderly had sewn creases into his pants but they had long since bagged out. The aluminum stars he wore had been taken from an Italian private.[50]

Together with his assistant division commander Teddy Roosevelt Jr., they were terrific fighters but lacked the instincts of good disciplinarians. As phrased by Omar Bradley,

> They looked upon discipline as an unwelcome crutch to be used by less able and personable commanders. Terry's own career as an army rebel had long ago disproved the maxim that discipline makes the soldier. Having broken the mold himself, he saw no need to apply it to his troops.[51]

Author Lewis Sorley tells the story of Abrams's 37th Tank Battalion (TB) encountering a German military warehouse stocked with sheepskin coats. Coming out of Bastogne, Abrams's column passed through Luxembourg City, home of Patton's HQ, where the MPs were used to enforcing Patton's regulations. The MPs noticed the tankers wearing unauthorized, sharp-looking, cozy, warm coats.

> [The] MPs stopped the column and told Abrams to order his troops to get rid of the sheepskin coats. "You take them off," Abrams told the rear echelon cops, signaling the column to get moving again. "The MPs knew this was one they couldn't win," reported [war correspondent] Jimmy Cannon.[52]

There is no evidence to suggest that the troops under Ulysses Grant, Creighton Abrams, Terry Allen, or Douglas MacArthur were less capable fighters because of the lax enforcement of dress codes or the unkempt appearance of their commanders.

FLAMBOYANT GENERALS

When a general's behavior and personalized uniform takes a turn toward the strutting peacock, it should raise the red flag for narcissism. Vazire et al. documented that when ordinary people make snap judgments of others based only on appearance, they can diagnose narcissism in strangers with impressive accuracy. The cues they used included expensive clothing and markers of excessive personal grooming.[53] For the military, one need only look at the individual's deviations from the dress code.

Brevet Maj. Gen. George Armstrong Custer, who finished last in his class of 1862 at West Point, spent his life seeking publicity. He went through two famous court-martials and took great pains about his appearance and great pride in his cascading golden locks, which were perfumed with cinnamon oil. His uniform was made of black velvet embossed in gold lace. He wore a distinctive, large sombrero, with a red scarf around his neck. Author and psychoanalyst Dr. Charles K. Hofling writes that Custer above all wanted fame and military glory. In his 1981 book, with the facts available to him (a minute fraction of the documents available on Patton), he diagnosed Custer with Narcissistic Personality Disorder.[54] It is probably significant that Custer had a doting mother.[55] It's also interesting that Custer was strangely halfhearted about the Battle at Little Big Horn, similar to Patton's attack on Fort Driant and his handling of the Hammelburg fiasco (see chapter 13).[56]

In chapter 8, I mentioned Gen. Douglas MacArthur's habit to "parade back and forth in front of a large mirror across from his desk, dressed in a Japanese silk dressing gown, an ivory cigarette holder clamped in his mouth, admiring his profile while orating."[57] The image of the corncob pipe, aviator glasses, and open collar and the sanctimonious oratory are red flags for MacArthur's narcissism. MacArthur's mother, like Patton's mother and Aunt Nannie, followed him to West Point and rented quarters across from campus just to be near him. MacArthur was a mama's boy write the psychologists R. Hogan and J. Fico. They also state,

> [President Bill] Clinton's mother personally enrolled him in college and found his lodging for him. Freud, who was fabulously indulged by his mother at the expense of his talented sisters, was fond of saying that any man who enjoyed the exclusive attention of his mother was destined to think of himself thereafter in heroic terms—as a Conquistador.[58]

In 1942, then Lt. Gen. Bernard Law Montgomery adopted the black beret, which he often wore with pullovers and baggy corduroys, a red flag for narcissism. He was notoriously egotistical, tactless, and an inveterate publicity seeker. But when Monty was a child, his mother routinely beat him severely, so he cut off all contact with her and refused to go to her funeral. Monty was also quite empathetic with his troops, so perhaps on further investigation his narcissism would not necessarily qualify as NPD.

VAIN TO THE END

Patton required reading glasses since the age of thirty-two,[59] but he was seldom photographed wearing them. His teeth were mottled and revealed a bit too much of the upper gums. Near the war's end, on March 14, 1945, Patton's vanity was on display when *Life* magazine photographer Margaret Bourke-White came to take his photograph. He insisted on her taking his profile from the left side. D'Este wrote,

> "Don't show my jowls," he complained. "And don't show the creases in my neck. Stop taking pictures of my teeth. Why are photographers always taking pictures of my teeth?" Tucking his head into his chest, Patton groused: "This is the only angle at which the little hair I have will show."[60]

In conclusion, Patton's vanity, need for excess admiration, and sense of entitlement were strong components (DSM-5 criteria 2, 4, and 5) of his NPD. When acting as a strict disciplinarian of his subordinates, he reaped a rich harvest of ego self-inflation from additional criteria (1 through 9). It is difficult to differentiate Patton the disciplinarian from Patton the bully, and thus it is doubtful that his actions were always for the betterment and well-being of his soldiers.[61]

• *12* •

Liberating Bastogne, Patton's Finest Moment

> The first thing that usually slows up operations is an element of caution, fatigue or doubt on the part of a higher commander. Patton is never affected by these.[1]
>
> —Eisenhower in a cable to Marshall, August 27, 1943

> The relief of Bastogne is the most brilliant operation we have thus far performed and is in my opinion the outstanding achievement of this war.[2]
>
> —Patton in a letter to Beatrice, December 29, 1944

"This was the sublime moment of his career," wrote Martin Blumenson.[3] It is 11:00 a.m. on December 19, 1944. The scene is a dingy former military barracks in Verdun, France, now being used as Bradley's 12th Army Group rear-echelon HQ, code-named "EAGLE MAIN." The second-floor room has a map on the wall and it is cold—heated only by a potbellied stove. Assembled around a long table are Generals Eisenhower, Bradley, Patton, and Devers, Air Marshal Tedder, and their aides.

THE MOMENT

The Allies have come from afar to plan a strategy for dealing with the sudden counterattack on December 16 by the Germans. The latter came thundering westward out of the early-morning fog through Allied lines with some twenty divisions (and five more in reserve), eight of them armored,[4] and into the Ardennes Forest along a sixty-mile front. Crawling out from the security of his West Wall ("Siegfried Line"), ready to spend his manpower and gasoline reserves, Hitler bet everything on this roll of the dice. The Allies had no clue that the Germans had that kind of offensive power left and were caught with their pants down. The front along Germany's western border was attacked in the sector most sparsely manned by the Americans. It belonged to the VIII Corps of the US First Army, headed by the prickly Mississippian, Maj. Gen. Troy H. Middleton. His units were either in rest and recuperation mode or in training. The German attack was intended to drive past the Meuse River, to divide American and British forces, and to recapture the deep-water port of Antwerp. Loss of the Allies' most important supply line could reverse the tide of the war.

The tension in the conference room was palpable. Some of the American troops had broken and run in panic, and others deserted.[5] Brig. Gen. Kenneth Strong, Ike's G-2 (intelligence officer) gave a pessimistic briefing. The 110th Infantry Regiment of the 28th "Bloody Bucket" Division from Pennsylvania had been all but wiped out. The bulk of one division, the 106th Infantry, was surrounded on the Schnee Eifel hogback, and later that day would surrender nearly seven thousand men—the largest surrender of US forces since Bataan.[6]

After a column from Kampfgruppe Peiper was reported to have approached within six miles of Spa, Belgium, the site of Gen. Courtney Hodges's First Army headquarters, Hodges was so upset that he couldn't function for several days. Nearly relieved of command,[7] Hodges was absent from the meeting, moving his HQ to greater safety in Liege, Belgium. General Strong also revealed that the Germans had reached Bastogne, which was in imminent danger of being overrun[8] (though it was not yet encircled). Now, after three days of steady German advances in force, a penetration forty miles deep and thirty miles wide,[9] all present in the room agreed that the situation was critical.

Sensing the gloom, Eisenhower speaks. "The present situation is to be regarded as one of opportunity for us and not disaster. There will be only cheerful faces at this conference table."

Patton replies: "Hell, let's have the guts to let the sons of bitches go all the way to Paris. Then we'll really cut them off and chew 'em up."

Some laugh, but Ike says, "George, that's fine. But the enemy must never be allowed to cross the Meuse."[10] Ike's strategy was essentially to hold the Germans at the Meuse and then counterattack.[11] Only Patton had arrived at the meeting full of confidence, with specific plans tailored to each of three options.[12]

Later in the discussion, as recounted by Rick Atkinson,

> Peering down the long table at Patton, Eisenhower asked in his booming voice, "George, how soon can you get an attack off?" "On December 22,"[13] Patton replied, "with three divisions—the 4th Armored, the 26th, and the

80th." Leaning forward, Eisenhower quickly calculated space, time, and divisions on his fingers. The maneuver required making a sharp left turn with a full corps, then moving nearly a hundred miles over winter roads. "Don't be fatuous, George. If you try to go that early, you won't have all three divisions ready and you'll go piecemeal," he said. "I'd even settle for the 23rd if it takes that long to get three full divisions."[14]

Lt. Col. Paul D. Harkins, Patton's deputy chief of staff for operations, recalled these words being exchanged:

Patton said: "I'll make a meeting engagement in three days and I'll give you a six-division coordinated attack in six days." Well, that brought a bit of a chuckle. Ike's staff didn't think that was possible. General Patton turned to me and said, "We can do that," and I said "Yes, sir."[15]

Carlo D'Este describes the reaction to Patton's promise:

Codman [Boston-bred pilot, wine expert, and Patton aide Maj. Charles R. Codman] witnessed a "stir, a shuffling of feet, as those present straightened up in their chairs. In some faces skepticism. But through the room the current of excitement leaped like a flame." John Eisenhower writes: "Witnesses to the occasion testify to the electric effect of the exchange."[16]

In this perilous situation, Patton did not feel the anxiety of the others in the room. Instead, it was the perfect springboard for the military glory that he had lived for since he was a child. Because of his NPD, aided by his belief in reincarnation, he was fearless—only attracted to and excited by the situation.

Turning the Third Army ninety degrees north on a limited network of crowded, icy roads in wintry weather was a logistical nightmare, largely because of all the supply dumps now oriented toward the Saar campaign. The onrushing Germans had already captured some gasoline dumps, and the rest had to be moved westward as soon as possible. Rick Atkinson wrote:

The feat was prodigious, requiring most of Third Army to swing sharply left while keeping the Saar front secure. The maneuver also required distributing fifty-seven tons of new maps, uprooting and reinstalling an extensive signal-wire network, and stockpiling fuel and ammunition, including shells for twelve hundred guns in the army's 108 artillery battalions.[17]

"Altogether it was an operation that only a master could think of executing," said Blumenson.[18] Earlier on December 19, Patton had met with Col. Karl R. Bendetsen,[19] Bradley's chief combat liaison officer. He told Bendetsen that he needed to move north his supplies of petroleum, oil, lubricants, ammunition, ordnance, transport, replacements, rations, etc., and he had a favor to ask. "I need a freight train. I'm not going to be satisfied unless the Third Army can have its own freight train for this temporary period. . . . I want one and I call upon you to provide it by all means, fair or foul." In a few days, Bendetsen had stolen a freight train for Patton and had gotten away with it.[20]

Swashbuckling with his cigar, Patton went to the map and illustrated his plans for dealing with the "Bulge." For an hour he worked out the divisions to be employed, new boundaries, how Devers's Sixth Army Group would partly move north to take over for the Third Army—all details resolved on Patton's own terms. He answered all questions adeptly. As written by D'Este,

> Simply put, it was perhaps the most remarkable hour of Patton's military career. Bradley later acknowledged that this was a "greatly matured Patton," and that the Third Army staff had pulled off "a brilliant effort."[21]

PREPARATION FOR COUNTERATTACK

Immediately after the Verdun meeting, Patton called his chief of staff, Maj. Gen. Hobart R. Gay,[22] at HQ in Nancy, France, with a prearranged code to let him know which of several plans had been adopted.[23] What only Patton and Bradley and their aides knew at the meeting was that about one-third of their 4th Armored Division (Combat Command B, or CCB) had already been on the road toward Arlon, Belgium, since 00:30 a.m. that day. The other two combat commands, CCA and CCR (where "R" means "reserve"), were not many hours behind, and the 80th Infantry Division had started that morning toward Luxembourg.[24] The 26th would start northward the next day, December 20. The road from just north of Nancy to Arlon would be clogged for days with a hundred-mile-long column of the 4th Armored Division's 1,500 tanks and vehicles alone.[25] Thus, Patton was not exaggerating when he promised three divisions ready to attack in less than seventy-two hours.

The jump-start idea had been proposed at a meeting the previous day, December 18, when Patton and some staff members drove up from Nancy to meet with Bradley at his new 12th Army Group HQ ("EAGLE TAC") in Luxembourg City. A full briefing at the latest map confirmed Patton's belief in the seriousness of the German attack.[26] While Patton was en route to Nancy, Bradley called Gay to ask if any of the combat commands would be ready to move that night, December 18. Gay replied that CCB was ready to move late that night. Brad asked to have Patton call him at 8:00 p.m. from Nancy. In that conversation, Bradley told Patton that the situation was far more serious than reported earlier in the day and that his units needed to move with greater speed.[27]

Patton had been convinced by his own Third Army intelligence briefing of December 17 that the war was taking a new direction and that he would have to drop his much-anticipated December 19 Saar offensive.[28] Together with his G-3, Col. Halley G. Maddox, however, he was thinking of action much more grandiose—pushing east to cut off the Germans and trap them west of the Rhine.[29] At the December 18 meeting, he eagerly offered Bradley the three aforementioned divisions (26th, 80th, and 4th Armored) in short order. These divisions were going to join Gen. John Millikin's III Corps, "the Rescuers," and would thus remain under the control of Patton, who would play the hero in the show. Bradley told Patton that Middleton's VIII Corps, "the Surrounded," would soon also come under Patton's command.[30]

INTELLIGENCE ON THE "BULGE"

How Allied intelligence could have been so taken aback at the Battle of the Bulge, the greatest American intelligence breakdown since Pearl Harbor,[31] has long been debated. How the Germans could have amassed twenty-five divisions along their western border without Allied military noticing is very surprising in view of their ability to intercept and decode ULTRA messages. Did Patton really foresee it, as sometimes claimed? Since the attempt on Hitler's life on July 20, 1944, German security had been considerably tightened up. Operation WACHT AM RHEIN, the German code name for the Ardennes offensive, was known to very few high-level officers. Bad weather interrupted the Allies' normal schedule of surveillance flights. German suspicion of the Allied code breakers was growing, and fewer electronic communiqués were broadcast, meaning fewer ULTRA intercepts. But there were enough ULTRA intercepts and other evidence to have raised Allied suspicion of the coming German counteroffensive.[32]

Many critics felt that Patton's staff was second rate,[33] full of sycophants, but its performance in the early days of the Ardennes offensive was nothing short of spectacular. Patton's superb intelligence officer (G-2), bespectacled Col. Oscar W. Koch, was a stickler for details. His analytical mind probed tirelessly into the plans of the German High Command. As described by author Leo Barron, "Koch had an innate ability to understand the enemy."[34] When Patton claimed to have a "sixth sense" about the enemy, one might assume that Colonel Koch played more than a small role. According to D'Este, Koch was alone among his peers in predicting the Bulge and planning how to deal with it.[35] Most of the US Army's intelligence was defense oriented—warning about bad things to come. Patton's intelligence was offense oriented—what opportunities lurk here? Not that Patton had always listened to Colonel Koch's predictions.[36] Earlier in the war, Patton had been skeptical of military intelligence, but now he was hungry for ULTRA and any other sources of information. He had even established his own, private intelligence team, partly to avoid the delays coming through the supreme headquarters, allied expeditionary force (SHAEF).

Patton had to know if there was a weak spot on his left flank. What would he do if the German Army came rushing through? As noted by author Don Fox, "On November 25, Patton made a portentous, nay, almost prescient entry in his diary: . . . the First Army is making a terrible mistake by leaving the VIII Corps static, as it is highly probable that the Germans are building up east of them."[37]

On December 9, Koch briefed Patton, showing the German units lined up against Middleton's VIII Corps on Patton's left flank. As written by Leo Barron,

> At the time, the corps had three infantry divisions and one armored division, which was not at full strength. Arrayed against them were four enemy infantry divisions, while behind those were two panzer divisions and another three infantry divisions. Even worse was the amount of ground the VIII Corps had to defend—nearly 80 miles of thick forest and deep gullies.[38]

Patton believed Koch was probably right, but it was still a theory. Without further confirmation, on December 9, Patton intended to continue with his planned December 19 attack on the Saar, then the Rhine, and eventually Frankfurt. Meanwhile, and this might have been the most important decision he ever made, "he ordered Koch and the rest of his staff to prepare for a contingency plan to stop a German offensive in the VIII Corps' area of operation."[39] Patton also moved the 6th Armored and 26th Infantry Divisions into Millikin's III Corps[40] because, as Patton wrote in his diary, "If the enemy attacks the VIII Corps of the First Army, as is probable, I can use the III Corps to help."[41]

PATTON GOES INTO ACTION

After the Verdun meeting on December 19, Patton sent his aide, Major Codman, back to Third Army HQ in Nancy. Patton, however, did not return, serving as a whirlwind one-man headquarters for the next few days until the new "Lucky Forward" had been moved to Luxembourg City. Accompanied by his very fast driver, M.Sgt. John L. Mims, Patton spent the first night with XX Corps in Metz and then visited seven divisions on December 20.[42] Late that day, Patton was joined by his deputy chief, Lieutenant Colonel Harkins.[43]

On December 20, Patton issued a written directive to formalize his previous verbal orders. The first nine commands included some rather grandiose ambitions to "seize crossings of the Rhine River," and "to attack . . . in the direction of St. Vith . . . in the direction of Bitburg."[44] These commands did not mention Bastogne, a situation reminiscent of the Lorraine campaign, where Patton was often focused on the Rhine rather than the task at hand.[45] If Patton's focus on Bastogne had slipped, fortunately General Middleton was intimately familiar with the town that had been his VIII Corps HQ for months. He understood what an important crossroads town it was, as described by D'Este:

> The afternoon of December 20 Patton met Middleton at Arlon and greeting him with the admonition: "Troy, of all the goddam crazy things I ever heard of, leaving the 101st Airborne to be surrounded in Bastogne is the worst!" A friend of long standing, Middleton was never in the least intimidated by Patton or his blustery remarks, and rejoined: "George, just look at that map with all the [six] roads converging on Bastogne. Bastogne is the hub of the wheel. If we let the Boche [Germans] take it, they will be on the Meuse in a day."[46]

So credit Middleton with influencing the decision to save Bastogne at all costs, even if it were surrounded. The remainder of December 20 and 21, Patton patched together his new army, improvising in a hundred ways to get ready for the promised attack on December 22. Maj. Gen. John Millikin would not have been Patton's first choice to command his new III Corps into the Bulge. A former cavalryman, Millikin had never led troops into combat.[47] Thus Patton, against his own principles, took most of the lead in the organization and conduct of the coming battles.

On December 21, Patton and Harkins were in Luxembourg reorganizing units for the next day's attack. As described by Hirshson, "[The] troops, Harkins remembered, were badly jumbled, antiaircraft units, for example, being scrambled with the infantry. Patton first created task forces, small, aggressive units named after their commanders, such as Task Force Jones or Task Force Gregory. Years later Harkins lavishly praised Patton's creativity,"

> I don't think if you sat down in Fort Leavenworth and tried to figure out how you could save that thing, you could have done better than he did. He just had a knack of what should go together and what they should do. In the first place, he just turned them all around and sent them north. It was absolutely fantastic, and when we got all straightened out, in two or three days, and the divisions started coming up and taking over and absorbing

these little task forces. They, the task forces, really held the enemy off while the divisions moved up. As I say, it was fantastic, quite a job.[48]

Carlo D'Este wrote,

What the Battle of the Bulge demonstrated is that, while possessed of tremendous vision—the ability to anticipate and react with impeccable foresight to an enemy move or countermove—Patton's greatest strength was not so much as a tactician but as an organizer, a mover and shaker.[49]

THE "PRE-LIBERATION" OF BASTOGNE SIX DAYS EARLY

On December 20, Task Force Ezell from the 4th Armored came cruising into Bastogne, unopposed by the enemy, with orders from the First Army to help defend the town. They went for instructions to the acting 101st Airborne Division commander, Brig. Gen. Anthony C. McAuliffe, who referred them to Col. William L. Roberts, commander of CCB of the 10th Armored. A few hours later, they were recalled, escaping just before the Germans slammed the door on Bastogne.

How could such a bizarre event have happened? And if the task force had stayed, could it have prevented the encirclement of the town? The story of this episode[50] has been told by one of the leading eyewitnesses, Brig. Gen. Albin F. Irzyk, commander of the 8th Tank Battalion of CCB of the 4th Armored.[51] General Irzyk believed that neither Task Force Ezell nor CCB were powerful enough to have enabled keeping open an exit road, such as the Bastogne–Neufchâteau road (N85). The "pre-liberation" of Bastogne was a wasteful bureaucratic foul-up caused by the rapid movement and reshuffling of troop units but did not in fact cause any serious harm.

A CHAIN OF DOGFIGHTS (DECEMBER 22–26)

Starting early on December 22, Patton's promised northward attack by Middleton's III Corps took place, with the 4th Armored on the left, the 26th Infantry in the middle, and the 80th Infantry on the right. This would involve five days of tough slogging against superior numbers of well-entrenched Germans in terrain unfavorable for tank attacks. Patton seemed to feel that he had to liberate Bastogne by December 25. His greeting to McAuliffe on December 24, "Xmas Eve present coming up. Hold on," was ill advised and only raised false hopes.[52] Patton had clearly underestimated the difficulty of getting there. General Eisenhower wrote,

> It was the kind of fighting that General Patton distinctly disliked. It was slow, laborious going, with a sudden break-through an impossibility. Several times during the course of this attack General Patton called me to express his disappointment because he could go no faster.[53]

Most of the III Corps units were understrength, both men and equipment tired and beaten up. Most of the tanks had been driven hard and were well beyond their service lifetimes. A fully equipped combat command should have had fifty-three M4 medium (Sherman) tanks and seventeen M5 light (Stuart) tanks (see below).[54] The number of combat-ready Shermans on December 22 was reported for CCA, between thirty-seven and forty-two, for CCB, eighteen to thirty-one, and for CCR, twenty-eight to thirty-one.[55]

Scale drawings of US medium five-man (Sherman) and light four-man (Stuart) tanks (adapted from http://www.taskforcebaum.de).

Near the top of map 12.1 lies the town of Bastogne, connected to major highways N85, leading southwest to Neufchâteau, and N4, leading south to Arlon (neither town shown). The Sauer River slices horizontally across Belgium and forms part of the Belgium/Luxembourg border. US combat engineers from the famous 299th Battalion (first on Omaha Beach, where they took more than 30 percent casualties) had methodically blown the bridges across the Sauer on December 21 in order to stop any German attacks. They had also blown massive craters in highways, such as N4. It would cost precious time to repair these demolitions.

4TH ARMORED, CCA BATTLES

CCA (see map 12.1) arrived in a blinding snowstorm on the morning of December 22 up highway N4, led by the 51st Armored Infantry Battalion (AIB, Maj. Dan Alanis, commander). They had to wait several hours while engineers repaired a giant crater in the highway near the Perle junction. They were followed by the 35th Tank Battalion (Lt. Col. Delk M. Oden, commander). Fighting their way into Martelange, CCA discovered two more blown bridges across the Sauer, which delayed them nearly twenty-four hours while engineers rebuilt them.

Warnach was stoutly defended by the Germans, and the battle turned into an intense street brawl—attack following counterattack, made particularly difficult by Patton's orders to fight all night. Warnach was finally taken by CCA, but at the expense of sixty-eight casualties, four Stuart tanks, and two half-tracks.[56] Tintange, though not on the N4 path to Bastogne, needed to be cleaned out to protect the right flank of the advance. Manpower was augmented by a 450-man battalion detached from the 80th Infantry. They spent Christmas Eve huddled in an open, snowy field. At 2:30 a.m. they received instructions, and at 7:00 a.m. traveled to Tintange. At 8:00 a.m., they waded through a creek at the bottom of a deep gorge into the teeth of German machine gun fire and hand grenades.

After a furious battle, they secured the town of Tintange at 4:00 p.m. on Christmas Day, at a cost of 326 casualties from the 80th Infantry Division.[57] Later that day, the 51st AIB pushed farther north along N4 with some help from American P-47 fighter-bombers. They suffered sixty-two casualties on Christmas Day and stopped for the night just outside the village of Hollange.[58]

4TH ARMORED, CCB BATTLES, CHAUMONT, DECEMBER 22–23

Brig. Gen. Holmes E. Dager's experienced CCB was expected by many to get to Bastogne first (see map 12.1).[59] Assigned to a secondary, dirt road, more like a logging trail, running north from Louftremont (not shown on map 12.1), Fauvillers-Burnon-Chaumont and then north to Bastogne, they expected to catch the Germans off guard.[60] Starting at 4:30 a.m., Irzyk's Eighth

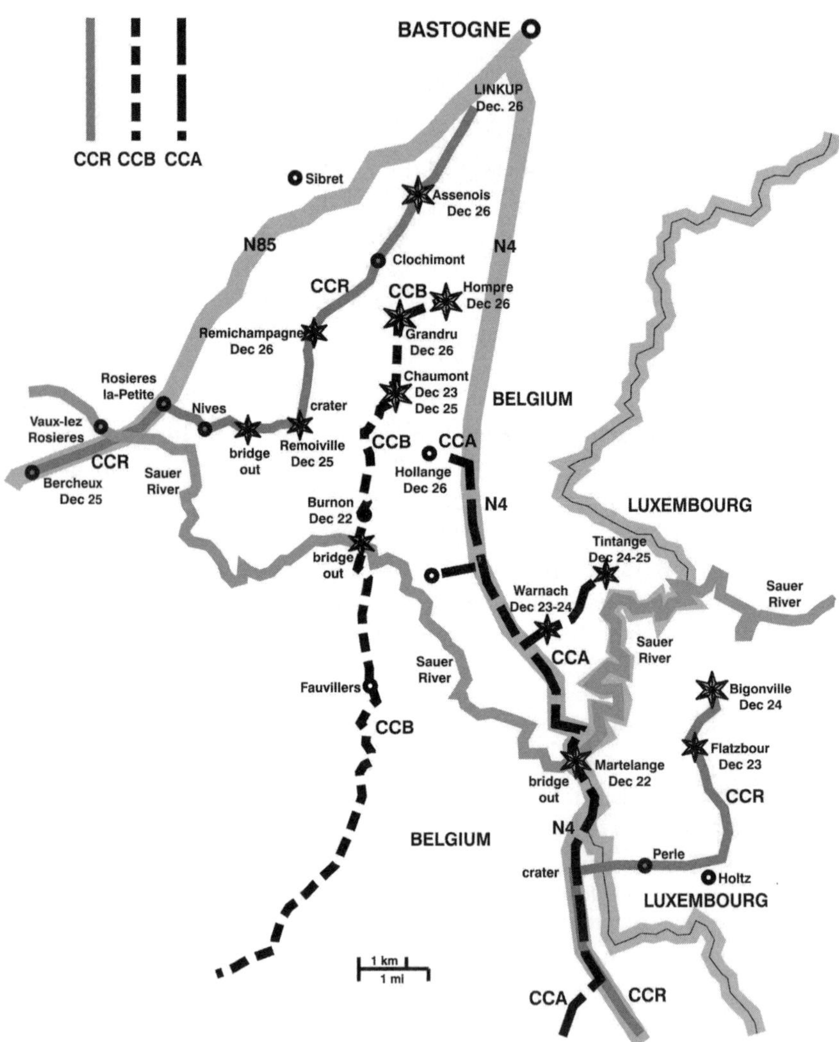

Map 12.1. Relief of Bastogne, December 22–26, 1944.

Brig. Gen. Albin F. Irzyk, 2006.
Courtesy of Ivan Steenkiste.

Tank Batallion (TB) headed over snow-covered, icy roads in hazy conditions, reaching Fauvillers at 10:15 a.m. against light German resistance.

Reaching the Sauer River just south of Burnon, Irzyk discovered the bridge had been blown at noon the previous day by the 299th Combat Engineer Battalion. "This was a shocker," recalled Irzyk, "because at the rate we were going, we thought we would be in Bastogne the next day."[61] With suppressive artillery fire, the 24th Combat Engineer Battalion built a thirty-six-foot treadway bridge, finishing just after sundown. CCB stopped for the night a bit north of Burnon for the dicey business of bringing up and guarding tanker trucks for refueling.[62]

At 9:00 p.m., just as CCB had established its bivouac positions, an order originating from Patton was received: "Move all night." The details of the order were fleshed out in writing at CCB headquarters in Fauvillers and were to be picked up by 1st Lt. William J. Marshall, Irzyk's S-2. Marshall and another officer got into a jeep heading for Irzyk's command post but before long, Irzyk's radio crackled:

> "Lieutenant Marshall, the S-2 for the 8th Tank Battalion, was captured two kilometers east of checkpoint 49 at around 2030 hours with orders for this evening. Break. . . . He had the checkpoint list and other data." . . .

It was worse than that. Marshall had the passwords for the next four days and the unit locations for the previous day. Now the Germans had them.[63]

It was after midnight by the time CCB was ready to push north again. Part of the 25th Armored Cavalry, mostly jeeps supported by Stuart tanks, took the lead. They advanced slowly through the dark, against the drifting snow and the gnawing uncertainty about the enemy ahead.[64] Sunrise was at 8:34 a.m.[65]

In the predawn light, the leading Stuart tanks and jeeps began a descent into the small village of Chaumont. As they rounded a slight jog in the road to the right, all hell broke loose! The Germans, who had been lying in ambush, destroyed one Stuart tank and blew three jeeps sky high with their 75 mm self-propelled assault guns (StuG IIIs). This was followed by German artillery and a charge by paratroopers armed with Panzerfausts (a disposable, one-shot, bazooka-like antitank weapon). The Shermans soon got into the fight, dispatched one of the StuGs, and chased the German troops back into the woods.[66]

Wreckage from Stuart tank and three jeeps after dawn ambush at Chaumont, December 23. Body in foreground. Beech tree appears to be draped with clothing and body parts. US Army Signal Corps.

It had taken seven hours to cover one mile since they received Patton's order to "move all night," which cost CCB's exhausted troops a night's sleep.[67] Now CCB pulled back behind the hill to consider its options. Chaumont was a town of some fifty dwellings, mostly half barn, half house, each with its own manure pile. Heights of land on all four corners surrounded Chaumont, which sat in the bottom of a saucer, with no way to travel north except through the town.

Major Irzyk surveyed the landscape and came up with a plan, which he explained in a meeting. The Eighth TB would attack with C Company (seven Sherman tanks) across a snowy field on the left, B Company (nine Shermans) down the main road, and A Company (six Shermans) down the ridge on the right, all accompanied by Lieutenant Colonel Cohen's 10th Armored Infantrymen riding piggyback on the various tanks.[68] Preceded by an hour of artillery bombardment and some fighter-bomber support, Irzyk sent the various task forces sequentially into the fray.

Things started badly. C Company got mired in a stream not shown on Irzyk's 1:100,000 scale maps and invisible under the snow, essentially taking them out of the battle. But A Company was moving forward, and B Company overcame vicious resistance inside the village, allowing the infantry to advance toward the town center.[69] One of the lead tanks was knocked out by an antitank gun. B Company of the 10th AIB (B/10 in shorthand) dislodged the German paratroopers in heroic house-to-house combat. An hour later, Irzyk sent in more armored infantry and tanks. By 4:00 p.m. on December 23, the last reserves of armored infantry had been committed. Irzyk said, "We got to the far end of Chaumont, and we felt that Chaumont now was ours."[70]

The German commander, Col. Heinz Kokott, was at his headquarters north of Chaumont in the village of Hompre. Like CCB, he was focused on attacking Bastogne, but the pressure of the elite 4th Armored Division in his rear flank was starting to make him uncomfortable. Just by luck, four fifty-eight-ton Tiger I tanks with their infamous 88 mm guns rumbled into town. Kokott ordered them to Chaumont with a half dozen other armored vehicles, including StuGs, and about five hundred infantrymen, many riding on the tanks.[71] The German force trudged up a dirt road on the back side of the hilltop (Hill 490) northeast of the village. From the ridge, they looked down on Chaumont and CCB like so many fish in a barrel, ready to change the tide of battle in dramatic fashion.

Suddenly, the Germans opened fire, and under cover of smoke and Tiger tank fire, German infantry and armored vehicles moved down the hill. Sherman tanks were brewing up, and the American infantry was in chaos.

With no chance to organize a defense, the order to retreat was issued. German fighter planes added to the mayhem, although two were shot down. B Company was decimated. Soldiers risked their lives to cover the retreat and to bring along the wounded and dying. As described by Fox,

> Those that made it back to the south end of the ugly, manure-strewn hell of a village were faced with the prospect of crossing over completely open, exposed ground, as they climbed back up the slope whence their attack had originated.

Major Irzyk, who had been trying to maintain control of the retreat, now realized that he too was in the crosshairs of those Tiger tanks, and started backing up through the streets of Chaumont. Since there was no room to turn around, driving in reverse meant Irzyk's gunners could keep firing, and it was better than exposing the thin armor of his rear. However, it was slow and awkward because of his poor visibility and the driver's delay in responding to his cues. Reaching the southern edge of the village, Irzyk's tank was more exposed than ever to the Tiger tanks across the valley. So for greater visibility, he turned the turret forward and the tank sped up in reverse. Then, not far from the crest of the hill, Irzyk reported,

> There was a low, loud, deafening, earsplitting sound, followed by a terrible, horrible, frightening blow. The tank was shoved violently forward. It was as though the tank had been hit in the back by a huge sledge hammer, and picked up and thrown forward by a super-human hand.

Don Fox said,

> The three men in the turret were thrown to the floor, amidst a cascade of gun shells that had broken loose from their mounting around the turret and were tossed around like matchsticks.[72]

The tank could still be driven in reverse, but soon Irzyk saw daylight through a crack in the turret. The Germans, fortunately, had no orders to pursue the Americans, and after CCB reached a safe place, Irzyk took stock of the damage. His tank survived because the shell happened to strike an extra plate of six-inch-thick armor about five inches square welded to the rear of the turret for reasons still unknown. He had lost eleven Sherman tanks, and Company A/10 alone had suffered more than sixty-five casualties, including all the officers.

PATTON'S MISMANAGEMENT

Patton made the mistake of micromanaging these battles for Bastogne and managing too many echelons down—something clearly against his own principles. He wrote, for example, that, "An Army Commander should command corps, and show on his battle map the locations of corps and divisions, but he should not command the division."[73] By giving orders to combat commands, he was meddling three levels below his echelon.[74] Because of his lack of trust in generals Millikin and Gaffey, neither of whom had previously led troops into battle, Patton was making an exception. But it was wrong and based on misinformation, which showed in some of the unrealistic orders: "Drive like hell. That we keep on attacking tonight," "Get them to bypass towns and get forward," "I want Bastogne by 1350 [on December 23]," and "Tell Millikin to get them going if he has to go down to the frontline platoon and move them."[75] Shades of Pinky Ward (Chapter 7)?

Few of these Belgian villages, such as Chaumont, could be bypassed. To have tanks attacking at night was not a part of tank doctrine in 1944 because it surrendered the advantage of long-range fire that tanks have over infantry.[76] Patton wrote in his diary, December 24,

> We have received violent counterattacks, one of which forced . . . the 4th Armored back some miles with the loss of ten tanks. This was probably my fault, because I had been insisting on day and night attacks. This is all right on the first or second day of the battle and when we had the enemy surprised, but after that the men get too tired. Furthermore, in this bad weather, it is very difficult for armored outfits to operate at night.[77]

A quote from Don Fox: "To his credit, he realized his mistake, and took responsibility for it."[78] But Patton also violated his own dictum in a battle near Ettelbruck, Luxembourg, to never attack through woods at night. Fox stated, "He would violate his own tenets on more than one occasion during the fight in the Ardennes, and never once showed a positive result for doing so."[79]

4TH ARMORED, CCB BATTLES, CHAUMONT, GRANDRU, HOMPRE, DECEMBER 25–26

After a day spent regrouping just north of Burnon on December 24, CCB received reinforcements of 350 men from the 80th Infantry Division. Prior to attacking Chaumont, Irzyk ordered the cleaning out of the large wooded area on his right flank, using bayonets against the fiercest resistors. Next, the troops cleaned out the unnamed woods just southeast of Chaumont in a long, hard battle, showing heroics such as those that earned Pvt. Paul Wiedorfer the Medal of Honor. The wooded heights (Hill 490) northeast of Chaumont, whence the Tiger tanks had fired so effectively two days earlier, were attacked next. Though hit at one point by "friendly" artillery fire, the stalwart 80th Infantry seized the hill, taking one hundred German prisoners. Another wooded hill was taken on the northwest side.[80] Artillery was exchanged to retake Chaumont village, and after ten hours of continuous fighting, CCB finally succeeded, bagging another hundred German prisoners. The battle was costly, with all infantry companies depleted—one down to only twenty-nine men.[81]

On December 26, CCB pressed forward into what became another slugfest, and by nightfall they had taken Grandru, Hompre, and increasing numbers of German prisoners. They were surprised to make contact on their left with the Sherman tanks of Lieutenant Colonel Abrams's CCR, which they had no idea had traversed that far west.[82]

4TH ARMORED, CCR BATTLES, FLATZBOUR, DECEMBER 23

Col. Wendell Blanchard's CCR was the last of the 4th Armored to get into battle, but they would not be "in reserve" for long. It was built around Lt. Col. Creighton Abrams's distinguished 37th TB, which was perilously low in Sherman tanks (down to twenty-eight). They were joined by Lt. Col. "Jigger"

Table 12.1. Organization of CCR during Relief of Bastogne

Abrams's 37th Tank Battalion		*Jacques's 53rd Armored Infantry Battalion*	
Full strength	53 Shermans 17 Stuarts	**Full strength**	1,001 men
Company	**Commander (Tanks)**	**Company**	**Commander**
A	Whitehill (Shermans)	**A**	Kutak
B	Leach (Shermans)	**B**	?
C	Boggess (Shermans)	**C**	Smith
D	Donahue (Stuarts)		

George L. Jacques's (pronounced "Jakes") 53rd AIB. Thirty or forty German panzers had been reported up the road somewhere beyond Flatzbour, which could potentially cut off and surround CCA. CCR's mission on December 23 was to drive to Bigonville and remove this potential hazard.[83] A hard freeze the previous night caused many of CCR's tanks to skid on the ice, some sliding into ditches. With B Company commander Capt. Jimmie Leach in the lead Sherman tank, "Blockbuster 3d," the attackers, as they moved toward the railway station in Flatzbour, saw evidence of German tank tracks. Leach called for an artillery barrage, but the Germans withdrew, and when they returned, their fire was even deadlier.

Lieutenant Colonel Abrams then brought Lt. John A. Whitehill's A Company into the battle.[84] A minefield buried under the snow crippled the track on the tank of Whitehill, who took over another Sherman. Suddenly, antitank gunfire erupted, and Whitehill's second tank was hit by three artillery shells, wounding several crewmen. Most of the crew bailed out, but Whitehill drove the tank back to the rear for use in evacuating the wounded. Another Sherman was hit, wounding its commander, leaving Whitehill with no other officers in A Company. With daylight fading, Abrams brought up Captain Trover's C Company between companies A and B and then swung east across the road to Bigonville. Trover, a Bronze Star recipient who had just volunteered to take the leadership of C Company, was going around the east side of Flatzbour, riding in his always-open command turret—a 37th TB tradition—when he was killed by a sniper's bullet.[85] Abrams, his CCR having lost two Shermans and fifty-nine infantrymen, decided to postpone the attack on Bigonville until the next day.[86]

BIGONVILLE, DECEMBER 24

The next morning, the Germans had drawn back from Flatzbour, but they had reinforcements and were dug in in Bigonville, waiting for the "Amis." First Lt. Charles P. Boggess, former executive officer of C Company, 37th TB, took over command of C Company after the death of Trover. Whitehill's A Company would make the main attack on Bigonville, with Leach's B Company protecting their left flank. S.Sgt. Walter P. Kaplin asked Leach if he could take command of a tank. Leach later said, "Since he had been out of tanks for a while, I was skeptical until he volunteered some professional fire commands and superb radio procedure. He was ready."[87]

Each side had two companies of infantry, but the Americans had far more tanks, artillery, and air support.[88] Six American batteries, three of which were 155 mm "Long Toms," began their predawn wake-up call on Bigonville with devastating effect.[89] Whitehill's tank struggled north straight into Bigonville, flanked by platoons of four Shermans each on his left and right. They were bombarded by German machine guns, mortars, and Panzerfausts. Leach, with two platoons totaling seven Shermans, entered Bigonville from the southwest, blasting the houses with machine gun fire to suppress the enemy. A sniper's bullet instantly killed another tank commander, but with his body underfoot in the turret, the crew rolled on. For Abrams, however, the overall advance was entirely too slow.[90] Then Leach was hit with a bullet that penetrated his helmet, knocking him out. He fell to the turret floor but was soon back on his feet. Abrams came up with a new plan. Instead of having Leach penetrate the town of Bigonville, he ordered him to seize the high ground on the north side, thus trapping the Germans.[91]

Knocking holes in the stone walls, the tankers used "bunker-buster" shells. Then they fired .50-caliber machine guns, which usually started fires inside. The house-to-house fighting, using the method of grenade and rush, progressed to the center of town. Leach's blocking north of town was established, although 1st Lt. Rob Cook, his platoon leader and executive officer, was seriously wounded. By about noon, the Germans had had enough of fighting,[92] and about four hundred surrendered. Among the dead in B/37 was Sergeant Kaplin, who had volunteered to take command of a Sherman tank. Col. Jimmie Leach remembered Sergeant Kaplin for the rest of his life with strong emotion.[93]

CCR BATTLES INTO BASTOGNE, DECEMBER 25–26

> "This is it!"
>
> —Abrams's last words in pep talk to Boggess and Dwight[94]

The mission of CCR in Bigonville, securing the right flank of the 4th Armored, had been accomplished, and the men looked forward to some Christmas relief. Instead, late Christmas Eve, Colonel Blanchard received orders from General Gaffey to move his CCR some sixteen kilometers west (thirty kilometers by the circuitous route required) to secure the division's left flank. This audacious maneuver (see map 12.1) would prove to be a stroke of genius, almost certainly by Gaffey, since Patton, no shrinking violet, did not claim it in his memoir.[95]

Arriving dog tired, like all of CCR, in the predawn hours of December 25 at Bercheux, Belgium, Colonel Abrams was summoned to a meeting by Colonel Blanchard. Blanchard's instructions involved driving CCR east to

Remoiville and then north toward Sibret, where the enemy was believed to be strengthening. CCR's main mission was to protect the left flank of Irzyk's CCB as they attacked Bastogne, though Blanchard had no information on the progress of CCB. Jump-off time was 11:00 a.m., with D/37 and their fast, highly maneuverable, Stuart tanks leading the way.[96]

Abrams's tactic on the first two villages was to blow right past the German engineer outposts, leaving the Shermans to clean them out. The engineers suddenly realized that they had been cut off from their units and quickly surrendered. Thus the villages of Vaux-lez-Rosieres, Rosieres la-Petite, and Nives were taken within three hours. Colonel Abrams had a close call that Christmas Day when his jeep hit a mine, totaling the vehicle and seriously injuring the driver.[97] In Cobreville (not on map 12.1), a small village east of Nives, Lieutenant Boggess, the new C/37 commander, led the way on foot while his infantry searched the houses. Then Boggess discovered a bridge over a small creek that had been blown by US engineers. The battalion tankdozer went quickly to work and filled in the creek with debris from a stone wall. By 2:50 p.m., the "C Team" (the C companies of the 37th TB and 53rd AIB) was on the march to Remoiville.[98]

Remoiville, where CCR was about to meet the main line of the German defense, was surrounded on four sides by ridges. After a furious barrage of artillery from four CCR batteries, Boggess's C Team occupied the west ridge looking down on the town. Leach's B Company occupied a position on a hill northeast of town, where it could block any attack from the north. Then Whitehill's A Team drove quickly into the center of town under covering fire from the C Team, keeping the Germans pinned down. Leading A Company's infantry was the fearless 1st Lt. Frank R. Kutak, who, while twice wounded, led from the front, getting his men fired up. The Shermans blasted the buildings point blank, while the armored infantry cleared them out one by one. C Team then entered the town, sealing off its west side. In two hours, CCR had eliminated as a fighting unit one battalion of German paratroopers. Soon Abrams's Stuart tanks were speeding off to Remichampagne, when they found a huge crater blocking the road. With darkness approaching, Abrams called a halt to the attack for the night and outposted the town to secure their gains, while engineers repaired the road.[99]

At 9:25 a.m. on December 26, CCR artillery began the bombardment of a forest and a road west of Remichampagne, where spotter aircraft had reported German tanks. The Stuart tanks of D Company, followed by Leach's B Team, led the advance over a frozen, open field east of the main north–south highway, while Boggess's C Team advanced on a parallel track west of the highway. Boggess reported German troops going into the woods on his left. A flight of sixteen P-47s arrived to help strafe and bomb the woods for fifty minutes, leaving the place a smoking graveyard. B Team, preceded by their own 105 mm assault gun fire,[100] entered the town of Remichampagne at 9:55 a.m. and, supported by tank fire from the C Team on their left, spent the next hour pushing through town toward Clochimont. At 10:55 a.m., Abrams reported to CCR that most of the town was secured. The price for success so far was that CCR was down to twenty combat-ready Sherman tanks, and Jacques's 53rd Armored Infantry had lost 230 men. CCR, however, had disregarded Patton's command to attack all night, every night since December 22 and were thus better rested than CCA or CCB.[101]

No sooner had Company A taken a position northwest of Clochimont looking down on Sibret than they began to receive serious 88 mm fire from a camouflaged position on their right rear. Abrams ordered Leach to take care of it, but Leach's 105 mm assault gun loader was out of high explosive (HE) shells. The assault gunner knocked out several other targets, but Abrams in his tank, "Thunderbolt VI," became impatient and rolled up close to Leach's tank. As described by Don Fox, "Abrams [came] riding high in the . . . turret, as was his custom. Abrams immediately barked out fire orders to his gunner, John Gatusky: 'Gunner—anti-tank—HE (x-range)—(gunner ready) fire.' And with one HE round from his 76 mm cannon, the enemy AT gun was sent skyward."

Leach wrote, "I recommended him for the DSC right there. After all, he's the Colonel—a lot of colonels stay back at the flagpole but not Abrams."[102] Whitehill, with the A Team, reported that he was not seeing any Germans in Sibret.[103]

CCR drove on toward Clochimont. The previous night, Abrams and Jacques had attended a meeting with Colonel Blanchard in which he ordered them to conquer Sibret—a step he thought necessary before Bastogne could be liberated. Now, at 3:00 p.m., time was running out, and they needed a plan. Abrams took inventory of his ammunition. Company B was out of 75 mm shells, and Company A was almost out.[104]

Over Bastogne, the skies were filled with hundreds of slow-flying C-47 transports, dropping supplies by glider or floating in on an array of brightly colored parachutes. German antiaircraft fire caught some of the planes, and they shattered and dived to earth, trailing smoke and flames. The spectacle of the courageous airmen gave fresh inspiration to Abrams. He suggested to Jacques that, against Blanchard's orders, they head for Bastogne via the shortest route, namely through Clochimont and Assenois. If the enemy was strong in Sibret, Abrams doubted they could win anyway with their depleted ammunition supply. Jacques agreed, and the plan moved into high gear.[105] Abrams could have been court-martialed if the plan had failed.[106]

The B Team guarded the heights of Clochimont. Abrams's choice for the unit he would send for the last, frenzied "Hail Mary" into Bastogne, ironically, was the only unit with enough tank ammo—the C Team. Coordination was required in order to avoid fratricide in the invasion and artillery show Abrams had planned. The 101st Airborne was warned, and batteries not only from CCR but also from neighborly CCB joined in a single-fire plan.

The C Team, similar to a task force, was headed up by Capt. William A. Dwight, Abrams's trusted, agile S-3 (operations officer). Following them, to clean out Assenois, would be the AB Team. Before the C Team pushed off at about 4:15 p.m., Abrams gave Dwight and Boggess a little briefing and pep talk to say, "Get to those men in Bastogne!" As Boggess reported later,

> We were going through fast, all guns firing, straight up that road to bust through before they had time to get set. . . . I thought of whether the road would be mined, whether the bridge in Assenois would be blown, whether they would be ready at their anti-tank guns. Then we charged, and I didn't have any time to wonder.[107]

At 4:34 p.m., Boggess was en route and radioed Abrams for artillery on Assenois. "Number nine, play it soft and sweet," was the coded euphemism relayed by Abrams. This brought down a curtain of hurt from thirteen artillery batteries on top of Assenois village and the woods on both sides, which were suspected of harboring antitank guns. Boggess led the way, all guns firing, into the smoking village in "Cobra King," his heavy, overarmored Sherman command tank. Somehow, "Cobra King" and its driver, Pvt. Hubert J. J. Smith, avoided any damage from the zigzag of incoming antitank rounds. Now it was time to raise the wall of artillery looming ahead. However, the artillery spotter's jeep had received a direct hit, killing the driver and throwing the spotter into a ditch before he could send the message. Boggess called for the artillery to be lifted but couldn't wait long enough and charged straight ahead anyway.[108]

The dust and smoke from the barrage reduced visibility for both sides. The armored infantry never stopped firing over the sides of their half-tracks, keeping the Germans from retaliating. Two of the Sherman tanks made a wrong turn and fell behind, and one of the half-tracks took a direct hit, wounding three. A half-track farther back in the column was pinned down by a falling telephone pole, stopping the column. Colonel Abrams and his crew dismounted from "Thunderbolt VI" and wrestled the pole out of the way, freeing the half-track.[109] There were other heroics in Assenois that afternoon. Pvt. James Hendrix, a nineteen-year-old rifleman, took on two 88 mm antitank guns by himself, killing one member of the crew and capturing the rest. Soon after, he braved enemy fire to rescue wounded comrades on two occasions from two different blown-up half-tracks. From these actions, Hendrix was one of only three members of the 4th Armored Division to receive the Medal of Honor.[110]

Roaring out of Assenois hell-bent for Bastogne, the C Team was now spearheaded by six vehicles: Boggess in front, followed by two other Shermans, a single half-track, and two more Shermans, the first of which was commanded by Dwight. The half-track for some reason fell three hundred yards behind, giving German soldiers in the adjacent woods time to place a string of a dozen Teller mines on the road. The half-track plowed right into a mine, transforming it into a flaming pile of twisted steel and rubber. Dwight dismounted and, helped by the survivors, started throwing the rest of the mines into a ditch. Boggess and his two companion Shermans kept driving full speed, firing all their guns right and left at all suspected enemy sites.

A green concrete pillbox loomed ahead. Loader Pvt. James Murphy and gunner Cpl. Milton Dickerman got off three quick 75 mm shots, caving in the pillbox and killing a dozen Germans. Bow gunner Pvt. Harold Hafner kept his sights on the woods near the pillbox as "Cobra King" moved slowly forward. Several men in uniform stood near the pillbox. They were American engineers who had been preparing to knock out the same pillbox. "Come here, come on out. This the 4th Armored," shouted Boggess. A man approached and said, "I'm Lt. Webster of the 326th Engineers, 101st Airborne Division. Glad to see you." These simple words at 4:50 p.m., December 26, 1944, meant an end to five days of bloody, bitter combat.

Although it would take another day before the corridor from Bastogne to Assenois was secure, it meant that General Patton had made good on his promise to liberate Bastogne and relieve the 101st Airborne. General McAuliffe soon appeared to greet Captain Dwight, and later, Colonel Abrams. "Gee, I am mighty glad to see you," were McAuliffe's words.[111] The 101st Airborne often liked to say about their enemies, "We're surrounded again, those poor sons-of-bitches." Many of the 101st even denied that they were ever in need of relief. True, they had been resupplied by air drops with food, ammo, and medicine, but their wounded were in dire need of evacuation, and they were beyond exhaustion.

SUMMARY

1. Patton did not liberate Bastogne by himself. But like the coach of a Super Bowl team, Patton had collected star players, many of them veterans, and rehearsed them until they could run their plays in their sleep. The players, in turn, knowing that they were in the biggest

game of the season, were willing to risk it all. It would be hard to pick the most valuable player. Lieutenant Colonel Abrams (who earned a DSC from the battle) and CCR, certainly. But what about Major Irzyk and CCB, who took on the brunt of the German defensive line, which enabled Abrams's winning end run? How about Oden and CCA, who drew first blood and helped wear down the defenders? Each of some thirteen hard-fought battles depicted on map 12.1 required its own set of tactics and its own sacrifices. There were many other stellar performances—from Koch, Gaffey, Harkins, Middleton, Boggess, Whitehill, Leach, Trover, Dager, Alanis, Cohen, Jacques, Kutak, Dwight, Kaplin, and Hendrix. The crews of "Thunderbolt VI," "Cobra King," and "Blockbuster 3d." The P-47 fighter-bomber pilots. The superbly coordinated artillery. The intrepid artillery spotters in their L-4 aircraft. The resourceful combat engineers, who could erect a new bridge under enemy fire almost as fast as they could destroy one.

2. Patton's execution regarding the battle was masterful but not perfect. He contradicted his own principles by commanding too far down the chain. These commands were deleterious (e.g., requiring the tankers to attack at night and the infantrymen to attack in the woods at night). Bridges and roads were blown prematurely in many cases, causing needless delays in rebuilding. The pre-liberation of Bastogne on December 20 by Task Force Ezell was understandable in view of the rapid and complex movement of the troops. The task force might easily have been trapped, but they got lucky.
3. The liberation of Bastogne was clearly Patton's finest hour. He anticipated the Ardennes offensive, he made contingency plans for it, he confronted it not with dread but with eager anticipation, he orchestrated very quickly and efficiently the intricate movement of resources to meet it headlong, and he carried out his battle plan to a successful conclusion. As expressed by Carlo D'Este,

> Bradley would offer the highest praise of Patton he would ever accord: "True to his boast at Verdun, Patton, having turned his Third Army ninety degrees, attacked on December 22. His generalship during this difficult maneuver was magnificent. One of the most brilliant performances by any commander on either side in World War II. It was absolutely his cup of tea—rapid, open warfare combined with noble purpose and difficult goals. He relished every minute of it, knowing full well that this mission, if nothing else, would guarantee him a place of high honor in the annals of the US Army."[112]

Bradley also offered strong praise for the maturation of Patton's logistics starting with the Bulge:

> Meanwhile, Patton, who in Sicily had brushed off supply as a bothersome detail, demonstrated how well he had learned his lessons during the September drought by stuffing his Third Army dumps with engineer bridging equipment to be used in spanning the Rhine. Fearful lest Devers ransack that hoard should it fall into his hands on the Army Group shift, George insisted that in rearranging his boundary we keep those dumps within his sector. Two months later that foresight paid off when George took the Rhine on the run and jumped Third Army across it on those bountiful engineer stores.[113]

Patton's performance in liberating Bastogne validated the high esteem with which Eisenhower held him back in September 1943, expressed in a letter to Marshall: "Under particular conditions boldness is ten times as important as numbers. Patton's great strength is that he thinks only in terms of attack as long as there is a single battalion that can keep advancing." Ike commented on the "extraordinary and ruthless driving power that Patton can exert at critical moments." He said that Patton remained "preeminently a combat commander" who was "never affected by doubt, fatigue, or caution; consequently, "his troops are not affected." He was a "truly aggressive commander" and had more drive on the battlefield than "any other man I know."[114]

• *13* •

The Hammelburg Raid—*Not* His "Only Mistake"

> Throughout the campaign in Europe I know of no error I made except that of failing to send a Combat Command to take Hammelburg. Otherwise, my operations were to me, strictly satisfactory.[1]
>
> —Patton, from his *War as I Knew It*

> Uncle George, however, never quite forgave himself for the Hammelburg disaster.[2]
>
> —Fred Ayer, from his *Before the Colors Fade*

During the final six weeks of the war, Patton's Third Army had crossed the Rhine, and German resistance was collapsing. Patton had a son-in-law, Lt. Col. John K. Waters, who had been a German POW since early 1942, and Patton's forces were approaching the prison camp at Hammelburg, Germany, about seventy miles east of Frankfurt, where Waters was believed to be held.[3] Although he would probably have been liberated within a week by other American forces, Patton could not resist pulling one last headline-grabbing stunt. So he sent an unauthorized, 314-man, nighttime raiding party from his 4th Armored Division to go fifty miles behind enemy lines in order to rescue Waters. The raid ended in disaster, with 25 of the raiders being killed and 245 being taken prisoner. The Hammelburg raid has often been called "Patton's one mistake."

PATTON GETS OUT OF THE "DOGHOUSE"

On March 16, 1945, General Eisenhower came to visit Patton's HQ in Luxembourg City. The war was going spectacularly well. On March 1, Patton's Third Army had captured Trier. On March 7, Hodges's First Army captured the first Allied bridgehead across the Rhine at Remagen. Also on March 7, Patton's 4th Armored Division reached the Rhine north of Coblenz. Soon the Third Army was across the Moselle and sweeping southeasterly through the Palatinate area and preparing to cross the Rhine.

At Patton's CP in Luxembourg City there was a festive dinner on March 16 in honor of General Eisenhower with a number of Red Cross donut girls present, including Jean Gordon. Ike had a very good time, and Patton and Ike stayed up drinking until 2:30 a.m.[4] The next morning, at a staff meeting, Patton received the first public praise he had ever heard in person from Eisenhower:

Rescue of Hammelburg POWs by 14th Armored Division ten days after failed Task Force Baum. US Army Signal Corps.

> The trouble with you people in Third Army is that you don't appreciate your own greatness. You're not cocky enough. Let the world know what you are doing, otherwise the American soldier will not be appreciated at his full value. George, you are not only a good general, you are a lucky general, and, as you will remember, in a General, Napoleon prized luck above skill.

Patton replied laughingly: "Well, that is the first compliment you have paid me since we served together."[5] This praise from Eisenhower, however ambiguous or ironic, was all Patton needed to feel released from the doghouse for the first time since the slapping incident two years earlier (see appendix A) and to start dreaming big. The knowledge that his son-in-law, Lt. Col. John K. Waters, had been in German captivity since February 14, 1942, had gnawed at him for some time. The release of approximately five hundred American prisoners from the Cabanatuan POW camp in the Philippines via the headline-grabbing raid by General MacArthur six weeks earlier may have confirmed Patton's decision to rescue his son-in-law.[6]

There was evidence that Waters was imprisoned at Oflag XIIIB, a prison camp for Allied officers in Hammelburg, Germany, some seventy-five miles east of Frankfurt—but it was not 100 percent certain. To perform the heroic act of rescuing Johnny Waters was probably the highest form of grandstanding Patton could imagine, particularly for the benefit of his own wife and daughter. For a man suffering from NPD, his cravings for a successful Hammelburg rescue were too much to resist. On March 23, the day the bulk of the Third Army crossed the Rhine, Patton wrote to Beatrice, "We are headed right for John's place and may get there before he is moved."[7] On the same day, Patton met with Lt. Gen. Alexander M. Patch to discuss the boundaries east of the Rhine.[8] On March 25, he wrote again to Bea, "Hope to send an expedition tomorrow to get John."[9]

These were the problems with the raid:

1. *Off mission.* Third Army had a critical mission at this juncture: to provide the southeastern half of the pincer which, together with the First Army on the northern half, would encircle the Ruhr valley, the industrial heartland of Germany.
2. *Inadequate combat power.* How many men and machines could be spared for Patton's raid (originally he had wanted a "combat command," around three thousand men and one hundred tanks from the 4th Armored Division) without seriously damaging the primary mission? The 4th Armored was exhausted from several days of continuous combat and was seriously understrength and underequipped.

3. *Out of bounds.* The camp lay within the boundaries that on March 26 or soon thereafter[10] were to be assigned to Lt. Gen. Alexander M. Patch's Seventh Army (see map 13.1).[11] Thus Patton's raid had to be done quickly and without the official consent of his superiors, Bradley[12] and Eisenhower.
4. *Fraudulent justification.* He would pretend that the goal of the raid was to liberate all the prisoners, not just his son-in-law. (He could truthfully deny knowing for certain that his son-in-law was at the camp. After the spectacular failure of the raid, Patton would declare that one of the purposes of its easterly movement was to serve as a feint for the northeasterly move of the Third Army. This was transparent fiction.)
5. *Too many prisoners.* The number of American POWs in the camp was estimated by American intelligence at 1,500,[13] but Patton kept using the more optimistic figure of 900[14] and sometimes 400 to 500.[15] The half-track, an armored personnel carrier normally designed to carry ten or twelve men, might be able to carry up to twenty-four prisoners home if necessary. The ten Sherman tanks and three assault guns assigned to the raid might be able to carry another dozen POWs each, riding on top.

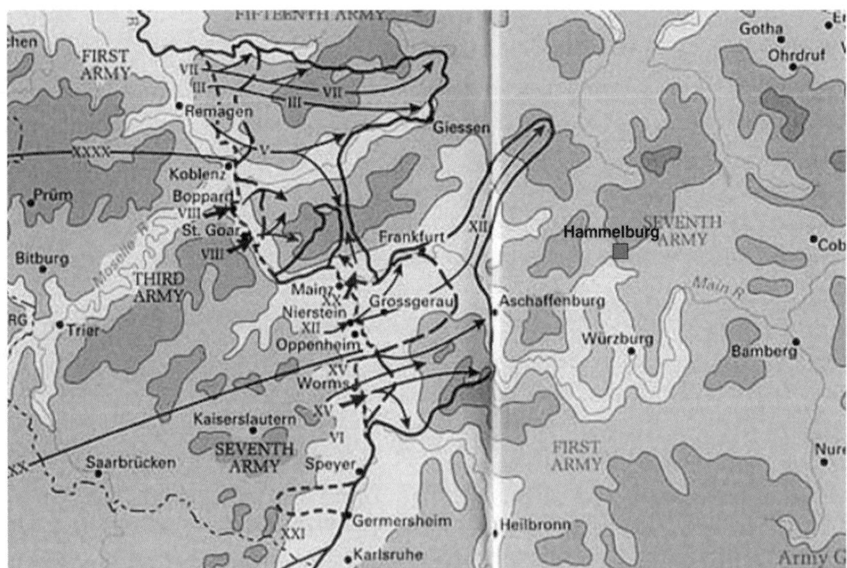

Map 13.1. Rhine crossing and start of Ruhr encirclement March 22–28, 1945. Note that Eddy's XII Corps moves NE while Hammelburg POW camp is in Seventh Army zone. From CMH brochure Pub 72, 4-5.

6. *Too far away.* The distance to the POW camp, fifty miles each way, would require refueling of all armored vehicles (tanks, assault guns, and half-tracks). The solution adopted to problems 5 and 6 was to send an extra ten half-tracks to carry fuel on the outbound leg and prisoners on the return leg (at best about four hundred prisoners could be accommodated by this plan). Capturing German fuel and vehicles were also advanced as possibilities.[16]
7. *Location unknown.* The exact location of Oflag XIIIB in Hammelburg was unknown and would hopefully be revealed by a German citizen if one could be captured.
8. *Waters' identity unknown.* None of the actual raiders had met John Waters. For this, Patton chose his longtime trusted aide, Maj. Alexander C. Stiller, a stocky, red-haired, leather-faced former Texas Ranger, to accompany the raid. Major Stiller came to stay with the XII Corps starting on March 21[17]—another indication of Patton's resolve at an early date to carry out the raid. Major Stiller tended to use as the number of American POWs in Hammelburg the most optimistic figure of three hundred, which then spread to the planners and raiders.
9. *Inadequate intelligence.* Intelligence estimates of enemy strength were also overly optimistic, reporting that the route would be weakly defended, mostly by *Volkssturm*, consisting of old men and young boys. The raid was not based on sound military judgment but had the look of haste, desperation, and narcissistic overconfidence.

Patton stressed the urgency of saving the American POWs from being killed by the Germans either by extermination or during battles of liberation. However, in subsequent weeks, he declined the opportunity to liberate much larger POW camps, such as Stalag VIIA at Moosberg.[18] The Hammelburg raid in Patton's mind was far from a humanitarian effort. As will be shown, there was no urgent reason for Patton to rescue the Hammelburg prisoners. In about a week's time, they would have been liberated anyway by Patch's Seventh Army along its assigned route. The only urgency was in Patton's craving for attention and glory, for which he was willing to sacrifice the lives of his men.

BRIDGEHEAD ACROSS THE RIVER MAIN

By March 25, the Third Army had reached the River Main, one of the last major barriers to reaching Hammelburg. Patton desperately wanted to capture a bridge over the Main intact. At Aschaffenburg there was a highway bridge, which the Germans blew up, dropping one Sherman tank and its five-man crew into the river below.[19] The 4th Armored Division, however, was able to capture a railroad bridge slightly south of there, at Nilkheim, just before it was to be demolished.

THE RAID TAKES SHAPE

Patton would still have many problems convincing his subordinates to carry out the unorthodox operation. He found great skepticism in the chain of command from Maj. Gen. Manton Eddy, his XII Corps commander, to Brig. Gen. William M. Hoge, his 4th Armored Division commander, to Col. Creighton W. Abrams, commander of Combat Command B (CCB), to Lt. Col. Harold Cohen, commander of the 10th AIB, who put the raid together, and Capt. Abraham Baum, the S-3 (operations officer) of the 10th AIB, who would lead the raid.

On March 24, Patton and some aides came to Eddy's command post, and they all went out on the new heavy pontoon bridge over the Rhine at

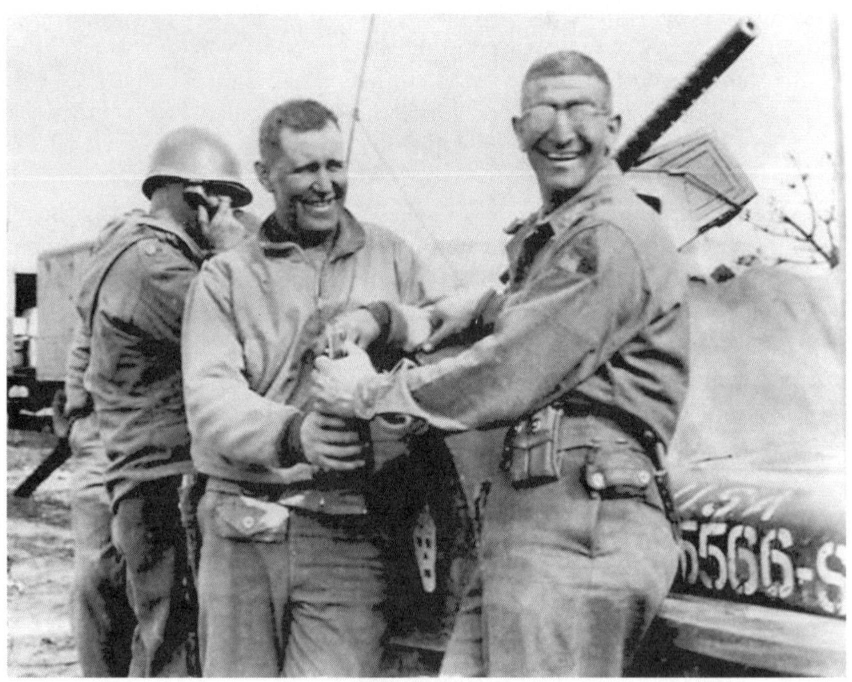

Abrams and Cohen celebrating capture of railroad bridge over the Main at Nilkheim.
National Archives.

Nierstein while Patton urinated in the river for the photographers. They had lunch together, according to Eddy's diary, during which it is reasonable to assume that Patton discussed his intention to order Eddy to send a combat command to Hammelburg to rescue the prisoners there. Eddy was highly focused on his existing orders to move northeast in order to attack Frankfurt and complete the surrounding of the Ruhr valley. Thus, he strongly opposed any diversion of a combat command for the rescue of prisoners.[20] As if to sweeten up the deal, Patton pinned the Bronze Star oak leaf cluster on Eddy for his pivotal role in crossing the Rhine. Patton persisted in seeking a combat command for the Hammelburg raid. Eddy argued that a smaller force would have greater mobility.

Later, on March 24, General Eddy called General Hoge to tell him to organize a task force of about three hundred men to liberate some nine hundred prisoners at Hammelburg. The fifty-one-year-old, straight-talking Hoge, who led the heroic capture of the railroad bridge over the Rhine at Remagen,[21] had been on the job as commander of the 4th Armored for only three days. He said that it was too dangerous to send such a small force, which could easily be surrounded and destroyed. Considering the exhaustion of his 4th Armored Division and their priorities up north, he told Eddy that the order was impossible to obey and assumed that that was the end of the matter.[22] Thus, Hoge risked charges of insubordination in his intention to put a halt to the raid.

Brig. Gen. William M. Hoge, commander, 4th Armored Division.
US Army Signal Corps.

Eddy called Patton to tell him Hoge's response, and Patton immediately got back on the phone to Hoge (violating the chain of command). "This is going to make the MacArthur raid on Cabanatuan look like peanuts, Bill," said Patton.[23] General Hoge was not about to say, "No," directly to Patton but called Eddy to unload his feelings about the order. His divisional front, which army guidelines said should not exceed six miles, was already stretched to twenty miles. The thirty-six-hour, nonstop race to the River Main had left his men exhausted. He asked, "What's so darned important about Hammelburg and a handful of prisoners of war?" Eddy listened, and said, "All right, Bill, I'll take it up with George."[24]

On the afternoon of March 25, Major Stiller arrived at Hoge's 4th Armored Division HQ with detailed orders from his boss, General Patton, for a task force to raid the Hammelburg prison camp. "But I thought the idea was shelved," said Hoge.

"No," said Stiller, "the General wants it to go on as planned, and I'm going to ride along." As soon as Stiller left, Hoge picked up the phone and called Eddy to ask him what was going on. Once again, Hoge was placated by Eddy. "Don't worry," he said. "I'll handle it personally."[25]

On the morning of March 26, Patton's motorcade, air horns blaring, skidded to a halt at General Eddy's XII Corps Command Post at Undenheim, Germany, a few miles west of the Rhine. Patton and an aide were saluted by bespectacled Brig. Gen. Ralph Canine, General Eddy's chief of staff. Patton shrieked, "Where the hell is Manton?"

"Sir, he's with the 6th Armored . . . he wasn't expecting," stammered Canine.

"Get Bill Hoge on the phone and tell him to get his ass to Hammelburg," shouted Patton.

"Pardon me, Sir, but General Eddy told me that if you gave me that order, I was to refuse it," said Canine. General Eddy thereby also risked a charge of insubordination. Canine waited for Patton's temper to erupt.

It didn't. Patton calmly said, "Get Hoge on the phone. I'll tell him myself."

A relieved General Canine cranked the field telephone and handed the receiver to General Patton. "Bill, I need you to organize that raiding party and get them to Hammelburg right now—today," said Patton. Hoge pointed out that his CCA was already in deep shit at the Hanau bridge. Now Patton started to grovel in a voice that Hoge found embarrassing. "Bill, I promise, I'll replace whatever you lose—every tank, every man."

Inexperienced men would be no replacement for his battle-hardened veterans but finally, Hoge could no longer resist. "All right, sir. I'll get Colonel Abrams right on it." Hoge then looked at Major Stiller, who had been standing by during the phone call, and asked him, "What's so damn important about the prison camp at Hammelburg?" Stiller replied that Patton wanted Hammelburg liberated because his son-in-law was a prisoner there. Hoge was dumbfounded.[26]

General Hoge called Colonel Abrams to ask if he had planned the Hammelburg mission yet. "Yes, sir," said Abrams.

"Who is going to lead it?" asked Hoge.

"I am, sir. I'll lead my Combat Command B," said Abrams. "A 300-man task force is too small to go 50 miles and return."

"No," said Hoge, "It has to be a small force. And Army says it has to go tonight. You are needed elsewhere. Who else can you get to lead it?"

"The best would be Col. Cohen, sir," said Abrams. "The only problem is that his piles are acting up really bad." In fact, Cohen, who had nearly passed out the previous day from inflamed hemorrhoids while making plans for the task force, was treated that morning by the medical staff, and they insisted on immediate hospitalization.

The next best choice of Abrams and Cohen was a twenty-four-year-old, six-foot tall, street-smart, Jewish guy from the Bronx named Capt. Abe Baum, who was the S-3 of Cohen's battalion. The crew cut and Errol Flynn mustache were befitting the amateur boxing champion who had won a chest full of medals during five campaigns, earning the nickname "Able." Abrams and Cohen called Baum in to give him orders for his biggest job so far—leading Task Force Baum.

Capt. Abe Baum, spring 1945. Photo courtesy of Abraham and Eileen Baum Living Trust.

Author Charles Whiting described the meeting, with Abrams saying,

> "There's a prisoner-of-war camp at Hammelburg. We want you to take a task force and liberate as many Americans as you can. We think there are about 300 officers at the Oflag." The colonel hesitated. "The division is not to follow you—you'll be on your own. We'll give you the best we have available. You're to get back to us whichever way you can. You understand?" Baum cracked to his battalion commander, "This is no way to get rid of me. I'll be back."[27]

Cohen and Abrams got out the map and outlined the mission for Baum. He was to take the most direct route to the camp and avoid fighting by bypassing any resistance. Major Stiller was present, and he was introduced to Captain Baum as someone from Patton's staff. He would be going along "just for laughs" but, outranking Baum, would not use his authority. Baum was suspicious. By now, Stiller had informed Abrams confidentially that Patton's son-in-law was probably in the Hammelburg prison camp. After Baum left, Cohen and Abrams were furious at the suicide mission they had just been forced to dispatch. Abrams pounded the table with his fist, shouting, "If this mission is accomplished, that guy [Baum] deserves a Congressional Medal of Honor!"[28] Later that night, about two hours into the mission, when Stiller informed Baum about the presence of John Waters in the prison camp, Baum was so incensed that he considered scrubbing the mission.[29]

Note the agreement among virtually everyone in the chain of command that to guarantee a successful raid would require a combat command of three thousand men and one hundred tanks. Virtually everyone also agreed that the Third Army could not afford to divert such a large force from its primary task of encircling the Ruhr valley—except Patton. Only General Patton, for personal reasons, favored some kind of raid—if only a limited one—and because of his authority, it went forward.

THE MEN AND EQUIPMENT

Task Force Baum was formed from one company of the 37th Tank Battalion (2nd Lt. William J. Nutto's C Company) and one company of the 10th Armored Infantry (Capt. Robert Lange's A Company) of the 4th Armored Division. In addition, 2nd Lt. William Weaver's D Company brought a platoon of five light tanks, Tech Sgt. Charles Graham brought three 105 mm assault guns, and 2nd Lt. Norman E. Hoffner brought a reconnaissance platoon with three jeeps. Task Force Baum ended up with 314 men, including eleven officers, and fifty-seven vehicles. The vehicles included ten medium (Sherman) tanks, six light (Stuart) tanks, three 105 mm assault guns, and twenty-eight half-tracks.[30] With normal spacing between vehicles in a single column, the task force would extend between one and two miles.

After a thirty-minute artillery barrage, the task force would take off just before midnight on March 26. The goal was to run as silently as possible through the night under "black-out conditions," with headlights off and taillights dimmed, reaching Hammelburg and liberating the prisoners before dawn, and returning the same day. A number of villages, foothills, and rivers would have to be traversed. Speed and stealth were essential.

THE RAID UNRAVELS

This chapter cannot describe in detail the tragic story of the raid collapsing—a subject that is covered in several excellent sources referenced herein.[31] Armed resistance popped up from almost everywhere during the first hours of the raid, putting the raiders behind schedule and ruining any chance of surprise. The single-shot German rocket-propelled grenade known as the Panzerfaust was used in great abundance against the American tanks by the defenders. The raiders, confirmed hotshots, tended to blast anything that moved, such as trains, trucks, barges, and any stationary target likely to harbor the enemy, also helping to destroy the element of surprise.

A key bridge was blown in the Americans' faces at Gemünden, forcing a fifteen-mile detour to the north across foothills, valleys, and rivers. Baum and Nutto were wounded and others killed near Gemünden. The task force was located by a German spotter plane and later by a hilltop observation tower. A freight train arrived in Hammelburg just at the right moment for the Germans, bringing ten brand-new Hetzers (Czech-made tank destroyers). Their German crews quickly set up an ambush across the valley from the road the task force, like ducks in a shooting gallery, would have to traverse. KA-BOOM! went several vehicles, including half-tracks carrying extra fuel. Task Force Baum finally got up the hill south of Hammelburg and knocked down the Oflag XIIIB fence. They were astonished to find 1,500 hungry, jubilant American prisoners, not three hundred, ready for liberation—far more than the task force could bring home. To make matters worse, during the camp surrender, Colonel Waters was shot in the lower spine by a confused German guard and could not be moved.

An efficient and ruthless Nazi officer, Hauptman (Captain) Walter Eggeman, arrived on the scene to organize a counterattack. On the second night of the raid, the liberators camped at the base of the small mountain called Reussenberg or Hill 427. They were surrounded, with every escape route blocked. Early in the morning, the Germans blitzed the task force with an overwhelming, accurate bombardment of high-explosive Hetzer and mortar fire—accurate because the Americans were camped on an army base firing range, with all distances perfectly zeroed in. Captain Baum, already wounded, was forced to call, "Every man for himself." Scattering into the surrounding woodlands, the American liberators were now fugitives hunted by police dogs, and soon the majority were added to the roll of POWs.

The weather was satisfactory for air support during the raid, but there was no air support, evidently because Patton did not want to attract attention to the raid from top brass. Author Spires writes,

> Given the impressive air-ground coordination evident by late March, 1945, one must ask why Third Army planners failed to provide for air support in this operation. . . . Even the bad weather on March 29–30 would not have prevented Weyland from sending his aircraft to help. . . . Such a contingency seems not to have been considered by Patton, who apparently planned and executed the operation without consulting his air commander.[32]

The final toll of Task Force Baum was that twenty-five of the raiders and an unknown number of prisoners were killed, 245 of the raiders became German prisoners,[33] and the rest escaped, most arriving at American lines after about a week. Among the wounded, several required leg amputations. On April 6, the 14th Armored Division from Patch's Seventh Army liberated the camp, including the wounded John Waters and the thrice-wounded Abe Baum. Waters was airlifted out by order of Patton and eventually made a full recovery and a four-star generalship. In an army field hospital, Baum was presented with the DSC by Patton, who told him that the raid had been classified top secret and to use caution in saying anything about it. All raid members were required to sign a document pledging their silence. The cover-up worked pretty well until May 1948, when the *Saturday Evening Post* ran a story[34] revealing the Hammelburg raid, "General Patton's Mistake," to the general public.

All the task force equipment and vehicles were lost or captured. At a cost of $33,500 for each Sherman tank in 1942[35] and perhaps half of that for each half-track, the total cost to the taxpayer just for the lost equipment was probably in excess of $10 million in 2015 dollars. The Hammelburg raid was an embarrassment—the first complete rout suffered by an element of the vaunted 4th Armored Division—one of only two divisions during World War II to receive the Presidential Unit Citation. Author Charles Whiting wrote, "Patton's decision to attack Hammelburg to rescue Colonel Waters must be without parallel as the most selfish action of a commanding general in the entire course of World War II. . . . [Not] one word of regret ever crossed his lips for the men who had died to achieve his purpose."[36]

Instead of admitting his fault for carrying out such a selfish, poorly planned, unethical raid and instead of praising the men who tried to discourage the raid, Patton variously blamed Bradley, Eddy, and Hoge[37] for talking him out of sending a full combat command. When Patton admitted to Hammelburg as his "one mistake,"[38] it sounds like an anomaly that could be overlooked. But his NPD, which motivated the Hammelburg raid, was not anomalous and drove his grandiosity (criterion 1), feelings of invincibility (criterion 2), need for excessive admiration (criterion 4), sense of entitlement (criterion 5), exploitation of others (criterion 6), lack of empathy (criterion 7), and envy (criterion 8) of MacArthur. The Hammelburg fiasco put Patton's character on full display, and I believe it is key to understanding his psyche. Those who may cling to previous hypotheses must explain how dyslexia, ADD, PTSD, or traumatic brain injury could have produced the kind of focus, drive, fearlessness, risk-taking, and need for glory required to conceive and order a Hammelburg raid.

• 14 •

Patton and Leadership

> I have it—but I'll be damned if I can define it.[1]
>
> —Patton in letter to his son

> Regard your soldiers as your children, and they will follow you into the deepest valleys; look upon them as your own beloved sons, and they will stand by you even unto death.[2]
>
> —Sun Tzu, from *The Art of War*

> At times I felt that Patton, however successful he was as a corps commander, had not yet learned to command himself.[3]
>
> —Gen. Omar N. Bradley, from his *A Soldier's Story*

In this chapter, I will attempt to show how military leadership is defined and to point out where Patton excelled, where he was deficient, and how his leadership was influenced by his NPD.

In his own words, chronological order:

1. Patton lecture, March 1918: "In battle as in fistfights or football, man cannot reason. What he does for good or evil he does automatically—subconsciously. . . . It is by discipline alone that all your efforts, all your patriotism, shall not have been in vain. Without it Heroism is futile. You will die for nothing. With DISCIPLINE you are IRRESISTIBLE."[4]
2. Instructions to himself, 1921: "Try to make fenatics [*sic*] of your men. It is the only way to get great sacrefices [*sic*]."[5]

3. Lecture, "The Cavalryman," 1921: "And we shall expect that a man . . . shall, in an instant, the twinkling of an eye, direct [divest] himself of all restraint of all caution and hurl himself on the enemy, a frenzied beast, lusting to probe his foe-man's guts with three feet of steel or shatter his brains with a bullet. . . . Therefore, you must school yourself to savagry [*sic*]. You must imagine how it will feel when your sword hilt crashes into the breast bone of your enemy."[6]
4. Lecture "On Leadership," Hawaii, 1925: Patton categorically fixed the foremost trait of a military leader as "the possession of a superiority complex. . . . What other traits are necessary[?]"[7]
5. The reader may recall from chapter 3 Patton's 1927 lecture, in which he stated that "superiority in all endeavors, particularly in war, was hereditary. A man's class would show in gentlemanly behavior and sacrifice and leadership. The lower classes had to be schooled to instant and unquestioning obedience to authority."[8] (This is NPD criterion 9 at work, demonstrating arrogant or haughty attitudes.)
6. On the cavalry charge, Patton wrote in 1929: "To charge effectively a man must be in a frenzy; you cannot have controlled frenzy."[9]
7. November 30, 1942, *Life* magazine article: "According to Patton himself, a soldier fought primarily for two reasons—hero worship of his commanding officer and desire for glory. Patriotism was not enough, for patriots could defend, but glory hunters could attack. Patton was not interested in defense. His motto was: go forward."[10] (Patton's desire for glory and to be hero-worshiped come right out of NPD criterion 2, fantasies of unlimited success, and criterion 4, need for excessive admiration, respectively.)
8. June 6, 1944, letter to son George: "All men are timid on entering any fight. Whether it is the first fight or the last fight, all of us are timid. Cowards are those who let their timidity get the better of their manhood. . . . In Sicily I decided as a result of my information, observations, and a sixth sense that I have that the enemy did not have another large scale attack in his system. I bet my shirt on that and I was right. . . . What success I have had results from the fact that I have always been certain that my military reactions were correct. Many people do not agree with me; they are wrong."[11] (Invincibility, sixth sense, fits right into NPD criterion 2; grandiose claims from Sicily, self-inflating, some people not agreeing with his greatness, fit criterion 1.)
9. January 1945, letter from Patton to his son told by Blumenson: "'Leadership,' said Patton, 'is the thing that wins battles. I have it—but I'll be damned if I can define it. Probably it consists in knowing

what you want to do and doing it and getting mad if any one steps in the way. Self-confidence and leadership are twin brothers.' The sublime irony is that Patton's self-confidence was an act, forced and assumed, put on, riveted to his exterior. Yet his leadership was real and inspiring, almost palpable. It worked."[12]

10. Postwar memoir: "Never tell people *how* to do things. Tell them *what* to do and they will surprise you with their ingenuity."[13] (Great advice, except that Patton frequently, because of his impetuous nature, could not resist telling his subordinates *when* to do things, which sometimes caused them great problems. They often had to struggle with other realities, such as the next item, 11.)
11. Postwar memoir: "Haste and Speed: There is a great difference between these two words. Haste exists when troops are committed without proper reconnaissance, without the arrangement for proper supporting fire, and before every available man has been brought up. The result of such an attack will be to get the troops into action early, but to complete the action very slowly."[14]
12. Postwar memoir: "This habit of commanding too far down, I believe, is inculcated at schools and at maneuvers. Actually, a General should command one echelon down, and know the position of units two echelons down. For example, an Army Commander should command corps, and show on his battle map the locations of corps and divisions, but he should not command the division."[15] (Patton was in violation of this, his own principle, at various times including the liberation of Bastogne.)

AMERICAN GENERALSHIP BY EDGAR F. PURYEAR JR.

Mr. Puryear interviewed over one hundred American generals and admirals during the thirty-five-year period of 1965–2000, trying to answer the question, "What is effective military leadership?"[16] The book also incorporates information from several earlier books regarding Generals Marshall, MacArthur, Eisenhower, and Patton. The subtitle of his book is revealing: *Character Is Everything: The Art of Command.*

"Are leaders born?" asks Puryear. "No. They might have some natural attributes," said most veteran officers, but leadership skills can be learned. One definition of leadership is "the unconscious expression of the character and personality of the leader." What then is character? Character involves integrity, decisiveness, honesty, judgment, reliability, loyalty, stamina and patience in adversity, capacity for self-sacrifice, and the courage to stand up for your convictions.[17] The rest of the book goes into detail with case histories and chapters on selflessness, decision, feel or "sixth sense," aversion to "yes men," importance of reading, mentorship, consideration, delegation, and "fix the problem, not the blame" (proactivity).

Selflessness is the most important quality in Eisenhower's judgment, and he resented anyone who did not have it. Gen. George Marshall got high marks for selflessness, having turned down the much-prized command of SHAEF and a fifth star in favor of sending Ike to Europe during World War II, with himself remaining in Washington, DC, for the good of the country.[18] Puryear did not consider the effect of narcissism upon character and personality, but it is clear that a narcissistic officer would be sorely lacking in selflessness. Although Patton's fantasy was to die a hero in battle, ostensibly an unselfish act, he was totally selfish in competition for rank, command posts, men, armaments, gasoline, and headlines.

The officers differed on whether or not there is a "sixth sense." Gen. "Lightnin'" Joe Collins said that any "sixth sense" is actually based on the information.[19] Gen. Colin Powell believed in gathering all the available information and finally testing his decision to see if it "felt" and "smelled" right.[20] General McAuliffe, famous for replying, "Nuts," to a German demand for surrender at Bastogne, points out that it helps to be a psychologist of men. Although there is no way of proving how often Patton's legendary "sixth sense" proved to be true, Gen. Omar Bradley offered anecdotal evidence to at least one instance. During the Palatinate campaign in March 1945, Patton halted the Third Army attack, sensing a strong German counterattack, which indeed struck the next day.[21] There is no way to prove that this was not due to luck, coincidence, or information known to Patton but not Bradley. I have already pointed out under item 8 how a narcissist like Patton, due to his fantasies of success and brilliance, believes he has a sixth sense (criterion 2), and is likely to boast about the superiority of his military reactions (criterion 1).

Gen. Matthew Ridgway visited his subordinates by air in Korea before issuing orders so that he could get a feeling for how they would be received.[22] General Eisenhower made frequent unannounced visits to the frontline troops during World War II. He surprised the men with his humility and his common touch, asking them about their concerns and worries and about their jobs and families back home.[23] He said that talking with the troops frankly gave him inspiration.[24] Ike felt that making eye contact with them and never losing touch with the feel of the troops were the most important parts of his job.[25] This must be contrasted with Patton's stage-managed, conspicuous forays toward the front, with all horns blaring.[26] Patton's visits may have made some of the soldiers feel safer to know that a general was present among them, but the visits were largely for Patton's benefit—an exercise in criterion 4, narcissistic need for excessive admiration.

In his chapter on "Feel or Sixth-Sense," Puryear included a section on showmanship in which he referred specifically to Patton's immaculate appearance and MacArthur's dramatic acting. He made the point that showmanship can be an important part of the leadership style of individuals like Patton and MacArthur. He also mentioned the "Ike jacket" worn by Eisenhower "and Ike's smile that Bradley said was worth several divisions."[27] In no way, however, did Puryear's research identify showmanship as a universal quality of great military leaders.[28]

In an interview for his chapter "Fix the Problem, Not the Blame," Puryear quoted Eisenhower as saying, "Leadership is nothing more than taking responsibility for everything that goes wrong and giving your subordinates credit for everything that goes right." One example of Ike's sincerity in this credo is the famous note he penned on D-Day accepting full personal responsibility in case the invasion should fail.[29] Puryear was generous to point out that Patton sometimes shared the credit for victories with his staff, his subordinates, and his troops.[30] But in less guarded moments, as I have shown in chapter 9, Patton's NPD could not resist taking personal credit for the achievements of the entire Third Army or, as shown in chapters 7 and 13, blaming the subordinates whom he deemed to be at fault for any failures.

Gen. Norman Schwarzkopf, in an interview with Puryear, talked about his motivation: "There's nothing better than leading a bunch of winners and to have a group of people who, through the success of your organization, come to think of themselves as winners and are proud of themselves. . . . Then to be able to say, 'I made it happen; the organization made it happen, but I was the catalyst that caused it to come about.'"[31]

Puryear writes, "The outstanding generals of WWII . . . had character; they possessed the feeling of belonging to something greater than themselves; they believed in the code, 'Duty, Honor, Country.' . . . Ambition can be good or bad. . . . There can be ambition for power, popularity, money, and prestige. . . . Duty is a life not centered on oneself. These men saw their duty and they did it, which required sacrifice—the loss of personal comforts, money, health, and sometimes their lives."[32] A narcissist like Patton, living as he did through a false self, needy as he was for personal admiration, unquenchable as was his need for glory, would have found it impossible to live up to such high standards of selflessness, self-sacrifice, duty, integrity, or character. Not even patriotism motivated Patton until the last few months of World War II.[33]

A SAMPLE OF SON CAPT. GEORGE S. PATTON IV'S LEADERSHIP

In March 1953, George Patton IV, almost seven years out of West Point, was assigned command of A Company, 140th TB, in the Korean War. The son of the legendary general, Patton IV felt that at first the troops resented his presence. As relayed by author Brian Sobel,

> They were probably saying, "Who is this SOB coming in here? He is going to get us all killed, he's ambitious, young and a West Point hotshot from the Armor School." . . . They don't have to tell you, you can just sense that tension . . . Some also felt I was there in order to get credit or get a medal or something and then as soon as I did I would leave for some hotshot staff job. . . . I made the rounds and it took me all day. I had three platoons on line and one platoon in reserve. . . . I was checking the tank crews, looking over their maintenance and their positions.[34]

Sobel continued,

> Patton asked the usual questions. . . . "How is the mail? How is the food? Seen any Chinese or North Koreans lately?" Most answers were positive, but the troops did not look good. They were short of water for shaving and needed clean fatigues . . . they were bored and tired. . . . There was no mess tent, mail service was very poor, the soldiers were not receiving hot meals when deployed on the line, and, as Patton says, "the officers were sitting on their asses in the CP" . . . and the troops were eating in the rain. Remembering that Napoleon had once said, "An army travels on its stomach," he resolved to fix the food problem first. Patton called in his . . . executive officer . . . and said, "I want these people fed a hot meal." [The exec] said, "Sir, I think that's impossible; there's too much exposure." Patton . . . said, "I appreciate your comments, but I'm going to do it personally, with a jeep and a trailer. . . . We'll start in the morning with the lunch meal and we'll finish when we finish."[35]

General George Patton IV recalled years later that he could tell by looking in the eyes of the tank crews in the company that what he was doing hit the mark. "The message was, here was a CO who was interested in serving a hot meal for his troops . . . at some risk to himself because he felt it was important. [One tanker] said, 'Captain, this is the first hot meal I have had in three weeks . . . [and] I appreciate what you are doing.'"[36]

A SAMPLE OF LT. COL. CREIGHTON ABRAMS'S LEADERSHIP

In March 1945, near the Kyll river, just short of Bitburg, Germany, a totally exhausted 37th TB of the 4th Armored Division was looking forward to a day of rest and maintenance. Author Lewis Sorley describes what happened next:

> Then came the bad news. Lt. Col. Hal Pattison, the combat command executive officer, had the job of delivering it. An enemy counterattack was boring in from the northeast, he told Abrams, and the 37th had to deal with it. . . . Abrams gave them [his assembled company commanders and staff] the order, and he chewed them out in the harshest terms one could imagine. He said they were lazy, and not worth a damn, worthless, in fact, and that if they had done their job properly it wouldn't be necessary to drag their soldiers out at this time of day to go finish it up. After the chastened officers trooped out Pattison looked over at Abrams. The commander was sitting there with his head sort of hanging down, and Pattison could see tears streaming down his face. After a bit Abrams looked up. "Goddamn it, Pat, those poor bastards are dead tired. I had to kick them in the ass to get them out of here. Otherwise they just wouldn't have been able to do it."
>
> Later Pattison reflected on the experience. Not too many people ever saw that side of Abe, I think—the soft side—because he kept it pretty well concealed. In my view Abe was a great commander. First of all, he was a brilliant tactician—he knew what had to be done. Secondly, his people were always prepared. In the third place, he had the humanitarian side to him.[37]

Perhaps nobody ever described Abrams more succinctly than Lt. Col. Delk Oden of the 4th Armored: "God damn what a leader!"[38]

US ARMY LEADERSHIP MANUAL

This excellent, comprehensive discussion of military leadership is available either on the World Wide Web in document Army Doctrine Publication (ADP 6-22), published by the Department of the Army, August 2012[39] or available from Amazon.com. Admittedly, the world and the US Army have changed since World War II. For one thing, winning "hearts and minds" in regional conflicts around a world having twenty-four-seven media coverage requires greater sensitivity to ethnic and cultural differences. But in appendix B I will examine how Patton measures up in terms of strengths and weaknesses to today's leadership. See appendix B, and then return here.

SUMMARY

General Patton's leadership in World War II falls short in several respects from the standards expected in today's US Army. Patton appears to have been deficient in character, deficient in developing talent in subordinates, deficient in being a good follower, deficient in being candid with superiors, and deficient in the quality of his leadership (sometimes toxic or negative). He was superior in personal courage, superior in presence, superior in situational leadership, and superior in getting results. I believe that Patton's strengths and weaknesses as a leader are, to a large extent, manifestations of his NPD.

• *15* •

Epilogue

No great genius has ever existed without some touch of madness.[1]

—Aristotle (384–322 BC)

In this book, I have tried to prove that General Patton suffered from pathological, overt narcissistic personality disorder and to show how the disorder influenced his worldview, his words and deeds both in combat and in his personal life.

OBVIOUS DIAGNOSIS?

Some readers may shrug and say that the diagnosis is obvious, even though, to the best of my knowledge, it's never previously been written about in any detail. Others may be furious that anyone could dare to risk tarnishing the image of the man so highly revered and celebrated around the world. This despite the fact that Patton's character has already been sullied by biographers, including family members—even himself, with labels such as "prima donna," "egomaniac," "conceited," "self-centered," "arrogant," and "prejudiced."

Anyone who still maintains that Patton suffered only from dyslexia, ADD, traumatic brain injury, PTSD, bipolar disorder, or various combinations thereof, to be credible should either *show how those problems independently led to the same profile as NPD behaviors* (e.g., grandiosity, vanity, social climbing, exhibitionism, sense of entitlement, exploitation of others, lack of empathy, envy, and snobbishness) or *refute the NPD diagnosis*. It is not at all obvious, for example, how repeated blows to the head would produce a lack of empathy, or how ADD would lead to snobbishness, how PTSD would cause a need for excessive attention, or how dyslexia would induce delusions of grandeur.

To show that a person suffers from diabetes, cancer, dyslexia, or PTSD is not to condemn that person. One diagnosed with NPD, however, which has been called "morally reprehensible" by at least one philosopher, should be judged by each reader in light of the sufferer's overall contribution to society.[2] For example, General MacArthur's narcissism is offset in the eyes of many due to the remarkable job he did in rebuilding Japan after World War II.[3] Likewise, many people are probably willing to forgive any abuses of General Patton because of his substantial contribution to winning World War II.

I have purposely avoided discussing some of Patton's more damning alleged deeds such as the "Biscari massacre" of about eighty people, mostly Italian prisoners,[4] and the destruction of German villages as retribution against civilians.[5] Even if there were ironclad proof that Patton authorized or incited these acts, it would add little to the list of NPD criteria already met. Patton was afflicted by NPD due to some combination of his genetics, the parenting he received, and his environment. NPD might well have been both Patton's greatest asset and greatest curse. Who else but a narcissistic General Patton would have worked so tirelessly at becoming one of America's greatest trainers and motivators of troops and arguably our greatest broken-field running general? Who else would have had so much drive, passion, determination, willpower, fearlessness, acceptance of casualties, and, well, *intestinal fortitude*? A deeper understanding of Patton's psyche cannot diminish his victories or the force of his personality—in fact, it may make them all the more remarkable.

PATTON'S NARCISSISM IGNORED

I have been astonished to find in the spate of recent books about NPD the omission of General Patton—hardly a passing reference. It is as if one of the prime examples has been hiding in plain sight. A psychobiography of General Custer by the psychoanalyst Dr. Charles K. Hofling diagnoses Custer with NPD.[6] In the book by Professor Ghaemi,[7] Patton and generals often mentioned as narcissists, such as MacArthur,[8] were overlooked. However, some of them might have been perfect examples of his main thesis: that it is often the mentally disturbed leader who is most effective and rises to the top in times of crisis. Instead, Ghaemi chose Gen. William T. Sherman, Ted Turner, Winston Churchill, Abraham Lincoln, Mahatma Ghandi, Martin Luther King Jr., Franklin Roosevelt, John F. Kennedy, and Adolf Hitler. All of Ghaemi's nine leaders were said to be bipolar, which (in some cases, provided they were optimally medicated) helped to engender the four qualities of *creativity, realism, resilience, and empathy.*[9]

Ghaemi dismissed NPD out of hand for his theory, stating that "narcissism has never been empirically validated as a psychiatric diagnosis or mental illness using scientific methods."[10] By this he means specifically tested for (a) symptoms, (b) course of illness, (c) family history, and (d) treatment response. The authors of DSM-5 evidently do not require these particular tests for personality disorders, and it is not clear that they would even apply to NPD. For example, there is little reason to think that NPD is genetic,[11] and few of its sufferers ever seek treatment.[12]

SUPPORT FOR GHAEMI'S HYPOTHESIS

Except for the exclusion of NPD from Professor Ghaemi's theory and his choice of *empathy* as a necessary criterion, I give my enthusiastic support to his primary thesis. Using World War II as an example of the crisis, we recall how Pearl Harbor caught America sleeping, costing us our battleship fleet. How Poland, Belgium, and France went down in weeks, how the U-boats were winning the Battle of the Atlantic, and how invincible the German Wehrmacht appeared to be.

In such a climate of terror and uncertainty, we as a nation cut our military leaders an extraordinary amount of slack. Our most confident generals rose to the top, and we listened eagerly to their big ideas, no matter how risky. If fire must be fought with fire, we were willing to put our narcissistic generals, Patton, Montgomery, and MacArthur, up against their narcissistic leaders, Hitler and Mussolini. We tolerated the bizarre things our narcissistic generals sometimes said and did as long as their battlefield victories continued. We were willing at the time to pay for their excesses, be they heavy casualties, insubordination, outrageous behavior, or diplomatic *faux pas*. They gave us what we so desperately needed—heroes and hope. In return, we gave them what they needed—glory. Perfect symbiosis.

A military leader as narcissistic as Patton could rise to the fore once again in a future crisis. More recent generations of American military leaders, such as Norman Schwarzkopf, Colin Powell, Wesley Clark, and Mike Mullen, seem to be endowed with far more emotional stability, wisdom, diplomacy, and empathy. But a thoroughbred like Patton might be useful in certain conflicts *not of an ideological nature*, such as our current war with ISIS, but of a strictly military nature. And he might perform brilliantly—*but only if he is kept on a tight rein by his handlers.* If someone suffering from NPD should ever become the chief executive in a democracy—a man who respects no rules except his own—a man who prefers bullying and intimidation over civility and rational discourse, it would certainly pose a threat to the democracy itself.[13]

THE FINAL DEFLATION

After the victory in Europe had been secured, General Patton was spent, both mentally and physically. He had achieved his goal of military glory and felt empty and anachronistic. "The effort he had expended all his life against his inner nature had absorbed enormous energy," wrote Blumenson.[14] General MacArthur and others had spurned his offers to fight in the Pacific against the Japanese, and there seemed to be no place left for him in a peacetime America.

During Patton's triumphal war bond tour with ticker tape parades and crowds in the millions in Boston and Los Angeles in June 1945, his last visit to America, the old fire in his belly was gone. His mood was subdued, closer to tears than usual. At a cocktail party, when a relative said, "Oh George, we're all tired of the war, let's talk about something else," he simply blushed and went silent.[15] He had a strong premonition of his imminent death and before returning to Europe, told his two daughters, "I'm never going to see you again. I know this. I am going to be buried in foreign soil."[16]

In about five months, his premonition came true after his neck was broken in a freakish, low-speed truck and auto collision on December 9, 1945, near Mannheim, Germany. Paralyzed from the neck downward, he was taken to a hospital in Heidelberg, and a top medical expert was flown in from America along with Patton's wife. General Patton died of pulmonary edema and congestive heart failure[17] on December 21 and his body was buried on December 24 in the Luxembourg American Cemetery and Memorial at Hamm, Luxembourg. In accord with Beatrice's wishes, her grave dating from 1953 at the family home, Green Meadows, lies empty since 1957 when her ashes were brought to Luxembourg by family members and scattered on General Patton's grave.[18]

Appendix A

PATTON'S CAREER MOOD SWINGS, 1920–1945

Table A.1. Patton's Changing Moods with Changing Circumstances, 1920 to December 9, 1945

	In the doghouse	*Out of the doghouse*
Unleashed (hot pursuit)	F - (Aug 1, 1944–Sept 29, 1944) France H - (Nov 8, 1944–Mar 16, 1945) France, Belgium, Luxembourg, Germany	C - (Nov 8, 1942–Aug 20, 1943) No. Africa & Sicily I - (Mar 17, 1945–May 9, 1945) Ike praised Patton Rhine Crossing, Hammelburg, Czech, Austria
Leashed (no gas or no battle)	E - (Jan 26, 1944–Jul 31, 1944) England, pre-Normandy G - (Sep 30, 1944–Nov 7, 1944) France, out of gas	B - (Jan 15, 1942–Nov 7, 1942) United States training J - (May 10, 1945–Sep 30, 1945) Germany, postwar
No Command	D - (Aug 21, 1943–Jan 25, 1944) Sicily, busted K - (Aug 1, 1945–Dec 9, 1945) Germany, postwar, busted again	A - (1920–Jan 14, 1942) Between World War I and World War II

A. Between World War I and World War II, when Patton had no troops to command and wasn't sure if he ever would, his personal behavior was at its worst. He was drinking to excess and was moody and volatile, with great fits of depression, aggression, and envy toward those around him.

B. With war declared against both Japan and the European Axis powers, Major General Patton received command of the 2nd Armored Division, which he had to build and train from the ground up. Hitler's Blitzkrieg had shown the world the importance of tank warfare. Patton was gaining national attention, and his spirits were improving.

C. Commanding the ground forces of the Western Task Force of Operation TORCH, the invasion of North Africa, made Major General Patton's spirits soar. Commanding the American ground forces of Operation HUSKY, the invasion of Sicily, raised now Lieutenant General Patton's ego as high as it could be. All that unrestrained power plus the horse race with Monty to Messina may have helped provoke the "slapping incident," which brought Patton down and nearly ended his career.

D. During Patton's lengthy stay in Palermo, he was in limbo and "in the doghouse" of Generals Eisenhower and Marshall. Patton felt chastised and somewhat contrite, and he distracted himself by travelling around ancient sites in the Mediterranean.

E. Summoned to England, Patton learned that he would be commanding the Third Army sometime after D-Day. Meanwhile, he played the part of commanding the fictitious First US Army Group to deceive the Germans as to the actual site of the D-Day invasion. Patton was still on probation from the "slapping incident" and the "Knutsford incident" referred to earlier.

F. With the activation of the Third Army in Normandy, Patton was back where he longed to be—in a war and in command. Still on probation, he restrained himself initially from throwing too much of his weight around. For example, he was uncharacteristically silent about the "Falaise Gap" controversy. This was the Third Army at its best, charging rapidly across France against a disorganized German enemy. The victorious Arracourt tank battles took place between September 18–29, just before the Third Army ran seriously out of gas.

G. Having outrun their supply lines, the Allies' advance came to a halt. During the October lull, Patton used the "rock soup" method mentioned earlier to deceive his commanders into giving him resources with which to continue attacking, which he sometimes called "reconnaissance in force." The attacks on hardened fortifications were some of Patton's most foolish and most wasteful in terms of resources and human lives.

H. With resupply complete, the stage is set for Patton's November 8 Lorraine offensive. The first month starts badly, mostly due to bad weather. The Battle of the Bulge, starting December 19, is Patton's finest moment (see chapter 12). With a few exceptions early on, such as his neglect of the 94th Infantry Division in their battle against the "Siegfried Switch" (January 13–February 25), his drive through Germany in February and the first half of March is triumphant.

I. On March 17, during Ike's visits to Patton's CP, Ike publicly compliments Patton and the Third Army on the job they have been doing. Patton now feels that he is out of the doghouse and conceives a very high-risk stunt—a raid that would rival MacArthur's well-publicized raid at the Cabanatuan prison camp in the Philippines. This became the unauthorized rescue of his son-in-law from a German POW camp at Hammelburg, Germany, fifty miles behind enemy lines (see chapter 13). When the raid starting on March 26 failed, Patton might well have been disciplined, if not relieved of command, except for the fast-moving conclusion of the war, including the death of President Roosevelt on April 12. Instead, Patton was promoted to four-star full general on April 14, 1945.

J. World War II comes to a conclusion. General Patton wants to continue fighting in the Pacific, but General MacArthur will not have him. Without a war to fight, Patton's spirits fall. He is assigned to be the military governor of Bavaria, for which he is ill suited. He gets in trouble over de-Nazification and various other political gaffes.

K. Patton is relieved of command of the Third Army and given an assignment commanding an army of historians. He is humiliated and depressed during the months leading up to the low-speed auto collision on December 9, 1945, near Mannheim, Germany, that breaks his neck and leads to his death twelve days later.

General Patton's mood swings may superficially resemble some aspects of bipolar disorder. However, as reported by Simonsen and Simonsen,[1]

> Bipolar disorders are reported in 5% to 11% of patients with NPD, while NPD is seen in 0% to 8% of patients with euthymic [fairly happy mood] bipolar I and II disorder.[2] What distinguishes the narcissistic patients from individuals experiencing hypomanic episodes is narcissistic patients' need for admiring attention, devaluation of others, and profound envy of others.[3]

My understanding is that one who suffers from bipolar disorder can win a million dollars in the lottery and go straight into a blue funk. The biochemical underpinnings of bipolar disorder do not usually allow the kind of correlation with the changing circumstances that are observed in Patton's life.

CONCLUSION

General Patton's moods and behaviors were not constant during his life but varied in a predictable way according to the opportunities and powers available for him to achieve his destiny (i.e., to cover himself with military glory). According to the "balloon model" of NPD (chapter 8), his mood rose and fell depending on his "narcissistic supplies"—whether he was gaining or losing ground in his struggle to become his grandiose, heroic, unreal self. Patton seemed to do his best work while *unleashed* but *in the doghouse*. When he was *unleashed* and *out of the doghouse*, he tended to get into trouble. Bottom line: A thoroughbred commander like Patton needs careful scrutiny and close supervision by his superiors.

Appendix B

PATTON VERSUS US ARMY LEADERSHIP MANUAL

The following are excerpts from the twenty-page ADP 6-22 document published in 2012, with Patton's strengths (author's judgment) underlined and weaknesses (author's judgment) in bold type. Italics are left in place.

General of the Army Omar Bradley once remarked: "Leadership in a democratic army means firmness, **not harshness**; understanding, not weakness; generosity, **not selfishness**; pride, not **egotism**."

Purpose of Leadership

Leadership is the process of influencing people by providing purpose, direction, and motivation to accomplish the mission and improve the organization. While personality and innate traits affect a process, the Army endorses the idea that good leadership does not just happen by chance but is a developable skill. Leadership serves a motivational purpose: to energize others to achieve challenging goals.

Components of Leadership

Leaders must balance successful mission accomplishment with **how they treat and care for organizational members**. Taking care of people involves creating and sustaining a positive climate through open communications, trust, cohesion, and teamwork. Given the hierarchical structure of the Army, every Army leader is also a follower. Learning to be a good leader also needs to be associated with **learning to be a good follower—learning loyalty, subordination, respect for superiors**, and even when and how to lodge candid disagreement.

Applying Influence

The degree of commitment or compliance affects initiative taken, motivation to accomplish missions, and the degree of accepted responsibility. Commanders expect subordinate leaders and Soldiers to commit to successful mission accomplishment. Trust, commitment, and competence enable mission command and allow the freedom of action to be operationally agile and adaptive [except when Patton insisted on carrying out actions exactly when he wanted]. Leaders can mitigate resistance by **anticipating what others value, their reactions to influence, their shared understanding of common goals** [Patton's goals were not always shared, e.g., the Hammelburg Raid, chapter 13], and their commitment to the general organization or the purpose of the mission and their trust in the organization and the leader.

One form of negative leadership is toxic leadership. **Toxic leadership is a combination of self-centered attitudes, motivations, and behaviors that have adverse effects on subordinates, the organization, and mission performance. This leader lacks concern for others and the climate of the organization, which leads to short- and long-term negative effects. The toxic leader operates with an inflated sense of self-worth and from acute self-interest. Toxic leaders consistently use dysfunctional behaviors to deceive, intimidate, coerce, or unfairly punish others to get what they want for themselves. The negative leader completes short-term requirements by operating at the bottom of the continuum of commitment, where followers respond to the positional power of their leader to fulfill requests. This may achieve results in the short term, but ignores the other leader competency categories of *leads* and *develops*. Prolonged use of negative leadership to influence followers undermines the followers' will, initiative, and potential and destroys unit morale.**

Encouragement and inspiration characterize leadership whereas coercive techniques run counter to Army leadership principles.

Leaders and Courage

It takes personal courage to take the initiative to make something happen rather than standing by or withdrawing and hoping events will turn out well. Leaders require personal courage when confronting problems of discipline or disorderly conduct, when innovation and adaptation are needed to try something that has never been done before, when leading soldiers in harm's way, **when being candid with a superior about a risky or improper course of action** [e.g., the Lorraine "rock soup" method, the Hammelburg raid], when deferring to a more technically competent subordinate, or when freeing units and personnel to solve problems. Leaders must have the courage to make tough calls, to discipline or demand better when required. Consistent and fair leaders will earn the respect of their followers.

Situational Leadership

Leaders adjust their actions based on the situation. A situation influences what purpose and direction are needed. Situations include the setting, the people and team, the adversary, cultural and historical background, and the mission to be accomplished. The effectiveness of influence methods also vary with the situation and the time available for action. Education, training and experience are vital to develop the knowledge necessary to lead.

Leadership Requirements

Character is the essence of who a person is, what a person believes, how a person acts. **Empathy is identifying and understanding what others think, feel and believe** [unlikely with NPD].

Leader Attributes

Character Leadership is affected by a person's character and identity. **Integrity** is a key mark of a leader's character. It means **doing what is right, legally and morally** [unlikely with NPD]. **Leaders of integrity adhere to the values that are part of their personal identity and set a standard for their followers to emulate** [unlikely with NPD]. **Identity is one's self-concept, how one defines him or herself** [weak with NPD].

Presence The impression a leader makes on others contributes to success in getting people to follow. This impression is the sum of a leader's outward appearance, demeanor, actions and words and the inward character and intellect of the leader. Presence entails the projection of military and professional bearing, holistic fitness, confidence and resilience. Strong presence is important as a touchstone for subordinates, especially under duress. **A leader who does not share the same risks could easily make a decision that could prove unworkable given the psychological state of soldiers and civilians affected by stress.** [Patton was not empathetic to subordinates who did not share his quest for military glory or his enthusiasm to die a hero in battle.]

Intellect The leader's intellect affects how well a leader thinks about problems, creates solutions, makes decisions and leads others. People differ in intellectual strengths and ways of thinking. There is no one right way to think. Each leader needs to be self-aware of strengths and limitations and apply them accordingly. Being mentally agile helps leaders address changes and adapt to the situation and the dynamics of operations. Critical and innovative thought are abilities that enable the leader to be adaptive [but at times Patton was too dependent on hunches, sixth sense, *deja vu* and other paranormal influences or historically based solutions]. **Sound judgment** [not always possible with NPD] enables the best decision for the situation at hand.

Leader Competencies

Leads *Builds trust* is an important competency to establish conditions of effective influence and for creating a positive environment. Leader actions and words comprise the competencies of *leads by example* and *communicates.* Actions can speak louder than words and excellent leaders use this to serve as a role model to set the standard.

Develops Leaders *develop others* to assume greater responsibility or achieve higher expertise. **They must ensure that they themselves are developing, that they are developing subordinates, and that they are sustaining a positive climate and improving the organization. Leaders choose when and how to coach, counsel and mentor others.** [Patton was too self-centered and envious of subordinates to have protégés[1] or to groom or mentor subordinates to move up in the Third Army. A number of top talents, such as Bruce C. Clarke and Holmes E. Dager of the 4th Armored Division, took promotions elsewhere.] Leaders often have the freedom to place people in the best situation to maximize their talent. [General Creighton Abrams was especially admired for this—for example, reassigning good people who were otherwise about to be fired.[2]]

Achieves "*Gets results*" is the single "*achieves*" competency and relates to actions to accomplish tasks and missions on time and to standard. [Patton usually got the job done no matter what the cost or long-term damage to the unit.]

Please return to the end of chapter 14 for a summary of this analysis.

Appendix C

Chronology

Table C.1. Brief Military Chronology of Patton

1885, Nov 11	Born, San Gabriel, CA
1897, Sep	Student, Clark's School for Boys, Pasadena, CA
1903, Sep	Cadet, Virginia Military Institute, Lexington, VA
1904, Jun 16	Cadet, US Military Academy, West Point, NY
1909, Jun 11	Graduated, 2nd lieutenant, 15th Cavalry
Sep 12	Fort Sheridan, IL
1911, Dec 3	Fort Myer, VA
1912, Jul	Modern Pentathlon, Olympics, Stockholm, Sweden
1913, Jul–Sep	Studied swordsmanship, Saumur, France
Sep 23	Mounted Service School, Fort Riley, KS
1915, Sep 15	8th Cavalry, Fort Bliss, TX
1916, May 14	Rubio Ranch affair
May 23	1st lieutenant
1917, May 15	Captain, Fort Bliss, TX
May 28	Sailed for Europe with Pershing's HQ
Nov 10	Detailed to Tank Service
Dec 16	Opened Light Tank Center and School, Langres, France
1918, Jan 23	Major
Feb 22	Moved Tank Center and School to Bourg, France
Apr 3	Lieutenant colonel
Sep 12	Saint-Mihiel offensive
Sep 26	Wounded, Meuse-Argonne offensive, Cheppy, France
Oct 17	Colonel
Dec 16	Awarded Distinguished Service Cross
1919, Mar 25	Camp Meade, MD
Jun 16	Awarded Distinguished Service Medal
1920, Jun 30	Reverted to captain
Jul 1	Major

(contiued)

Table C.1. (*continued*)

Oct 3	Fort Myer, VA
1923, Jan 10	Field Officers Course, Fort Riley, KS
Sep	Command and general staff college, Fort Leavenworth, KS
1925, Mar 31	Reached Hawaii by sailboat; G-1 and G-2 Hawaiian Division
1928, May 7	Office of Chief of Cavalry, Washington, DC
1931, Sep	Army War College, Washington, DC
1932, Jul 8	Fort Myer, VA
1934, Mar 1	Lieutenant colonel
1935, Jun 8	Arrived Honolulu; G-2 Hawaiian Division
1937, Jul 25	In hospital, Beverly, MA, with broken leg
1938, Feb 8	Fort Riley, KS
Jul 1	Colonel
Jul 24	Fort Clark, TX
1940, Apr	Umpire, spring maneuvers, Fort Benning, GA
May	Control officer, maneuvers, Fort Beauregard, LA
Jul 26	CO, 2nd Armored Brigade, 2nd Armored Division, Fort Benning, GA
Oct 2	Brigadier general
Nov	Acting CO, 2nd Armored Division
1941, Apr 4	Major general
Apr 11	Commanding general, 2nd Armored Division
Jun	Tennessee maneuvers
Aug–Sep	Louisiana-Texas maneuvers
Oct–Nov	Carolina maneuvers
1942, Jan 15	Commanding general, I Armored Corps
Apr 10	Commander, Desert Training Center
Jul 10	Washington, DC, to prepare for Operation TORCH
Aug 5–12	London, England, to prepare for Operation TORCH
Nov 8	TORCH landings in French North Africa
1943, Mar 6	Commanding general, II Corps in Tunisia
Mar 12	Lieutenant general
Apr 15	Gave up II Corps for Operation HUSKY (Sicily) planning
Jul 10	Commanding general, Seventh Army, Sicilian invasion
Aug 17	Capture of Messina
1944, Jan 26	Commanding general, Third Army
Feb 3	Revoked; acting commanding general, Third Army
Mar 26	Commanding general, Third Army
Jul 6	Arrival in Normandy
Aug 1	Third Army becomes operational
Dec 16	German Ardennes counteroffensive
1945, Apr 14	Promoted to general
May 9	End of war in Europe
Jun 4–Jul 4	War bond drives in Boston, Los Angeles
Oct 6	Relieved command Third Army; commander, Fifteenth Army
Dec 9	Auto accident near Mannheim, hospitalization in Heidelberg
Dec 21	Death
Dec 24	Buried at Hamm, Luxembourg

Note: See more detailed chronologies in MB1, 965–970 and MB2, 863–864.

Abbreviations

48HR: Whiting, Charles. *48 Hours to Hammelburg*. New York: PJB Books, 1982. First published 1970.

ABE: Sorley, Lewis. *Thunderbolt: General Creighton Abrams and the Army of His Times*. New York: Simon & Schuster, 1992.

AEF: Allied Expeditionary Force

AFHQ: Allied Force Headquarters

AM: Miller, Alice. *The Drama of the Gifted Child: The Search for the True Self.* New York: Basic Books, 2007.

BMS: Sobel, Brian M. *The Fighting Pattons*. New York: A Dell Book, 1997.

BRAD: Bradley, Omar N. *A Soldier's Story*. New York: Henry Holt, 1951.

CDE: D'Este, Carlo. *Patton, A Genius for War*. New York: HarperCollins, 1995.

CMH: US Army Center of Military History

CMP: Province, Charles M. *Patton's Third Army: A Daily Combat Diary*. New York: Hippocrene Books, 1992.

COMBAT COMMAND: A combat command was a brigade-sized, task-oriented force built around one tank battalion and one armored infantry battalion. This normally consisted of about three thousand men and one hundred armored vehicles.

CP: Command post

DOC: Province, Charles M. *I Was Patton's Doctor: The Reminiscences of Colonel Charles B. Odom, MD*. Oregon City, OR: Charles M. Province, 2011.

DRAGOON: Operation code name for invasion of southern France.

DSM-5: *American Psychiatric Association. Diagnostic and Statistical Manual of Mental Disorders*. 5th ed. Arlington, VA: American Psychiatric Publishing, 2013.

DUKW: Six-wheel-drive, 2.5 ton amphibious truck, commonly called "Duck."

EFP: Puryear, E. F. *American Generalship: Character Is Everything; The Art of Command.* New York: Presidio Press, 2000.

ENIGMA: Allies' code name for the German encryption machine

ETOUSA: European Theater of Operations, US Army.

FA: Ayer, Fred. *Before the Colors Fade.* Boston: Houghton Mifflin, 1964.

FOX: Fox, Don M. *Patton's Vanguard: The United States Army 4th Armored Division.* Jefferson, NC: McFarland, 2003.

GN: Ghaemi, Nassir. *A First-Rate Madness: Uncovering the Links between Leadership and Mental Illness.* New York: Penguin Books, 2011.

GSP: Patton, George S., Jr. *War as I Knew It.* New York: Bantam, 1980.

HGP: Phillips, Henry Gerard. *The Making of a Professional: Manton S. Eddy, USA.* Westport, CT: Greenwood Press, 2000.

HNPD: Campbell, W. Keith, and Joshua D. Miller, eds. *The Handbook of Narcissism and Narcissistic Personality Disorder: Theoretical Approaches, Empirical Findings, and Treatments.* Hoboken, NJ: Wiley, 2011.

HNS: Schwarzkopf, H. Norman. *It Doesn't Take a Hero.* New York: Bantam Book, 1992.

HQ: Headquarters.

HUSKY: Operation code name for invasion of Sicily.

IKE1: D'Este, Carlo. *Eisenhower: A Soldier's Life.* New York: Henry Holt, 2002.

JK: Kluger, Jeffrey. *The Narcissist Next Door.* New York: Riverhead Books, 2014.

JNR1: Rickard, John Nelson. *Patton at Bay: The Lorraine Campaign, September to December, 1944.* Westport, CT: Praeger, 1999.

JNR2: ———. *Advance and Destroy: Patton as Commander in the Bulge (American Warriors).* Lexington: University Press of Kentucky, 2011.

JW: Wellard, James. *Gen. George S. Patton Jr.: Man under Mars.* New York: Dodd, Mead & Co., 1946.

LEO: Barron, Leo. *Patton at the Battle of the Bulge: How the General's Tanks Turned the Tide at Bastogne.* New York: NAL/Caliber, 2014.

LNG: Lengel, E. G. *To Conquer Hell: The Meuse-Argonne, 1918; The Epic Battle That Ended the First World War.* New York: Henry Holt, 2008.

MARKET GARDEN: Operation code name for airborne invasion of Netherlands and north Germany.

MAST: Masterson, James F. *The Search for the Real Self: Unmasking the Personality Disorders of Our Age.* New York: Free Press, 1988.

MB1: Blumenson, Martin. *The Patton Papers, 1885–1940.* Boston: Houghton Mifflin, 1972.

MB2: ———. *The Patton Papers, 1940–1945*. Boston: Houghton Mifflin, 1974.

MB: ———. *Patton: The Man Behind the Legend, 1885–1945*. New York: Quill, William Morrow, 1985.

OVERLORD: Operation code name for Normandy invasion.

PLUNDER: Operation code name for Allies crossing the Rhine at Rees on March 23, 1945.

PREF: Prefer, Nathan N. *Patton's Ghost Corps: Cracking the Siegfried Line*. Novato, CA: Presidio Press, 1998.

RAID: Baron, Richard, Abraham Baum, and Richard Goldhurst. *Raid! The Untold Story of Patton's Secret Mission*. New York: Dell Books, 1981.

RA1: Atkinson, Rick. *An Army at Dawn: The War in North Africa, 1942–1943*. New York: Henry Holt, 2002.

RA2: ———. *The Day of Battle: The War in Sicily and Italy, 1943–1944*. New York: Henry Holt, 2007.

RA3: ———. *The Guns at Last Light: The War in Western Europe, 1944–1945*. New York: Henry Holt, 2013.

RHP: Patton, Robert H. *The Pattons: A Personal History of an American Family*. Washington, DC: Brassey's, 1994.

RE: Totten, Ruth Ellen Patton. *The Button Box: A Daughter's Loving Memoir of Mrs. George S. Patton*. Columbia: University of Missouri Press, 2005.

SH: Hotchkiss, Sandy. *Why Is It Always about You? The Seven Deadly Sins of Narcissism*. New York: Free Press, 2002.

SHAEF: Supreme Headquarters for Allied Expeditionary Force.

SLAM: Marshall, S. L. A. *Men against Fire: The Problem of Battle Command*. Norman: University of Oklahoma Press, 1947.

SPH: Hirshson, Stanley P. *General Patton: A Soldier's Life*. New York: HarperCollins, 2002.

STN: Steinberg, L. D. *The Ten Basic Principles of Good Parenting*. New York: Simon & Schuster, 2004.

TORCH: Operation code name for invasion of North Africa.

TR: Royle, Trevor. *Patton: Old Blood and Guts*. London: Weidenfeld & Nicholson, 2005.

TRSC: Truscott, Lucian K. *Command Missions*. New York: E. P. Dutton, 1954.

ULTRA: Allies' code name for the intercepted and decoded ENIGMA messages.

USMA: United States Military Academy at West Point, New York.

WACHT AM RHEIN: German code name for the Ardennes offensive.

WEST POINT: United States Military Academy at West Point, New York.

Notes

PREFACE

1. GN.
2. MB2, 676.
3. CDE, 797.
4. Ibid., 557.
5. LNG, 63.
6. CDE, 815.
7. Ibid.
8. D. K. R. Crosswell, "The Madness of General George," in *Imponderable but not Inevitable*, ed. Malcolm H. Murfett (Santa Barbara, CA: Praeger, 2010), 41–71.
9. MB, 16–17.
10. CDE, 45.
11. G. Jeansonne, F. C. Haney, and D. Luhrssen. "George S. Patton: A Life Shaped by Dyslexia," June 23, 2016. http://warfarehistorynetwork.com/daily/wwwii/a-life-shaped-by-dyslexia.
12. GN, 8.
13. DSM-5.
14. DSM-5, 25.
15. One of the few surviving voice recordings is on a YouTube video from the Los Angeles Coliseum: https://www.youtube.com/watch?v=SSySTnGS1M4.
16. N. Dixon, *On the Psychology of Military Incompetence* (London: Cape, 1976), 18.
17. For example, TV commentator Bill O'Reilly claimed that if General Patton were here today, he could defeat ISIS in one week. FOX TV, March 25, 2015. Presidential candidate Donald Trump echoed this remark on numerous occasions.
18. D. A. Lande, *I Was with Patton: First-Person Accounts of WWII in George S. Patton's Command* (St. Paul, MN: MBI Publishing), 2002.

CHAPTER 1

1. MB1, 336.
2. Frank B. Elser, "Cardenas' Family Saw Him Die at Bay; Shot Four Times." *New York Times*, May 23, 1916.
3. MB1, 328–338; CDE, 172–178; SPH, 73–78.
4. SPH, 77.
5. James W. Hurst, *Pancho Villa and Black Jack Pershing: The Punitive Expedition in Mexico* (Westport, CT: Praeger, 2008).
6. "He parked himself on a chair outside Pershing's office for almost forty continuous hours," waiting for Pershing to notice him (EFP, 199).
7. Elser, "Cardenas' Family Saw Him Die at Bay."
8. SPH, 76.
9. MB1, 744.
10. Ibid., 336.
11. SPH, 74.
12. List of Medal of Honor Recipients, Wikipedia, https://simple.wikipedia.org/wiki/List_of_Hispanic_Medal_of_Honor_recipients#World_War_II.

CHAPTER 2

1. MB1, 616.
2. Ibid., 442–443.
3. MB1, 583–597; CDE, 226–247.
4. SPH, 126.
5. Geoffrey Perret, *Old Soldiers Never Die: The Life of Douglas MacArthur* (Holbrook, MA: Adams Media, 1996), 92–104.
6. JW, 16.
7. Robert H. Ferrell, *Collapse at Meuse-Argonne: The Failure of the Missouri-Kansas Division* (Columbia: University of Missouri Press, 2004), 108.
8. American Battle Monuments Commission. *American Armies and Battlefields in Europe* (1938; repr. Washington, DC: United States Army Center of Military History, US Army, 1992), 167–175.
9. CDE, 254.
10. LNG, 110.
11. Ibid., 86.
12. Ferrell, *Collapse*, 28.
13. MB1, 612.
14. LNG, 111.
15. MB1, 613–617.
16. See also RHP, 183.
17. LNG, 6.

18. MB1, 616; CDE, 257.
19. MB1, 613–617.
20. CDE, 260.
21. MB1, 629.
22. Ibid., 704–705.
23. Ibid., 536.
24. Sometimes it makes sense to advance in the face of indirect fire from high-trajectory armaments such as mortars and artillery, but what military dogma advises an infantry charge into direct, concentrated machine gun fire?
25. MB1, 630.
26. Ferrell, *Collapse*, 35.
27. CDE, 259.
28. MB1, 628.
29. In 1938, Beatrice, accompanied by her son, George Patton IV, her daughter, Ruth Ellen, and the most expert French guide available, searched in vain for the spot of General Patton's wounding (RE, 292). The site was described as "a little plain between two hills." Evidently George IV had more success finding the exact spot on a later trip accompanied by his son, Benjamin, and biographer Martin Blumenson (BMS, 356).
30. GSP, 372.
31. CDE, 262.
32. Ibid., 411.
33. MB2, 539.
34. MB1, 624.
35. Ibid., 644.
36. Ibid., 665.
37. Ibid., 732.
38. *Congressional Medal of Honor, the Distinguished Service Cross and the Distinguished Service Medal Issued by the War Department Since April 6, 1917*, Office of the Adjutant General, 2012.
39. Arlington National Cemetery website: http://www.arlingtoncemetery.net/hhsemmes.htm.
40. Perret, *Old Soldiers*, 108–109.
41. HNS, 119–127.
42. Ibid., 170.
43. Ibid., 185.
44. Ibid., 267.
45. Ibid., 130.

CHAPTER 3

1. "General Patton's Niece Ends Life Surrounded by His Pictures," *Washington Post*, January 9, 1946, 8.

2. Federal Reserve Bank of Minneapolis Website: https://www.minneapolisfed.org/community/teaching-aids/cpi-calculator-information/consumer-price-index-1800. Consumer Price Indices. 1909, 27; 1911, 28; 1913, 29.7; 1917, 38.5; 1919, 52.1; 1927, 52.2; 1943, 52.0; 2015, 720 (CPI 2015 / CPI 1919 = 720 / 52.1 = 13.8).
3. SPH, 153, 184, 186, 192.
4. This calculation is with similar CPI values in 1919 and 1927: {[19.2 / 7 Ayer sibs] + [(0.394 + 0.692)/ 2 Patton sibs]} / {[2 spouses sharing] x [(0.394 + 0.692)/ 2 Patton sibs]} = 3.02.
5. SPH, 47.
6. (CPI 2015 / CPI 1909 = 720 / 27 = 26.7).
7. RHP, 133.
8. SPH, 327–328.
9. RHP, 143.
10. CDE, 196.
11. MB1, 404.
12. David Irving, *The War Between the Generals* (New York: Congden & Lattes, 1981), 196.
13. RE, 260.
14. Irving, *War between Generals*, 388.
15. Ibid., 418.
16. RHP, 234.
17. CDE, 316, 337, 364, 369.
18. RHP, 225, 230.
19. MB1, 412, 421, 425, 428, 429.
20. Ibid., 657.
21. RE, 109.
22. MB1, 625, 629, 653, 656, 672.
23. CDE, 253.
24. MB1, 237.
25. SPH, 222.
26. Ibid., 232–233.
27. RHP, 97.
28. CDE, 806.
29. *Washington Post*, January 9, 1946, 8.
30. CDE, 157–158.
31. SPH, 79.
32. CDE, 164.
33. SPH, 70.
34. MB1, 312.
35. Ibid., 707.
36. SPH, 148.
37. MB1, 857.
38. Ibid., 774.
39. Ibid., 939.
40. Ibid., 944.

41. CDE, 135.
42. MB1, 515.
43. Ibid., 902–903.
44. Ibid., 776.
45. Ibid., 874.
46. CDE, 352–353.
47. Ibid., 354.
48. SPH, 209.
49. MB1, 899–900.
50. Ibid., 938–939.
51. Ibid., 427–428.
52. Ibid., 561.
53. Ibid., 654.
54. Ibid., 685.
55. Ibid., 711.
56. GSP, 10–20.
57. MB1, 817–818.
58. RE, 190.
59. CDE, 107.
60. MB, 70.
61. CDE, 131.
62. RHP, 163.
63. CDE, 134.
64. Ibid., 135.
65. Ibid., 140–142.
66. MB1, 712.
67. JW, 26.

CHAPTER 4

1. MB1, 32.
2. RHP.
3. RE.
4. MB1, 32.
5. RHP, 117.
6. Ibid., 223.
7. FA, 19.
8. CDE, 181.
9. MB1, 28.
10. RHP, 78.
11. MB1, 30.
12. RE, 71.
13. RHP, 78.

14. RE, 71.
15. RHP, 106.
16. Ibid., 209–210.
17. FA, 55.
18. CDE, 33; Mary Scally stayed in touch with the family and Patton by letter and outlived him.
19. MB1, 29.
20. RHP, 82.
21. Ibid., 87.
22. Ibid., 82.
23. CDE, 109.
24. JW, 24.
25. CDE, 464. At the time, Georgie was unaware of the rank of four-star general, and the rank of five-star general did not exist.
26. RHP, 94–95.
27. STN, 27.
28. Ibid., 87–88.
29. Ibid., 91.
30. STN, 28.
31. RHP, 91; Roger H. Nye, *The Patton Mind: The Professional Development of an Extraordinary Leader* (Garden City Park, NY: Avery, 1993).
32. RHP, 50.
33. Ibid., 58–59.
34. Ibid., 63, 73.
35. CDE, 40.
36. RHP, 103.
37. MB, 16–17; CDE, 45.
38. SPH, 24–25.
39. The Yale Center for Dyslexia and Creativity, *Setting People Straight About Dyslexia*, 2016. http://dyslexia.yale.edu/EDU_dyslexiastraighttalk.html.
40. MB, 16–17.
41. I have been unable to find in the psychology literature any direct link, correlation, or causal relationship between dyslexia, ADD, or delayed literacy and narcissistic personality disorder (NPD). What is evident (see chapter 6) is that at least in Georgie's case, his humiliation at the Clark School due to his lack of reading proficiency, whatever its origin, was the "narcissistic wound" that drove him deeper into narcissism. A reading disorder, such as dyslexia, by itself should not create arrogance, vanity, a sense of entitlement, or a lack of empathy—in fact, it should tend to do the opposite. Thus it seems rare that dyslexia and NPD would coexist.
42. For example, Albert Einstein, Winston Churchill, J. F. Kennedy, Benjamin Franklin, Leonardo da Vinci, and writers Jane Austen, Agatha Christie, William Faulkner, F. Scott Fitzgerald, Ernest Hemingway, and the dyslexic John Irving. Online courses website http://www.onlinecollegecourses.com/2012/01/24/15-famous-thinkers-who-couldnt-spell/, January 24, 2012.
43. RHP, 126.

44. Ibid., 104–108.
45. RE, 134.
46. CDE, 816.
47. MB1, 783.
48. CDE, 171–172.
49. RHP, 96–97.
50. M. Blumenson, my interview, Washington, DC, November 27, 2004, with author Joe W. Wilson Jr. present.
51. MB2, 759–760.
52. CDE, 762–763; MB2, 786–788.
53. GSP, 49; MB2, 243.
54. MB2, 295; MB2, 315.
55. MB2, 712; RE, 344.
56. RHP, 259.
57. RE, 200; TR, 99.
58. CDE, 489.
59. MB2, 82.
60. Ibid., 500.
61. Ibid., 315.
62. RE, 179.
63. Ibid., 314.
64. CDE, 370.
65. FA, 114.
66. CDE, 362.
67. MB, 136.
68. GSP, 160.
69. Joe W. Wilson Jr., *The 761st "Black Panther" Tank Battalion in World War II* (Jefferson, NC: McFarland, 1999); Kareem Abdul-Jabbar and Anthony Walton, *Brothers in Arms: The Epic Story of the 761st Tank Battalion, WWII's Forgotten Heroes* (New York: Broadway, 2004).
70. CDE, 726.
71. Ibid., 163.
72. CDE, 172.
73. MB2, 296.
74. FA, 61–62.
75. RE, 286–287.
76. Ibid., 273.

CHAPTER 5

1. MB1, 30.
2. RE, 306.
3. RHP, ix.

4. Benjamin Spock, *The Common Sense Book of Baby and Child Care* (New York: Duell, Sloan and Pearce, 1946).

5. M. D. S. Ainsworth, "Object Relations, Dependency and Attachment: A Theoretical Review of the Infant-Mother Relationship," *Child Development* 40 (1969): 969–1025.

6. Margaret S. Mahler, Fred Pine, and Anni Bergman. *The Psychological Birth of the Human Infant: Symbiosis and Individuation* (New York: Basic Books, 1975).

7. K. Lyons-Ruth, "Rapprochement or Approchement: Mahler's Theory Reconsidered from the Vantage Point of Recent Research on Early Attachment Relationships," *Psychoanalytic Psychology* 8 (1991): 1–23.

8. E. Partanen et al., "Learning-Induced Neural Plasticity of Speech Processing before Birth," *Proceedings of the National Academy of Sciences USA* 110 (2013): 15145–15150.

9. STN, 16.

10. *Life's First Feelings*. WGBH Educational Foundation, 1986. Film.

11. RHP, 208.

12. CDE, 339.

13. MB1, 809–810.

14. CDE, 340.

15. MB1, 839.

16. RHP, 211.

17. MB1, 889.

18. RHP, 96.

19. John Bradshaw, *Bradshaw on the Family: A Revolutionary Way of Self Discovery* (Deerfield Beach, FL: Health Communications, 1996), 26.

20. Robert Karen, *Becoming Attached: First Relationships and How They Shape Our Capacity to Love* (New York: Oxford University Press, 1998), 93.

21. AM, 27–28.

22. STN, 29.

23. MB1, 30.

24. RHP, 95.

25. Ibid., 88.

26. MB1, 11.

27. CDE, 135.

28. Bradshaw, *Bradshaw on the Family*, 3 and 11.

29. Ibid., 3.

30. J. Bradshaw, *Healing the Shame That Binds You* (Deerfield Beach, FL: Health Communications, 2005), 7.

31. MB1, 515.

32. Ibid., 8.

33. RE, 388.

34. RHP, 255–258.

35. MB, 13.

36. RE, 89.

37. RHP, 141–142.

38. MB, 69.
39. MB1, 493.
40. Ibid., 625–626.
41. Alice Miller. *The Drama of the Gifted Child: The Search for the True Self* (New York: Basic Books, 2007), 7.
42. Bradshaw, *Healing the Shame*, xvii.
43. CDE, 287–288.
44. RE, 150–151.
45. Ibid., 158.
46. Ibid., 161.
47. RHP, 217–218.
48. RE, 155.
49. CDE, 345.
50. MB, 160.
51. BMS, 344.
52. Ibid., 119.
53. Ibid., 336–359.
54. Benjamin Patton, *Growing Up Patton* (New York: Berkley Caliber, 2012).
55. BMS, 347.
56. Patton, *Growing Up Patton*, 31–84.
57. RHP, 300.
58. ABE; BMS, 276–280; Patton, *Growing Up Patton*, 87–106.
59. RHP, 261.
60. Ibid., ix.
61. CDE, 40.
62. RHP, 149.
63. FA, 264–265.
64. RHP, 223.

CHAPTER 6

1. "Jeffrey Kluger's 7 Facts about Narcissists," http://www.mprnews.org/story/2014/10/23/daily-circuit-jeffrey-kluger.
2. SH, 123.
3. World Health Organization, *The ICD-10 Classification of Mental and Behavioural Disorders: Clinical Descriptions and Diagnostic Guidelines* (Geneva: WHO, 1992).
4. According to the DSM-5, the "significant functional impairment" or "subjective distress" is supposed to belong to the NPD sufferer (p. 672), not to those affected by the NPD sufferer. When the NPD sufferer is high-functioning, very rich or powerful, and seemingly successful, such as President Trump, it is easier to observe the impairment or distress inflicted on those around him than on the sufferer (Morris, A. "Trump and the Pathology of Narcissism." *Rolling Stone*, April 5, 2017). Some men-

tal health professionals, such as Prof. Joshua D. Miller of the University of Georgia, believe that the DSM-5 is wrong in this restrictive definition, because, for example, Trump's great wealth tends to shield him from the bankruptcies, unethical behavior, compulsive lying, and marital infidelities that would normally count as impairment for lesser mortals. Other psychiatrists simply ignore the restriction, as they publicly diagnose Trump with NPD (e.g., H. Alford, "Is Trump Actually a Narcissist? Therapists Weigh In." *Vanity Fair*, November 11, 2015) or the more damaging "malignant narcissism" (NPD combined with antisocial behavior, paranoia, and sadism; Prof. John Gartner in A. Morris, *Rolling Stone*). Whether the restriction is correct or not, I will show that despite his power and wealth, Patton exhibits significant impairment in his military failures, political gaffes, love life, and parenting. His distress is usually well concealed behind the mask of the Cowboy General, but as I will show, between the wars and at the end of World War II it will be laid bare.

5. Aaron James, *Assholes: A Theory* (New York: Anchor Books, 2012), 36n4. This entertaining but serious book describes from a philosopher's viewpoint what I am describing from a psychological viewpoint, except that I focus on one individual and Dr. James looks globally. He names the names of both contemporary and historical figures. In trying to define the person we all know as an asshole, with all the rich variety of species, subspecies, and mutants, Dr. James admits that the *DSM* criteria of overt NPD are essentially identical to the criteria for "assholeness."

6. K. N. Levy, W. D. Ellison, and J. S. Reynoso, "A Historical Review of Narcissism and Narcissistic Personality," in *HNPD*, 3–13.

7. Jeffrey Kluger, *The Narcissist Next Door* (New York: Riverhead Books, 2014), 21–25.

8. Ibid., 10.

9. D. K. Lapsley and P. C. Stey, "Adolescent Narcissism," in *Encyclopedia of Adolescence* (New York: Springer, 2012).

10. SH, 93; JK, 83.

11. SH, xv.

12. J. M. Twenge and W. K. Campbell, *Living in the Age of Entitlement: The Narcissism Epidemic* (New York: Free Press, 2009).

13. Twenge et al., *Age of Entitlement*, 30–31.

14. J. D. Foster and J. C. Brennan, "Narcissism, the Agency Model, and Approach-Avoidance Motivation," in *HNPD*, 89.

15. Foster and Brennan, "Narcissism, Agency Model," in *HNPD*, 96.

16. R. Hogan and J. Fico, "Leadership," in *HNPD*, 396.

17. A. B. Brunell et al., "Leader Emergence: The Case of the Narcissistic Leader," *Personality and Social Psychology Bulletin* 34 (2008): 1663–1676.

18. R. Hogan and J. Hogan, *Hogan Development Survey Manual*, 2nd ed. (Tulsa, OK: Hogan Assessment Systems, 2009).

19. SH, 147.

20. For example, obsequiousness to powerful people could have been categorized under criterion 8, a manifestation of envy, as placed by Sandy Hotchkiss (SH, 17), rather than our criterion 6, part of interpersonal exploitation. For another example,

belittling others or taking credit for their successes fits well in many criteria besides number 7.

21. O. Rank, "A Contribution to Narcissism." *Jahrbuch fur Psychoanalytische und Psychopathologische Forschungen* 3 (1911): 401–426.

22. Levy, Ellison, and Reynoso, "A Historical Review of Narcissism and Narcissistic Personality," in *HNPD*, 3–13.

23. AM, 52.

24. Twenge et al., *Age of Entitlement*, 35–36.

25. J. J. Bourgeois, M. J. Hall, R. M. Crosby, and K. G. Drexler, "An Examination of Narcissistic Personality Traits as Seen in a Military Population," *Military Medicine* 158 (1993): 170–74.

26 Grijalva, E., D. A. Newman, L. Tay, M. B. Donnellan, P. D. Harms, R. W. Robins, and T. Yan. "Gender Differences in Narcissism: A Meta-Analytic Review." P.D. Harms Publications, paper 5 (2014).

27. Otto F. Kernberg, MD, *Borderline Conditions and Pathological Narcissism* (Northvale, NJ: Jason Aronson, 1975).

28. T. Millon, *Disorders of Personality: DSM III: Axis II* (Chichester, UK: John Wiley 1981), 165.

29. H. Kohut, *The Restoration of the Self* (Madison, CT: International Universities Press, 1977).

30. A. Rothstein, "The Theory of Narcissism: An Object-Relations Perspective," *Psychoanalytic Review* 66 (1979): 35–47.

31. L. J. Otway and V. L. Vignoles, "Narcissism and Childhood Reflections: A Quantitative Test of Psychoanalytic Predictions," *Personality and Social Psychology Bulletin* 32 (2006): 104–116.

32. M. S. Mahler et al., *Psychological Birth of the Human Infant* (New York, 1975).

33. Mahler, *Psychological Birth*, 5.

34. MAST, 27.

35. SH, 39.

36. M. Botkin, "Separation-Individuation," in *International Encyclopedia of Marriage and Family*, ed. James J. Ponzetti Jr (New York: Macmillan Reference USA, 2003).

37. MAST, 30.

38. Ibid., 96.

39. SH, 42.

40. STN, 66.

41. Botkin, "Separation-Individuation."

42. SH, 43.

43. Ibid., 45.

44. MAST, 101.

45. RHP, 95.

46. MAST, 103.

47. Bradshaw, *The Family*, 27–42.

48. Bradshaw, *Healing the Shame*, 8–9; Parents. *The Age of Reason*. http://www.scholastic.com/parents/resources/article/stages-milestones/age-reason.
49. SH, 41.
50. D. K. Lapsley and P. C. Stey, “Adolescent Narcissism,” in *Encyclopedia of Adolescence* (New York: Springer, 2012).
51. SH, xvii.

CHAPTER 7

1. RA1, 402.
2. CDE, 541.
3. SH, 11.
4. CDE, 466.
5. RA1, 446.
6. Ibid., 325, 446–449.
7. In the first engagement of World War II between Allied and Axis forces in North Africa in which US forces took part, the surprise attack on February 19–22, 1943, at this Atlas Mountain pass in Western Tunisia was led by German Field Marshal Erwin Rommel. It inflicted about ten thousand casualties equally on the Americans and Brits.
8. RA1, 279.
9. Ibid., 449.
10. Ibid., 450.
11. MB2, 198.
12. RA1, 388.
13. E. N. Harmon, Milton MacKaye, and Ross MacKaye, *Combat Commander: Autobiography of a Soldier* (Englewood Cliffs, NJ: Prentice-Hall, 1970), 123–124; SPH, 332–333.
14. CDE, 533–535.
15. IKE1, 439.
16. Harmon, *Combat Commander*, 202.
17. RA1, 405.
18. Audie L. Murphy Memorial website: http://audiemurphy.com/biography.htm.
19. The Perilous Fight; America’s World War II in color website. The Mental Toll: http://www.pbs.org/perilousfight/psychology/the_mental_toll/.
20. US Department of Veteran’s Affairs. National Center for PTSD: http://www.ptsd.va.gov/public/PTSD-overview/basics/how-common-is-ptsd.asp.
21. RA2, 171–172.
22. Dwight Macdonald, *The Responsibility of Peoples, and Other Essays in Political Criticism* (Westport, CT: Greenwood Press, 1974), 65.
23. RA2, 148.
24. CDE, 538–539.

25. EFP, 200.
26. MB2, 379.
27. GSP, 382.
28. A recent report claims that Patton was present at the bombing but had to cover up that fact due to Ike's warning for him to avoid showing off his bravery and to stay out of harm's way. Kevin H. Hymel, "The Bravest and Best: Patton and the Death of Capt. Richard Jenson in North Africa," in *Army History* (US Army Center of Military History, Spring 2014), 30–40.
29. MB2, 202.
30. Ibid., 203.
31. HGP, 96.
32. RA1, 455.
33. GSP; Eddy was mentioned seventy times by name, with many additional references to him as XII Corps.
34. HGP, 17–88.
35. H. G. Phillips, *El Guettar: Crucible of Leadership* (Penn Valley, CA: Henry Gerard Phillips, 1991).
36. HGP, 96.
37. RA1, 453.
38. SLAM, 119.
39. RA2, 158.
40. BRAD, 301.
41. Lt. Col. George Dyer, *XII Corps: Spearhead of Patton's Third Army* (Baton Rouge, LA: Military Press, 1947), 180.
42. Ibid., 187.
43. Col. Thomas R. Henry, "The Avenging Ghosts of the 9th," *Saturday Evening Post*, July 6, 1946, 24.
44. CDE, 636–637.
45. David N. Spires, *Air Power for Patton's Army: The XIX Tactical Air Command in the Second World War* (Washington, DC: Air Force History and Museums Program, 2002); *www.afhso.af.mil/shared/media/document/AFD-100924-003.pdf.*
46. IKE1, 495.
47. ENIGMA is the Allies' code name for the German encryption machine; ULTRA is the Allies' code name for the intercepted and decoded Enigma messages; Michael Smith, "How It Began: Bletchley Park Goes to War," in Jack Copeland, ed., *Colossus: The Secrets of Bletchley Park's Codebreaking Computers* (Oxford: Oxford University Press, 2006).
48. CDE, 637.
49. BRAD, 298.
50. ABE, 95–96.
51. RA3, 345.
52. MB2, 570.
53. Eddy diary, November 7, 1944.
54. GSP, 163, 386.
55. JNR; Bradley called it "a ghastly war of attrition," CDE, 664.

56. JNR, 186.
57. CMP, 79.
58. CDE, 672.
59. A. H. Ganz, "Patton's Relief of General Wood," *Journal of Military History* 53 (1989): 257–73.
60. Stephen E. Ambrose, *Citizen Soldiers: The US Army from the Normandy Beaches to the Bulge to the Surrender of Germany/June 7, 1944, to May 7, 1945* (New York: Simon and Schuster, 1997), *162.*
61. Russell F. Weigley, *Eisenhower's Lieutenants* (Bloomington: Indiana University Press, 1981), 389.
62. JNR, 40.
63. Ibid., 86.
64. Ibid., 186.
65. Col. Thomas R. Henry, *Saturday Evening Post*, 1946.
66. CDE, 663.
67. GSP, 238.
68. Ibid., 388.
69. Dwight D. Eisenhower, *Crusade in Europe* (Garden City, NY: Doubleday, 1948), 384.
70. CDE, 712.
71. GSP, 268.
72. Ibid., 389.
73. Ibid., 266.
74. Eddy diary, April 17, 1945.
75. HGP, 187.
76. GSP, 304.
77. SPH, 630.
78. Ibid., 811.
79. SH, 147.

CHAPTER 8

1. CDE, 135.
2. J. L. Tracy, J. T. Cheng, J. P. Martens, and R. W. Robins, "The Emotional Dynamics of Narcissism: Inflated by Pride, Deflated by Shame," in *HNPD*, 330–343.
3. SH, 11.
4. MB1, 624.
5. Ibid., 627.
6. MB2, 14–15.
7. CDE, 499.
8. MB, 174.
9. MB2, 141.
10. Ibid., 150.

11. Ibid., 690.
12. Ibid., 149.
13. Ibid., 219.
14. Ibid., 553.
15. CDE, 662.
16. MB2, 557.
17. Ibid., 558.
18. JNR, 204.
19. BRAD, 45.
20. In Knutsford, England, on April 25, 1944, Patton gave a speech about the postwar world which seemed to ignore our Russian allies, caused an uproar in the press, made Ike furious, and put Patton even deeper into the doghouse.
21. MB, 215–216.
22. JNR, 180.
23. M. Blumenson, "Bradley-Patton: World War II's 'Odd Couple,'" *Army,* December 1985, 56.
24. MB2, 486; D. P. Bolger, "Zero Defects: Command Climate in the First US Army, 1944–1945," *US Army in Military Review*, May 1991, 67–68.
25. BRAD, 225–226.
26. RA3, 441.
27. IKE1, 145–155.
28. MB2, 83.
29. MB, 176.
30. MB2, 480.
31. DOC, 11–12.
32. In her memoir, *Past Forgetting*, Kay Summersby Morgan admitted that, though she fell deeply in love with Ike, their relationship grew out of wartime stress and loneliness, and was never consummated.
33. DOC, 12.
34. Ibid., 32–33.
35. IKE1, 330.
36. CDE, 711.
37. DOC, 73.
38. This partitioning of postwar Europe was hammered out at the Yalta conference, February 1945, by the Big Three: Roosevelt, Churchill, and Stalin.
39. CDE, 740.
40. TR, 207–208.
41. GSP, 119–120.
42. MB2, 533.
43. Ibid., 535.
44. MB2, 608.
45. MB1, 8.
46. Hampton Sides, *Ghost Soldiers: The Epic Account of World War II's Greatest Rescue Mission* (New York: Anchor Books, 2001).

47. Wikipedia. Raid at Cabanatuan: https://en.wikipedia.org/wiki/Raid_at_Cabanatuan; Perret, G. *Old Soldiers*, 1996, 446.
48. CDE, 734–735.
49. R. M. Citino in HistoryNet. Mark W. Clark—a General Reappraisal: http://www.historynet.com/mark-w-clark-a-general-reappraisal.htm; the author then goes on to defend Clark's record and positive qualities.
50. CDE, 751.
51. E. P. Hoyt, *Backwater War: The Allied Campaign in Italy, 1943–45* (Westport, CT: Praeger Publishers, 2002), viii.
52. CDE, 494.
53. W. Murray and A. R. Millett, *A War to Be Won* (Cambridge: Belknap Press of Harvard University Press, 2000), 270.
54. IKE1, 225–226.
55. Ibid., 226–228.
56. MAST, 93.
57. IKE1, 234–235.
58. MB2, 411.
59. A beggar boils a rock in a pot full of water. The villagers ask why. "Wouldn't it taste better with some carrots?" which they donate. Other villagers donate more ingredients, and pretty soon the soup is quite nutritious.

CHAPTER 9

1. H. M. Wallace, "Narcissistic Self-Enhancement," in *HNPD*, 309–318.
2. One of the few surviving voice recordings is on a YouTube video from the Los Angeles Colliseum: https://www.youtube.com/watch?v=SSySTnGS1M4.
3. CDE, 712.
4. MB2, 661.
5. FA, 206.
6. BRAD, 342.
7. J. L. Tracy, J. T. Cheng, R. W. Robins, and K. H. Trzesniewski, "Authentic and Hubristic Pride: The Affective Core of Self-Esteem and Narcissism," *Self and Identity* 8 (2009): 196–213.
8. R. F. Baumeister and K. D. Vohs, "Narcissism as Addiction to Esteem," *Psychological Inquiry* 12 (2001): 206–210.
9. W. K. Campbell, A. S. Goodie, and J. D. Foster, "Narcissism, Confidence, and Risk Attitude," *Journal of Behavioral Decision Making* 17 (2004): 297–311.
10. B. Bizumic and J. Duckitt, "'My Group Is Not Worthy of Me': Narcissism and Ethnocentrism," *Political Psychology* 29 (2008): 437–453.
11. John Field, "Patton of the Armored Force," *LIFE*, November 30, 1942, 113–125.
12. MB2, 53; Patton did object in a letter to a *LIFE* editor and to the War Department about some features of a draft of the article, such as his wealth, his athletic

prowess, and his personal challenge to Rommel for a duel (MB2, 101). However, when the article appeared in print, Beatrice found it had been changed to her satisfaction, and she assumed he would like it too (MB2, 132).

13. John Field, *LIFE*, Nov. 1942, 113–125.
14. FA, 63.
15. John Field, *LIFE*, Nov. 1942, 113–125.
16. RHP, 89–90.
17. CDE, 87.
18. MB2, 654.
19. RHP, 262.
20. JW, 13–14.
21. TR, 48.
22. RE, 108.
23. FA, 96.
24. RHP, 168.
25. MB1, 462.
26. George S. Patton, "Form and Use of the Saber." *Cavalry Journal* (March 1913).
27. George S. Patton, *Saber Exercise, 1914* (Washington, DC: US Government Printing Office, 1914).
28. MB1, 346; see also CDE, 181.
29. K. J. Parker, "Cutting Edge Technology," *Subterranean Press Magazine* (Fall 2011).
30. J. Christoph Amberger, *The Secret History of the Sword: Adventures in Ancient Martial Arts* (Burbank, CA: Unique Publications, 1999).
31. Wikipedia. Model 1913 Cavalry Saber: https://en.wikipedia.org/wiki/Model_1913_Cavalry_Saber.
32. MB1, 446.
33. Ibid., 447, 450.
34. Ibid., 435–479.
35. Ibid., 526.
36. Ibid., 514.
37. Ibid., 550.
38. Ibid., 554.
39. Ibid., 560.
40. Ibid., 541.
41. MB, 153.
42. CDE, 387.
43. JW, vii.
44. J. D. Foster, J. W. Shenesey, and J. S. Goff, "Why Do Narcissists Take More Risks? Testing the Roles of Perceived Risks and Benefits of Risky Behaviors," *Personality and Individual Differences* 47 (2009): 885–889; J. D. Foster, T. A. Misra, and D. E. Reidy, "Narcissists Are Approach-Oriented toward Their Money and Their Friends," *Journal of Research in Personality* 43 (2009): 764–769.
45. MB1, 773.

46. Boston Globe. Metro. Seth Moulton underplays military service: https://www.bostonglobe.com/metro/2014/10/17/moulton-underplays-military-service/lY9FfmOrviwL2LAFHr61dO/story.html.

CHAPTER 10

1. Field, "Patton of the Armored Force," 114.
2. Sun Tzu, *The Art of War* (Barnes & Noble Classics Series) (New York: Barnes & Noble Classics, 2003), 21.
3. Cornelius Ryan, *A Bridge Too Far* (New York: Simon and Schuster, 1974), 78.
4. JNR2, 4.
5. CDE, 616.
6. RHP, 150.
7. JW, 200.
8. CDE, 379.
9. RHP, 151.
10. CDE, 312.
11. IKE1, 269.
12. TRSC, 228–234.
13. BRAD, 158.
14. A. N. Garland, H. M. Smyth, and M. Blumenson, "Sicily and the Surrender," Center of Military History, US Army, Washington, DC, 1965, 389.
15. MB2, 318.
16. TRSC, 235.
17. RA2, 162–163.
18. TRSC, 235.
19. Garland et al., "Sicily and the Surrender," 396.
20. Half-tracks were lightly armored personnel carriers used by armored infantry divisions to transport about twelve infantrymen (one squad) each. They used tank treads in the rear for traction but were steered by wheels in front. They were normally armed with a .50-caliber machine gun in front and a .30-caliber machine gun in back.
21. Garland et al. "Sicily and the Surrender," 396–403.
22. TRSC, 237–239.
23. RA2, 164.
24. CDE, 530; RA2, 169.
25. BRAD, 159–160.
26. TR, 204.
27. JNR, 45.
28. Ibid., 58–59.
29. Ibid., 128.
30. S. J. Zaloga, *Metz 1944: Patton's Fortified Nemesis* (Oxford: Osprey Publishing, 2012).
31. JW, 198.

32. Hugh M. Cole, *The Lorraine Campaign* (Center of Military History, US Army, Washington, DC, 1997), 264–275.
33. JNR, 126.
34. CDE, 666.
35. JNR, 127.
36. Ibid., 237.
37. C. K. Hofling, *Custer and the Little Big Horn: A Psychobiographical Inquiry* (Detroit, MI: Wayne State University Press, 1981), 84–99.
38. JNR, 235.
39. Ibid., 140.
40. Ibid., 145.
41. Ibid., 123.
42. PREF, 14.
43. Ibid., 18.
44. Ibid., 48.
45. Ibid., 73.
46. Ibid., 83.
47. Ibid., 37.
48. C. B. MacDonald, *The Last Offensive* (Center of Military History, Washington, DC, 1993), 117.
49. PREF, 46.
50. Ibid., 56.
51. MacDonald, *The Last Offensive*, 122.
52. Ibid., 123.
53. PREF, 76.
54. Combat command was a brigade-sized, task-oriented force built around one tank battalion and one armored infantry battalion. This normally consisted of about three thousand men and one hundred armored vehicles.
55. Ibid., 209.
56. Ibid., 214.
57. SPH, 277.
58. CDE, 578.
59. MB2, 657.
60. GSP, 213.
61. FA, 147.
62. MB, 11.
63. Ian V. Hogg, *The Biography of General George S. Patton* (n.p.: Magna Book, 1982), 153.
64. JNR, 238.
65. CDE, 636.
66. William C. Westmoreland, *A Soldier Reports* (New York: Da Capo Press, 1976), 21.
67. GSP, 178.
68. Ibid., 399.

69. Kenneth Koyen, *The 4th Armored Division, from the Beach to Bavaria: The Story of the 4th Armored Division in Combat* (Nashville, TN: Battery Press, 1946), 291–294.

70. GSP, 157; with typical exaggeration, Patton said that three shells came within thirty-five yards. We have plotted the blasts using Nancy historical records and Google Earth (J. L. Sudmeier and J. LeClerc, "The Shelling of Patton's Nancy HQ," in *After the Battle, Vol. 176* [2017], 32–46.) One shell landed about thirty-five yards away from his residence, the next closest shells landed approximately 160 and 380 yards away.

71. Lande, *I Was with Patton*, 155.

72. MB2, 566.

73. Fencing shown in photo, MB, 262.

74. Patton diary, March 26, 1945, Library of Congress.

75. GSP, 249.

76. Ibid., 306.

77. Ibid., 202.

78. Ibid., 322.

79. BRAD, 159–160.

80. MB2, 213.

81. Ibid., 216.

82. Ibid., 182.

83. ABE, 53–54.

84. Frank Woolner, *Spearhead in the West: 3rd Armored Division* (Frankfurt am Main, 1946), 3.

85. Andy Rooney, *My War* (New York: Public Affairs, 1995), 259.

CHAPTER 11

1. MB1, 135.

2. Dwight Macdonald, "My Favourite General," in *The Responsibility of Peoples and Other Essays in Political Criticism* (Westport, CT: Greenwood Press, 1974), 62.

3. EFP, 97–98.

4. MB1, 474.

5. Ibid., 559.

6. RHP, 82.

7. MB1, 31.

8. Ibid., 12.

9. RHP, 142–143.

10. RE, 238.

11. RHP, 116–117.

12. MB1, 128.

13. Ibid., 130.

14. Ibid., 134–135.

15. Patton, *Growing Up Patton*, 18.
16. MB1, 135.
17. Ibid., 144.
18. Ibid., 594.
19. Ibid., 129–130.
20. CDE, 462-464.
21. Westmoreland, *A Soldier Reports*, 21.
22. TRSC, 542.
23. CDE, 214.
24. BRAD, 52.
25. CDE, 478.
26. SPH, 318–319.
27. MB2, 225.
28. MB1, 500.
29. Marshall falsely claimed that he had earned a battlefield commission during World War I. He also may have exaggerated the statistics in his report that during World War II typically less than one infantryman in four ever fired his weapon in anger, while standing by his main point that the number of soldiers that fired was in the minority.
30. SLAM, 60–61.
31. Ibid., 162–163.
32. Ibid., 158–159.
33. GSP, 43–44.
34. Ibid., 80.
35. Ibid., 84.
36. SA, 334.
37. Paul Fussell, *Wartime: The Experience of War, 1939–1945* (New York: Oxford University Press, 1989), 80.
38. TR, 204.
39. SA, 335.
40. Rooney, *My War*, 193, 197–198.
41. CDE, 522.
42. Rooney, *My War*, 195–196.
43. CDE, 576.
44. FA, 72.
45. TRSC, 541.
46. MB2, 181.
47. IKE1, 269–270.
48. ABE, 126; BMS, 289.
49. TR, 66.
50. BRAD, 81.
51. BRAD, 110; Bradley's distaste for Allen and Roosevelt's style was certainly one of the reasons they got fired during the Sicilian campaign (RA2, 139).
52. ABE, 82.

53. S. Vazire, L. P. Naumann, P. J. Rentfrow, and S. D. Gosling, "Portrait of a Narcissist: Manifestations of Narcissism in Physical Appearance," *Journal of Research in Personality* 42 (2008): 1439–1447.
54. Hofling, *Custer and the Little Big Horn*, 84–99.
55. Ibid., 53.
56. Ibid., 33–34.
57. IKE1, 226–228.
58. Hogan and Fico, "Leadership," in *HNPD*, 397.
59. CDE, 182.
60. Ibid., 725.
61. TR, 81.

CHAPTER 12

1. MB2, 339.
2. Ibid., 608.
3. Ibid., 599.
4. LEO, 37.
5. CDE, 679.
6. RA3, 437.
7. SPH, 630.
8. Ibid., 575.
9. CMP, 118.
10. FOX, 302.
11. IKE1, 644.
12. CDE, 680.
13. Though other versions have Patton promising three divisions by the twenty-first, Atkinson's studies show that the majority of those present heard Patton say "on December 22nd."
14. RA3, 446.
15. SPH, 575, 577.
16. CDE, 680.
17. RA3, 466.
18. CDE, 681.
19. Bendetsen is best known as the architect of the internment of Japanese Americans in World War II (website: https://en.wikipedia.org/wiki/Karl_Bendetsen).
20. SPH, 574–575.
21. CDE, 681.
22. The ever-loyal General Gay, blinded in one eye due to a polo accident, was with Patton during the low-speed auto crash that led to Patton's paralysis in December 1945.
23. FOX, 304.
24. MB2, 600.

25. CDE, 682.
26. Late on December 16, Patton had balked when Bradley phoned him from Ike's HQ to have him relinquish his 10th Armored Division. It was urgently needed up north in Bastogne, Belgium, to assist the soon-to-be-surrounded VIII Corps. But Patton had his own big plans for the 10th Armored and suggested that the Germans were making a "spoiling" attack (or feint) and that Middleton could handle it by himself. The 10th Armored was sent to VIII Corps over Patton's objections and played an essential role in the defense of Bastogne.
27. FOX, 298.
28. CDE, 676.
29. FOX, 297.
30. FOX, 299; SPH, 274.
31. FOX, 293.
32. CDE, 675.
33. SPH, 701.
34. LEO, 36.
35. CDE, 676.
36. JNR, 58–59.
37. FOX, 295.
38. LEO, 37.
39. Ibid., 38.
40. FOX, 296, as happening on December 12; CMP, 114, as happening on December 14.
41. Brig. Gen. Albin F. Irzyk. HistoryNet. Firsthand Account 4th Armored Spearhead at Bastogne: http://www.historynet.com/firsthand-account-4th-armored-division-spearhead-at-bastogne-november-99-world-war-ii-feature.htm.
42. CDE, 682.
43. SPH, 577.
44. CMP, 121–122.
45. JNR, 174.
46. CDE, 683–684.
47. FOX, 305.
48. SPH, 577–578.
49. CDE, 702.
50. General Irzyk's account: http://www.historynet.com/firsthand-account-4th-armored-division-spearhead-at-bastogne-november-99-world-war-ii-feature.htm.
51. Albin F. Irzyk, *He Rode Up Front for Patton* (Raleigh, NC: Pentland Press, 1996). (The best first-person account I've ever read about what World War II tank warfare was like.)
52. Charles B. MacDonald, *A Time for Trumpets: The Untold Story of the Battle of the Bulge* (New York: Morrow, 1985), 525.
53. IKE, 358.
54. BRAD, 565; K. R. Greenfield, R. R. Palmer, and B. I. Wiley, *The Army Ground Forces: The Organization of Ground Combat Troops* (Center of Military His-

tory, US Army, Washington, DC, 1987), 319–320. Each tank battalion should have 729 men; each armored infantry battalion should have 1,001 men.

55. LEO, 72–73, 126; FOX, 337, 358, 378.
56. LEO, 201–202.
57. FOX, 351–353.
58. Ibid., 355–356.
59. For General Irzyk's first-hand narration and a slide show of the action on December 22–23, using mostly modern photos of the battle sites, go to Liberator of Chaumont revisits 1944 Battlegrounds: http://users.skynet.be/wielewaal/General_Albin_Irzyk.htm.
60. FOX, 370.
61. LEO, 98.
62. FOX, 372–373.
63. LEO, 111–112.
64. FOX, 375.
65. LEO, 79.
66. FOX, 376.
67. Ibid., 377.
68. LEO, 126.
69. Ibid., 124–125, 128–129.
70. Ibid., 129–130.
71. Ibid., 130–137.
72. FOX, 385.
73. GSP, 147.
74. LEO, 102.
75. Ibid., 121.
76. Ibid., 184.
77. MB2, 605.
78. FOX, 388.
79. Ibid., 389.
80. Ibid., 391–392.
81. Ibid., 393.
82. Ibid., 394–395.
83. LEO, 143–144.
84. FOX, 360–362.
85. Ibid., 363–364.
86. LEO, 169.
87. FOX, 365.
88. LEO, 204–209.
89. Ibid., 209–211.
90. Ibid., 211–213.
91. Ibid., 213–218.
92. Ibid., 219–223.
93. FOX, 366–369.
94. ABE, 78.

95. FOX, 413; GSP, 200.
96. Ibid., 397–398.
97. Ibid., 401; ABE, 75.
98. LEO, 289–290; FOX, 399.
99. FOX, 399–401; LEO, 290–291.
100. The 105 mm assault gun is a Sherman tank chassis fixed with the gun of a 105 mm howitzer for greater firepower.
101. FOX, 403–404; LEO, 295–296.
102. LEO, 298.
103. FOX, 405.
104. LEO, 298.
105. Ibid., 307.
106. ABE, 78.
107. FOX, 366–369.
108. Ibid., 406–407.
109. ABE, 79.
110. FOX, 408–409.
111. Ibid., 409–410.
112. CDE, 684.
113. BRAD, 469–470.
114. JNR2, 102–103.

CHAPTER 13

1. GSP, 331.
2. FA, 222.
3. K. Margry, "The Hammelburg Raid," in *After the Battle*, *Vol. 91* (London: Battle of Britain Prints, 1996), 1–39.
4. MB2, 656.
5. CDE, 711.
6. Wikipedia on MacArthur's Cabanatuan raid: https://en.wikipedia.org/wiki/Raid_at_Cabanatuan; Perret, *Old Soldiers*, 446.
7. MB2, 664.
8. CDE, 714.
9. MB2, 665.
10. Patton diary, March 26, Library of Congress: "Before Gen. Eisenhower arrived, Bradley and I came to a fairly satisfactory decision as to the boundary between the Third and Seventh Armies, which he hopes to be able to put over."
11. The US Army Campaigns of World War II. Central Europe: http://www.history.army.mil/brochures/centeur/centeur.htm.
12. Patton seems to have had a tacit understanding with General Patch to use his zone for raiding the Hammelburg POW camp, at least on March 26–28. During the brief meeting on the morning of March 26 between Patton and Bradley, Patton also

seems to have received tacit consent from Bradley, who stipulated that Patton not accompany the raid personally (Margry, *After the Battle*, 1). That Bradley and Patton discussed the raid is confirmed by the fact that Bradley is one of the people Patton blamed for not allowing a sufficiently large force (MB2, 671). However, it is doubtful that Bradley was informed about the presence of Waters at the POW camp. After the war, Bradley denied that he had given prior approval of the raid (BRAD, 542), although this is contradicted by the diary of his aide, Lt. Col. Chester B. Hansen (RAID, 3). Patton told General Hoge, "I've cleared this with Bradley" (RAID, 6), but his diary entry from March 31 is inconsistent by blaming Bradley for his "strenuous objections to making any [effort] at all" (MB2, 668).

13. MB2, 664.
14. Ibid., 665.
15. Ibid., 668.
16. RAID, 13.
17. Eddy diary, March 21, 1944.
18. 48HR, 68.
19. ABE, 91.
20. MB2, 665.
21. Ken Hechler, *The Bridge at Remagen: The Amazing Story of March 7, 1945—The Day the Rhine River Was Crossed* (Missoula, MT: Pictorial Histories, 1957).
22. RAID, 6.
23. 48HR, 58.
24. Ibid., 59.
25. Ibid., 60.
26. Ibid., 61–62.
27. Ibid., 73–74.
28. Ibid., 75.
29. RAID, 42–43.
30. P. Domes and M. Heinlein, Task Force Baum and the Hammelburg Raid: http://www.taskforcebaum.de.
31. 48HR; RAID; Margry, *After the Battle*, vol. 91.
32. D. N. Spires, *Air Power for Patton's Army* (Washington, DC: Air Force History and Museums Program, 2002), 273; *www.afhso.af.mil/shared/media/document/AFD-100924-003.pdf.*
33. Domes and Heinlein, http://www.taskforcebaum.de.
34. K. Koyen, "Gen. Patton's Mistake: Third Army, 4th Armored Division and the Hammelburg Affair," *Saturday Evening Post,* May 1, 1948, 1.
35. Website Answers. What was the cost of a sherman tank in World War 2 dollars?: http://www.answers.com/Q/What_was_the_cost_of_a_sherman_tank_in_World_War_2_dollars.
36. 48HR, 70.
37. CDE, 716.
38. GSP, 331.

CHAPTER 14

1. CDE, 699.
2. Tzu, *The Art of War*, 20.
3. BRAD, 52.
4. MB1, 500–501.
5. Ibid., 753.
6. Ibid., 757.
7. Ibid., 789.
8. Ibid., 817–818.
9. Ibid., 850.
10. MB2, 142.
11. Ibid., 463.
12. MB, 307–308.
13. GSP, 357.
14. Ibid., 349.
15. Ibid., 147.
16. EFP.
17. Ibid., 5–7.
18. Ibid., 20.
19. Ibid., 85.
20. Ibid., 69.
21. Ibid., 84.
22. Ibid., 90.
23. Ibid., 81.
24. Ibid., 78.
25. Ibid., 103.
26. BRAD, 159–160.
27. EFP, 345.
28. Ibid., 97–102.
29. Ibid., 285.
30. Ibid., 288–290.
31. Ibid., 332.
32. Ibid., 333.
33. RE, 388.
34. BMS, 116–117.
35. Ibid., 117–118.
36. Ibid., 119.
37. ABE, 84–85.
38. JNR2, 177.
39. US Army publications website: https://armypubs.us.army.mil/doctrine/index.html.

CHAPTER 15

1. Attributed by Seneca, Lucius Annaeus (c.3 BCE–AD 65) in "Moral Essays" *On Tranquility of Mind*, Sect. 17, Subsec. 10 [See earlier note about treatment from Classical texts.]
2. Aaron James, *Assholes: A Theory* (New York: Anchor Books, 2012), 12.
3. James, *Assholes: A Theory*, 33–34.
4. RA2, 117.
5. CDE, 723–724.
6. Hofling, *Custer and the Little Big Horn*, 84–99.
7. GN
8. IKE1, 225–226.
9. Finding empathy from General Sherman seems to have been based on a single, flowery letter to the mayor of Atlanta just prior to his troops' burning and pillaging of that city (GN, 33–34). Hitler's empathy for people was an even bigger stretch (GN, 205), having to do with love of several objects, including his dog, his mother, and his half niece Geli, with whom he had a controlling sexual affair that led her to death. If the pistol bullet through her lungs was not a suicide, the next most likely cause was murder by Hitler (R. Hayman, *Hitler and Geli* [New York, NY: Bloomsbury, 1997]).
10. GN, 224.
11. "There are no biological determinants for narcissism." (Jerome Kagan, Harvard), JK, 43.
12. Otto F. Kernberg, MD, *Borderline Conditions and Pathological Narcissism* (New York: Rowman & Littlefield, 1975), 243.
13. Alford, H. "Is Trump Actually a Narcissist? Therapists Weigh In." *Vanity Fair*, November 11, 2015. http://www.vanityfair.com/news/2015/11/donald-trump-narcissism-therapists.
14. MB, 280.
15. RHP, 258.
16. FA, 238.
17. CDE, 796.
18. CDE, 808.

APPENDIX A

1. S. Simonsen and E. Simonsen, "Comorbidity," in *HNPD*, 240.
2. G. Rosso, U. Albert, F. Bogetto, and G. Maina, "Axis II Comorbidity in Euthymic Bipolar Disorder Patients: No Differences between Bipolar I and II Subtypes," *Journal of Affective Disorders* 115 (2009): 257–261.
3. D. Stormberg, E. Ronningstam, J. Gunderson, and M. Tohen, "Brief Communication: Pathological Narcissism in Bipolar Disorder Patients," *Journal of Personality Disorders* 12 (1998): 179–185.

APPENDIX B

1. Patton once spoke to newsmen about Creighton Abrams: "There's a great young officer in the 4th [Armored Division]," he said. "But if you're going to write about him, you better do it right away. He's so good, he isn't going to live long." (ABE, 57).
2. ABE, 118–120.

Bibliography

BOOKS

Abdul-Jabbar, Kareem, and Anthony Walton. *Brothers in Arms: The Epic Story of the 761st Tank Battalion, WWII's Forgotten Heroes*. New York: Broadway, 2004.

Amberger, J. Christoph. *The Secret History of the Sword: Adventures in Ancient Martial Arts*. Burbank, CA: Unique Publications, 1999.

Ambrose, Stephen E. *Citizen Soldiers: The US Army from the Normandy Beaches to the Bulge to the Surrender of Germany/June 7, 1944, to May 7, 1945*. New York: Simon and Schuster, 1997.

American Psychiatric Association. *Diagnostic and Statistical Manual of Mental Disorders*. 5th ed. (DSM-5). Arlington, VA: American Psychiatric Publishing, 2013.

Atkinson, Rick. *An Army at Dawn: The War in North Africa, 1942–1943*. New York: Henry Holt, 2002.

———. *The Day of Battle: The War in Sicily and Italy, 1943–1944*. New York: Henry Holt, 2007.

———. *The Guns at Last Light: The War in Western Europe, 1944–1945*. New York: Henry Holt, 2013.

Ayer, Fred. *Before the Colors Fade*. Boston: Houghton Mifflin, 1964.

Baron, Richard, Abraham Baum, and Richard Goldhurst. *Raid! The Untold Story of Patton's Secret Mission*. New York: Dell Books, 1981.

Barron, Leo. *Patton at the Battle of the Bulge; How the General's Tanks Turned the Tide at Bastogne*. New York: NAL/Caliber, 2014.

Blumenson, Martin. *The Patton Papers, 1885–1940*. Boston: Houghton Mifflin, 1972.

———. *The Patton Papers, 1940–1945*. Boston: Houghton Mifflin, 1974.

———. *Patton: The Man behind the Legend, 1885–1945*. New York: Quill, William Morrow, 1985.

Bowlby, J. *A Secure Base: Parent-Child Attachment and Healthy Human Development*. London: Routledge, 1988.

Botkin, Meryl. "Separation-Individuation." In *International Encyclopedia of Marriage and Family*, edited by James J. Ponzetti Jr. Macmillan Reference USA: Thomson Gale, 2003. http://www.encyclopedia.com/doc/1G2-3406900380.html.

Bradley, Omar N. *A Soldier's Story*. New York: Henry Holt, 1951.

Bradshaw, John. *Bradshaw on the Family: A Revolutionary Way of Self Discovery*. Deerfield Beach, FL: Health Communications, 1996.

———. *Healing the Shame That Binds You*. Deerfield Beach, FL: Health Communications, 2005.

Campbell, W. Keith, and Joshua D. Miller, eds. *The Handbook of Narcissism and Narcissistic Personality Disorder: Theoretical Approaches, Empirical Findings, and Treatments*. Hoboken, NJ: John Wiley & Sons, 2011.

Cooper, Belton Y. *Death Traps: The Survival of an American Division in World War II*. Novato, CA: Presidio Press, 1998.

Crosswell, D. K. R. "The Madness of General George." In *Imponderable but Not Inevitable*, edited by Murfett, M. H. Santa Barbara, CA: Praeger, 2010, 41–71.

D'Este, Carlo. *Patton, A Genius for War*. New York: HarperCollins, 1995.

———. *Eisenhower: A Soldier's Life*. New York: Henry Holt, 2002.

Dixon, Norman. *On the Psychology of Military Incompetence*. London: Cape, 1976.

Dyer, Lt. Col. George. *XII Corps: Spearhead of Patton's Third Army*. Baton Rouge, LA: Military Press, 1947.

Eisenhower, Dwight D. *Crusade in Europe*. Garden City, NY: Doubleday, 1948.

Farago, Ladislas. *Patton: Ordeal and Triumph*. New York: Ivan Obolensky, 1963.

———. *The Last Days of Patton*. New York: McGraw-Hill, 1981.

Ferrell, Robert H. *Collapse at Meuse-Argonne: The Failure of the Missouri-Kansas Division*. Columbia: University of Missouri Press, 2004.

Foster, J. D., and J. C. Brennan. "Narcissism, the Agency Model, and Approach-Avoidance Motivation." In *The Handbook of Narcissism and Narcissistic Personality Disorder: Theoretical Approaches, Empirical Findings, and Treatments*, edited by W. Keith Campbell and Joshua D. Miller. Hoboken, NJ: Wiley, 2011, 89.

Fox, Don M. *Patton's Vanguard: The United States Army 4th Armored Division*. Jefferson, NC: McFarland, 2003.

Freud, Sigmund, and James Strachey. *The Complete Psychological Works of Sigmund Freud*, vol. 14. London: Hogarth Press, 1957, 67–104.

Fussell, Paul. *Wartime: The Experience of War, 1939–1945*. New York: Oxford University Press, 1989.

———. *The Boy's Crusade: The American Infantryman in Northwestern Europe, 1944–1945*. New York: Modern Library, 2003.

Ghaemi, Nassir. *A First-Rate Madness: Uncovering the Links between Leadership and Mental Illness*. New York: Penguin Books, 2011.

Harmon, E. N., Milton MacKaye, and Ross MacKaye. *Combat Commander: Autobiography of a Soldier*. Englewood Cliffs, NJ: Prentice-Hall, 1970.

Hayman, Ronald. *Hitler and Geli*. New York: Bloomsbury, 1997.

Hechler, Ken. *The Bridge at Remagen: The Amazing Story of March 7, 1945—The Day the Rhine River Was Crossed*. Missoula, MT: Pictorial Histories, 1957.

Hirshson, Stanley P. *General Patton: A Soldier's Life*. New York: HarperCollins, 2002.

Hofling, C. K. *Custer and the Little Big Horn: A Psychobiographical Inquiry*. Detroit, MI: Wayne State University Press, 1981.

Hogan, R., and J. Fico. "Leadership." In *The Handbook of Narcissism and Narcissistic Personality Disorder: Theoretical Approaches, Empirical Findings, and Treatments*, edited by W. Keith Campbell and Joshua D. Miller, 393–402. Hoboken, NJ: Wiley, 2011.

Hogan, R., and J. Hogan. *Hogan Development Survey Manual*. 2nd ed. Tulsa, OK: Hogan Assessment Systems, 2009.

Hogg, Ian V. *The Biography of General George S. Patton*. n.p.: Magna Book, 1982.

Horvitz, L. A., and C. Catherwood. *Encyclopedia of War Crimes and Genocide*. New York: Facts on File, 2006.

Hotchkiss, Sandy, LCSW. *Why Is It Always about You? The Seven Deadly Sins of Narcissism*. New York: Free Press, 2002.

Hoyt, E. P. *Backwater War: The Allied Campaign in Italy, 1943–45*. Westport, CT: Praeger Publishers, 2002.

Hurst, James W. *Pancho Villa and Black Jack Pershing: The Punitive Expedition in Mexico*. Westport, CT: Praeger, 2008.

Irving, David. *The War between the Generals*. New York: Congden & Lattes, 1981. http://www.fpp.co.uk/books/WarBetween/2010_edition.pdf.

Irzyk, Albin F. *He Rode up Front for Patton*. Raleigh, NC: Pentland Press, 1996.

———. *Gasoline to Patton: A Different War*. Oakland, CA: Elderberry Press, 2005.

James, Aaron. *Assholes: A Theory*. New York: Anchor Books, 2012.

Karen, Robert. *Becoming Attached: First Relationships and How They Shape Our Capacity to Love*. New York: Oxford University Press, 1998.

Kernberg, Otto F., MD. *Borderline Conditions and Pathological Narcissism*. Northvale, NJ: Jason Aronson, 1975.

Kluger, Jeffrey. *The Narcissist Next Door*. New York: Riverhead Books, 2014.

Kohut, H. *The Restoration of the Self*. Madison, CT: International Universities Press, 1977.

Koyen, Kenneth. *The 4th Armored Division, from the Beach to Bavaria: The Story of the 4th Armored Division in Combat*. Nashville, TN: Battery Press, 1946.

Lande, D. A. *I Was with Patton; First-Person Accounts of WWII in George S. Patton's Command*. Saint Paul, MN: MBI Publishing, 2002.

Lapsley, D. K., and P. C. Stey. "Adolescent Narcissism." In *Encyclopedia of Adolescence*. New York: Springer, 2012.

Lengel, E. G. To Conquer Hell: The Meuse-Argonne, 1918; The Epic Battle That Ended the First World War. New York: Henry Holt, 2008.

Levy, K. N., W. D. Ellison, and J. S. Reynoso. "A Historical Review of Narcissism and Narcissistic Personality." In *The Handbook of Narcissism and Narcissistic Personality Disorder: Theoretical Approaches, Empirical Findings, and Treatments*, edited by W. Keith Campbell and Joshua D. Miller, 3–13. Hoboken, NJ: Wiley, 2011.

Liedloff, Jean. *The Continuum Concept: Allowing Human Nature to Work Successfully*. Reading, MA: Addison-Wesley, 1985.

MacDonald, Charles B. *A Time for Trumpets: The Untold Story of the Battle of the Bulge*. New York: Morrow, 1985.

Macdonald, Dwight. *The Responsibility of Peoples and Other Essays in Political Criticism*. Westport, CT: Greenwood Press, 1974.

Mahler, Margaret S., Fred Pine, and Anni Bergman. *The Psychological Birth of the Human Infant: Symbiosis and Individuation*. New York: Basic Books, 1975.

Marshall, S. L. A. *Men against Fire: The Problem of Battle Command*. Norman: University of Oklahoma Press, 1947.

Masterson, James F. *The Search for the Real Self: Unmasking the Personality Disorders of Our Age*. New York: Free Press, 1988.

Miller, Alice. *The Drama of the Gifted Child: The Search for the True Self*. New York: Basic Books, 2007.

Millon, T. *Disorders of Personality: DSM III; Axis II*. Chichester, UK: Wiley, 1981.

Morgan, Kay Summersby. *Past Forgetting*. New York: Simon & Schuster, 1976.

Murray, W., and A. R. Millett. *A War to Be Won*. Cambridge: Belknap Press of Harvard University Press, 2000.

Nye, Roger H. *The Patton Mind: The Professional Development of an Extraordinary Leader*. Garden City Park, NY: Avery, 1993.

Oltmanns, Thomas F., and Erin M. Lawton. "Self-Other Discrepancies." In *The Handbook of Narcissism and Narcissistic Personality Disorder: Theoretical Approaches, Empirical Findings, and Treatments*, edited by W. Keith Campbell and Joshua D. Miller 309–318. Hoboken, NJ: Wiley, 2011.

Patton, Benjamin. *Growing Up Patton*. New York: Berkley Caliber, 2012.

Patton, George S., Jr. *War as I Knew It*. New York: Bantam, 1980.

Patton, Robert H. *The Pattons: A Personal History of an American Family*. Washington, DC: Brassey's, 1994.

Perret, Geoffrey. *Old Soldiers Never Die: The Life of Douglas MacArthur*. Holbrook, MA: Adams Media, 1996.

Phillips, Henry Gerard. *The Making of a Professional: Manton S. Eddy, USA*. Westport, CT: Greenwood Press, 2000.

———. *El Guettar*. Penn Valley, CA: Henry Gerard Phillips, 1991.

Prefer, Nathan N. *Patton's Ghost Corps: Cracking the Siegfried Line*. Novato, CA: Presidio Press, 1998.

Province, Charles M. *Patton's Third Army: A Daily Combat Diary*. New York: Hippocrene Books, 1992.

———. *I Was Patton's Doctor; The Reminiscences of Colonel Charles B. Odom, MD*. Oregon City, OR: Charles M. Province, 2011.

Puryear, E. F. *American Generalship: Character Is Everything; The Art of Command*. New York: Presidio Press, 2000.

Pyle, Ernie. *Brave Men*. New York: Henry Holt & Co., 1944.

Rickard, John Nelson. *Advance and Destroy: Patton as Commander in the Bulge (American Warriors)*. Lexington: University Press of Kentucky, 2011.

———. *Patton at Bay: The Lorraine Campaign, September to December, 1944*. Westport, CT: Praeger, 1999.

Rooney, Andy. *My War*. New York: Public Affairs, 1995.

Royle, Trevor. *Patton: Old Blood and Guts*. London: Weidenfeld & Nicholson, 2005.

Ryan, Cornelius. *A Bridge Too Far*. New York: Simon & Schuster, 1974.

Schwarzkopf, H. Norman. *It Doesn't Take a Hero*. New York: Bantam Books, 1992.

Sides, Hampton. *Ghost Soldiers: The Epic Account of World War II's Greatest Rescue Mission*. New York: Anchor Books, 2001.

Simonsen, Sebastian, and Erik Simonsen. "Comorbidity between Narcissistic Personality Disorder and Axis I Diagnoses." In *The Handbook of Narcissism and Narcissistic Personality Disorder: Theoretical Approaches, Empirical Findings, and Treatments*, edited by W. Keith Campbell and Joshua D. Miller, 239–247. Hoboken, NJ: Wiley, 2011.

Smith, David Andrew. *George S. Patton: A Biography*. Westport, CT: Greenwood, 2003.

Smith, Michael. "How It Began: Bletchley Park Goes to War." In *Colossus: The Secrets of Bletchley Park's Codebreaking Computers*, edited by Jack Copeland. Oxford: Oxford University Press, 2006. http://www.colossus-computer.com/contents.htm.

Sobel, Brian M. *The Fighting Pattons*. New York: A Dell Book, 1997.

Sorley, Lewis. *Thunderbolt: General Creighton Abrams and the Army of His Times*. New York: Simon & Schuster, 1992.

Spock, Benjamin. *The Common Sense Book of Baby and Child Care*. New York: Duell, Sloan and Pearce, 1946.

Steinberg, L. D. *The Ten Basic Principles of Good Parenting*. New York: Simon & Schuster, 2004.

Totten, Ruth Ellen Patton. *The Button Box: A Daughter's Loving Memoir of Mrs. George S. Patton*. Columbia: University of Missouri Press, 2005.

Tracy, J. L., J. T. Cheng, J. P. Martens, and R. W. Robins, "The Emotional Dynamics of Narcissism; Inflated by Pride, Deflated by Shame." In *The Handbook of Narcissism and Narcissistic Personality Disorder: Theoretical Approaches, Empirical Findings, and Treatments*, edited by W. Keith Campbell and Joshua D. Miller, 330–343. Hoboken, NJ: Wiley, 2011.

Truscott, Lucian K. *Command Missions*. New York: E. P. Dutton, 1954.

Twenge, Jean M., and W. Keith Campbell. *Living in the Age of Entitlement: The Narcissism Epidemic*. New York: Free Press, 2009.

Tzu, Sun. *The Art of War* (Barnes & Noble Classics Series). New York: Barnes & Noble Classics, 2003.

Wallace, H. M. "Narcissistic Self-Enhancement." In *The Handbook of Narcissism and Narcissistic Personality Disorder: Theoretical Approaches, Empirical Findings, and Treatments*, edited by W. Keith Campbell and Joshua D. Miller, 309–318. Hoboken, NJ: Wiley, 2011.

Weigley, Russell F. *Eisenhower's Lieutenants*. Bloomington: Indiana University Press, 1981.

Wellard, James. *Gen. George S. Patton Jr.: Man under Mars*. New York: Dodd, Mead & Co., 1946.

Westmoreland, William C. *A Soldier Reports*. New York: Da Capo Press, 1976.

Whiting, Charles. *48 Hours to Hammelburg*. New York: PJB Books, 1982. First published 1970.

Wilson, Joe W., Jr. *The 761st "Black Panther" Tank Battalion in World War II*. Jefferson, NC: McFarland, 1999.

Woolner, Frank. *Spearhead in the West: The 3rd Armored Division*. Frankfurt am Main, 1946.

Zaloga, S. J. *Metz 1944: Patton's Fortified Nemesis*. Oxford: Osprey Publishing, 2012.

GOVERNMENT DOCUMENTS

Congressional Medal of Honor, the Distinguished Service Cross and the Distinguished Service Medal Issued by the War Department Since April 6, 1917. Office of the Adjutant General, 2012.

Adjutant General's Office, Official Army Register, Vol. 1. Washington, DC: US Government Printing Office, January 1, 1946.

American Battle Monuments Commission. *American Armies and Battlefields in Europe*. Washington, DC: Center of Military History, US Army, 1992. Originally published 1938.

Army Doctrine Publication (ADP 6-22). Department of the Army, August 2012.

Army Regulations No. 600-40, Personnel, Wearing of Service Uniform. War Department, Washington, DC, March 31, 1944.

Cole, Hugh M. *The Lorraine Campaign*. Washington, DC: Center of Military History, US Army, 1997. http://www.ibiblio.org/hyperwar/USA/USA-E-Lorraine/index.html.

———. *The Ardennes: Battle of the Bulge*. Washington, DC: Center of Military History, US Army, 1993. http://www.ibiblio.org/hyperwar/USA/USA-E-Ardennes/index.html.

Garland, A. N., H. M. Smyth, and M. Blumenson. "Sicily and the Surrender." Washington, DC: Center of Military History, US Army, 1965. http://www.ibiblio.org/hyperwar/USA/USA-MTO-Sicily/index.html.

Greenfield, K. R., R. R. Palmer, and B. I. Wiley. *The Army Ground Forces: The Organization of Ground Combat Troops*. Washington, DC: Center of Military History, US Army, 1987.

MacDonald, Charles B. *The Siegfried Line Campaign*. Washington, DC: Center of Military History, US Army, 2001. http://www.ibiblio.org/hyperwar/USA/USA-E-Siegfried/index.html.

———. *The Last Offensive*. Washington, DC: Center of Military History, US Army, 1993. http://www.ibiblio.org/hyperwar/USA/USA-E-Last/index.html.

Patton, George S. *Saber Exercise, 1914*. Washington, DC: US Government Printing Office, 1914.

Spires, David N. *Air Power for Patton's Army: The XIX Tactical Air Command in the Second World War*. Washington, DC: Air Force History and Museums Program, 2002. http://www.afhso.af.mil/shared/media/document/AFD-100924-003.pdf.

World Health Organization. *The ICD-10 Classification of Mental and Behavioural Disorders: Clinical Descriptions and Diagnostic Guidelines*. Geneva: WHO, 1992.

PERIODICALS

Alford, Henry. "Is Trump Actually a Narcissist? Therapists Weigh In." Vanity Fair, November 11, 2015. http://www.vanityfair.com/news/2015/11/donald-trump-narcissism-therapists.

Blumenson, M. "Bradley-Patton: World War II's 'Odd Couple.'" Army, December 1985, 56.

Bolger, D. P. "Zero Defects: Command Climate in the First US Army, 1944–45." US Army in Military Review, May 1991, 61–73.

Field, John. "Patton of the Armored Force." *Life*, November 30, 1942, 113–125.

Henry, Col. Thomas R. "The Avenging Ghosts of the 9th." *Saturday Evening Post*, July 6, 1946, 24.

Hymel, Kevin H., "The Bravest and Best: Patton and the Death of Capt. Richard Jenson in North Africa." *Army History, US Army Center of Military History* (Spring 2014): 30–40.

Koyen, K. "Gen. Patton's Mistake: Third Army, 4th Armored Division and the Hammelburg Affair." *Saturday Evening Post*, May 1, 1948, 1.

Margry, K. "Battle of the Bulge." In *After the Battle*, Vol. 4. Battle of Britain Prints, London, 1974.

———. "The Hammelburg Raid." In *After the Battle*, Vol. 91. Battle of Britain Prints, London, 1996.

Morris, A. "Trump and the Pathology of Narcissism." *Rolling Stone*, April 5, 2017. http://www.rollingstone.com/politics/features/trump-and-the-pathology-of-narcissism-w474896.

Parker, K. J. "Cutting Edge Technology." *Subterranean Press Magazine* (Fall 2011).

Patton, George S., "Form and Use of the Saber." *Cavalry Journal* (March 1913).

Sudmeier, J. L., and J. Leclerc. "The Shelling of Patton's Nancy HQ." In *After the Battle*, Vol. 176. *Battle of Britain International*, Essex, 2017, 32–46.

JOURNALS

Ainsworth, M. D. S. "Object Relations, Dependency and Attachment: A Theoretical Review of the Infant-Mother Relationship." *Child Development* 40 (1969): 969–1025.

Baumeister, R. F., and K. D. Vohs. "Narcissism as Addiction to Esteem." *Psychological Inquiry* 12 (2001): 206–210.

Bizumic, B., and J. Duckitt. "'My Group Is Not Worthy of Me': Narcissism and Ethnocentrism." *Political Psychology* 29 (2008): 437–453.

Bourgeois, J. J., M. J. Hall, R. M. Crosby, and K. G. Drexler. "An Examination of Narcissistic Personality Traits as Seen in a Military Population." *Military Medicine* 158 (1993): 170–174.

Broucek, F. J. "Shame and Its Relationship to Early Narcissistic Developments." *The International Journal of Psycho-Analysis* 63 (1982): 369–378.

Brunell, A. B., et al. "Leader Emergence: The Case of the Narcissistic Leader." *Personality and Social Psychology Bulletin* 34 (2008): 1663–1676.

Campbell, W. K., A. S. Goodie, and J. D. Foster. "Narcissism, Confidence, and Risk Attitude." *Journal of Behavioral Decision Making* 17 (2004): 297–311.

Foster, J. D., T. A. Misra, and D. E. Reidy. "Narcissists Are Approach-Oriented toward Their Money and Their Friends." *Journal of Research in Personality* 43 (2009): 764–769.

Foster, J. D., J. W. Shenesey, and J. S. Goff. "Why Do Narcissists Take More Risks? Testing the Roles of Perceived Risks and Benefits of Risky Behaviors." *Personality and Individual Differences* 47 (2009): 885–889.

Ganz, A. H. "Patton's Relief of General Wood." *Journal of Military History* 53 (1989): 257–273.

Grijalva, E., et al. "Gender Differences in Narcissism: A Meta-Analytic Review." P. D. Harms Publications. Paper 5 (2014).

Kendall, R. E. "The Distinction Between Personality Disorder and Mental Illness." *British Journal of Psychiatry* 180 (2002): 110–115.

Kernberg, O. F. "Borderline Personality Organization." *Journal of the American Psychoanalytic Association* 15 (1967): 641–685.

Lyons-Ruth, K. "Rapprochement or Approchement: Mahler's Theory Reconsidered from the Vantage Point of Recent Research on Early Attachment Relationships." *Psychoanalytic Psychology* 8 (1991): 1–23.

Otway, L. J., and V. L. Vignoles. "Narcissm and Childhood Reflections: A Quantitative Test of Psychoanalytic Predictions." *Personality and Social Psychology Bulletin* 32 (2006): 104–116.

Partanen, E., et al. "Learning-Induced Neural Plasticity of Speech Processing before Birth." *Proc Natl Acad Sci USA* 110 (2013): 15145–15150.

Rank, O. "A Contribution to Narcissism." *Jahrbuch fur Psychoanalytische und Psychopathologische Forschungen* 3 (1911): 401–426 (in German).

Rosso, G., U. Albert, F. Bogetto, and G. Maina. "Axis II Comorbidity in Euthymic Bipolar Disorder Patients: No Differences between Bipolar I and II Subtypes." *Journal of Affective Disorders* 115 (2009): 257–261.

Rothstein, A. "The Theory of Narcissism: An Object-Relations Perspective." *Psychoanalytic Review* 66 (1979): 35–47.

Stinson, F. S., et al. "Prevalence, Correlates, Disability, and Comorbidity of DSM-IV Narcissistic Personality Disorder." *Journal of Clinical Psychiatry* 69 (2008): 1033–1045.

Stormberg, D., E. Ronningstam, J. Gunderson, and M. Tohen. "Brief Communication: Pathological Narcissism in Bipolar Disorder Patients." *Journal of Personality Disorders* 12 (1998): 179–185.

Tracy, J. L., J. T. Cheng, R. W. Robins, and K. H. Trzesniewski. "Authentic and Hubristic Pride: The Affective Core of Self-Esteem and Narcissism." *Self and Identity* 8 (2009): 196–213.

Vazire, S., L. P. Naumann, P. J. Rentfrow, and S. D. Gosling. "Portrait of a Narcissist: Manifestations of Narcissism in Physical Appearance." *Journal of Research in Personality* 42 (2008): 1439–1447.

NEWSPAPERS

Elser, Frank B. "Cardenas's Family Saw Him Die at Bay; Shot Four Times." *New York Times*, May 23, 1916.

"General Patton's Niece Ends Life Surrounded by His Pictures," *Washington Post*, January 9, 1946, 8.

FILMS

Life's First Feelings. WGBH Educational Foundation, 1986. Film.

Patton. Twentieth Century Fox, 1970. Film.

WEBSITE

The Yale Center for Dyslexia & Creativity, Setting People Straight About Dyslexia, 2016. http://dyslexia.yale.edu/EDU_dyslexiastraighttalk.html.

Index

About the Author

Jim Sudmeier is a scientist and writer originally from Minneapolis, Minnesota. He graduated from the military academy Shattuck School, received the BA degree cum laude from Carleton College, and earned the PhD in chemistry from Princeton University. He was an assistant professor at UCLA for five years, associate professor at UC Riverside for thirteen years, and NIH Special Research Fellow at Oxford University, England, and Chalmers Institute, Sweden. He was senior lecturer at Tufts Medical School in Boston for twenty-eight years until retirement in 2013. Dr. Sudmeier is author of some seventy papers in peer-reviewed scientific journals. In 2006, he won the first-place Platinum REMI Award at the Houston Film Festival for screenwriting the docudrama *Patton's Secret Mission*, and in 2017 he co-wrote "The Shelling of Patton's Nancy HQ" for *After the Battle*. He is married with two children and six grandchildren. He enjoys skiing, golf, bicycling, canoeing, and travel. See his website at jimsudmeier.com.